ACOUSTIC MUSIC SOURCE BOOK

MB21665

BY RICHARD MATTESON

OVER 200 OLD-TIME SONGS WITH MELODY LINE, LYRICS AND GUITAR CHORDS!

D1609034

BILL'S MUSIC SHELF

Visit us on the Web at www.melbay.com or www.billsmusicshelf.com

About the Author

Richard L. Matteson Jr. is a nationally recognized fingerstyle guitarist and author. He has written or been included in eleven books by Mel Bay publications in Pacific, Missouri. His ninth book for Mel Bay, "Right-Handed Arpeggio Forms For Acoustic Guitar," a classic guitar technique book, was published in 2002 and is still in print. His tenth book, Mel Bay's Bluegrass Picker's Tune Book (279 pages with 213 bluegrass songs with stories and info about the songs) was just published in May 2006. Seven of Matteson's books have been based on folk songs or early American gospel songs.

He was the acting President of the Piedmont Classic Guitar Society from 1989 until 2005. Matteson was the Program Director in 2006-2007. During his tenure managing the society, the PCGS has hosted concerts by most of the great solo guitarists of our time. Matteson has organized concerts with Manuel Barrueco, the dedication concert for Celedonio Romero , and Christopher Parkening.

He has written articles and been featured in workshops in such national publications as Fingerstyle Guitar Magazine, Acoustic Guitar Magazine, Soundboard Magazine, and Guitar Review Magazine.

Matteson has recorded 4 CD's of fingerstyle arrangements for solo guitar for Mel Bay Publications. He also has solo guitar recordings of three ragtime (Scott Joplin) tunes. In 1996 Matteson performed his ragtime piece, Tar-Heel Rag at half-time of the UNC basketball game in Smith Center before 14,000 fans. A solo recording of the Tar-Heel Rag is also available.

He has several other ensemble recordings available besides the 2 CD's with Bluegrass Messengers. A recording is available of Matteson's original works for guitar and string quartet was done at Salem College at a concert in the Piedmont Classic Guitar Society Fall series. A recording of Matteson's 1992 performance of three pieces for guitar, harmonica, and cello at the Chet Atkins concert in Reynolds Auditorium is available.

Besides his original compositions, Matteson recorded some of his original songs in "True Blue" in 1989 with his brother and harmonica player, Jeff Matteson. A later album of original songs with a Christian message was recorded in 1998 entitled "Stand on the Rock."

Matteson has performed with or shared the stage with Chet Atkins, regularly with jazz legend Charlie Byrd until his death. He has performed with Doc Watson with his bluegrass group, The Bluegrass Messengers. He has played such large festivals as the Merle Watson Festival in Wilkesboro and performed and done workshops at the Chet Atkins Appreciation Concerts in Nashville.

In 2007 Matteson taught guitar, bass, banjo, dulcimer, dobro, and fiddle at Duncan Music Teaching Studios in Winston-Salem, NC until he moved to Oquawka, Illinois in March 2007. He does folk/bluegrass research on his web-site: BluegrassMessengers.com as well as original art work. He has a commission to do a mural and is painting a series of acrylics based on folk songs.

Contact the Author: For more information about the songs visit the author's web-site: *BluegrassMessengers.com*

E-mail information is available there.

Introduction

Bill Bay asked me to write a follow up book to my last book, *"The Bluegrass Pickers Tune Book."* If you like Bluegrass music (232 songs) I'd recommend getting that book to add to your collection. The focus of this book, "The Acoustic Source Book" is on roots and old-time music. The book is focused on the time period from late 1800's until 1940's. There are a few songs from The Bluegrass Book that were too important to be left out. I decided not to use any patriotic and Christmas songs and came up with a list of about 400 songs which eventually was cut down to 241.

The Music

During the late 1800's and early 1900's there was an important evolution in American music; the birth of jazz, ragtime, and blues. This was also the period of the phonograph and early commercial recordings. Music from the Minstrel period as well as traditional songs were used as staple for the roots musicians. In the early 1900's there were rags, blues, gospel, Tin-Pan Alley, jug band, spiritual, old-time country and popular songs. I've tried to include some of the well-known songs from every genre to give you a big slice of Americana.

There are some great songs that are popular roots, bluegrass and old-time songs today that have never been published. There are also great songs that are not well known that should be played and enjoyed.

Styles Of Music

There are many different styles of music found in this book. Here's a brief description of the different styles and some of the songs included in the book that fit that style.

Traditional Ballads and Folk Songs- are the largest category of songs in this book. Folk songs (songs with no proven author) include blues type songs, work songs and ballads (songs telling a story). With the popularity of early country music recordings in the 1920's, many folk songs were copyrighted. *Man of Constant Sorrow* was claimed by Richard Burnett and appeared in his 1913 book but was also claimed by Emry Arthur. Alabama Bound was claimed to have been written by Jelly Roll Morton in 1905 but he had to use another title when he recorded it many years because it was already copyrighted in 1910. *Kumbaya* is a song claimed to have been composed by Reverend Marvin V. Frey (1918 – 1992) in the but the song was already collected previously and information about Frey's initial learning of the song has surfaced. Some of the many songs include *Ain't Gonna Rain No More, Careless Love; Pretty Little Pink* and ballads like *Banks of the Ohio; Barbara Allen;* and *Willie Moore.*

Shape-Note Hymns- were printed hymns that used shaped notes that were based on William Little and William Smith's book 'The Easy Instructor" published in 1798. Some of the main books were The Kentucky Harmony 1816, Southern Harmony, Sacred Harp and the Social Harp. Some of the old hymns found in this book are: *Amazing Grace* (New Britain) and *Green Pastures.*

Cowboy and Western Songs- Some great acoustic songs are cowboy and western songs. They include *I'll Be Working on the Railroad; Red River Valley; Home on the Range;* and *Streets of Laredo.*

Bluegrass Songs- Bluegrass music started around 1945 with Bill Monroe's classic band. Bluegrass songs were based on the old-time songs and popular songs from the late 1800's to the 1940's. Many of these songs are standard bluegrass songs like *Little Maggie* and *Roll In my Sweet Baby's Arms.*

Ragtime- From the word, "ragged time," ragtime is an American musical genre which enjoyed its peak popularity from the late 1800's to around 1920 that used syncopated rhythms and 16 measure forms. It has had several periods of revival since then and is still being composed today. Scott Joplin was one of the most famous composers. Some examples of songs played in ragtime style are: *Alexander's Ragtime Band; Alabama Jubilee; At a Georgia Camp Meeting*

Blues Songs- There were many songs called blues songs that were not in the standard twelve-bar form. Some were eight bars, some were called blues but were 16 measure songs and others were mountain blues performed mainly by white musicians. One important source of acoustic music is the country blues artists like Mississippi John Hurt. The country blues songs in this book include *My Creole Belle; John Henry; Frankie and Johnny; Spike Driver Blues; Hesitation Blues; Make Me A Pallet On Your Floor(Atlanta Blues)* and *Cannonball Blues.*

Twelve Bar Blues- The standard blues form was developed in the late 1800's and early 1900's from songs found in this collection like *Alabama Bound* and *Careless Love (Loveless Love).* The twelve bar form uses one lyric line and echo (repeating the first line) and an answering line that rhymes with the first lines. Some standard blues found in this book are: *Joe Turner Blues; Easy Rider; Corinna, Corinna; St. Louis Blues* and *Down Hearted Blues.*

Minstrel Songs- Minstrel music was developed in the late 1830s with the advent of the five-string banjo by Joel Sweeney of Appomattox Court House, Virginia. This new form of music became very popular as the performers, usually working usually in small groups, went from town to town or traveled with the circus. In 1843, Dan Emmetts "Virginia Minstrels" performed the first minstrel show with banjo, fiddle, bones, and tambourine. Some songs in this collection are: *Oh! Susanna, Camptown Race; Buffalo Gals; Jim Crack Corn; Angelina Baker;* and *Beautiful Dreamer.*

Old-time Songs- The word old-time is generally applied to songs that were popular between 1890 and 1930 although I consider music before bluegrass music (circa 1945) to be old-time music. All the songs could be considered old-time in this collection.

Old-time Gospel- The old-time country string bands played both gospel and secular songs. There are obscure songs like *Ain't Gonna Lay My Armor Down* to popular gospel songs like *Will the Circle Be Unbroken; Angel Band;* and *Amazing Grace.*

Spirituals- Traditional African-American Spirituals are an important source of acoustic music. Some songs like *"You Shall Be Free"* and a spiritual (depending on the lyrics) or a secular song. Some songs are: *All My Trials Lord; Down By the Riverside; Wade in the Water; Michael Row The Boat Ashore;* and *Kumbaya.*

Jazz and Dixieland Jazz- Dixieland jazz usually identified by brass developed in New Orleans in the early 1900's and eventually spread to other cities like Chicago and New York City and was quite popular among the general public. The term Dixieland became widely used after the advent of the first million-selling hit records of the Original Dixieland Jass Band in 1917. The music has been played continuously since the early part of the 20th century. Louis Armstrong's All-Stars was the band most popularly identified with Dixieland. Some songs are: *At a Georgia Camp Meeting; St Louis Blues; Down By the Riverside; When The Saints; Bill* Bailey and *Frankie and Johnny.*

Popular Standards From Late 1800 and early 1900's- The popular songs were the staple of many of the acoustic recording artists of the 1920's and 1930's like the Carter Family and Vernon Dalhart. Song in this book include: *The Band Played On; Bird in a Gilded Cage; In the Good Old Summertime; Shine On Harvest Moon* and *By the Beautiful Sea.*

Barbershop Quartet Songs- Barbershop singing originated in African-American communities around 1900, where barbershops were places of social gathering. The four-part harmony of the form has its roots in the black church, where close harmony has a long tradition. Some examples found in this book are: *Bill Grogan's Goat; In the Good Old Summertime* and *Shine On Harvest Moon.*

Old-Time Country- refers to the early country music recording artists like Fiddlin' John Carson; Uncle Dave Macon, Gid Tanner and His Skillet Lickers; Jimmie Rodgers and the Carter Family. The early recordings were done in the 1920's and are covered by country artists today. Songs include; *Ain't No Bugs on Me; Cat Came Back; She'll Be Coming Round the Mountain;* and *Don't Get Trouble in your Mind.*

Tin-Pan Alley Songs- are the name given songs that were published in New York City starting circa 1885. Many of the most popular songs came from Tin-Pan Alley writers like Harry Von Tilzer. Songs include *Alabama Jubilee; Take Me Out to the Ballgame* and *At A Georgia Camp Meeting.*

Jug Band Songs- The origins of jug bands can be traced to Louisville, Kentucky around the turn of the century. The early jug bands played a mixture of early jazz, country and pop that had its roots in ragtime. By 1910 there were several jug bands in Louisville, usually consisting of a jug, fiddle, banjo and sometimes a mandolin or guitar. One of the first jug bands to be recorded was Earl McDonalds Dixieland Jug Blowers in the early 1920s. The Memphis Jug Band and Canon's Jug Stompers were two other early popular bands. *Tear It Down; Ragged But Right;*

Song Notes

Each of the 240 songs has information about the songs, including the author (if it's not traditional), the date, some other names the song is known and a short list of important recordings. If you need help learning a song you can find most of the recordings on-line or at a CD store. If you want more information about the songs you can go to my web-site: BluegrassMessengers.com and click on lyrics.

Thank You

I would like to thank Bill Bay for suggesting I write this book. Many thanks to all the sources I used to compile my notes. The Mudcate Café (on-line) is one great source for information as is the late Gus Meade's book Country Music Sources.

Contents

7

After the Ball

Words and music by Charles K. Harris; Widely known. **ARTIST:** Early version by Vernon Dalhard; Bradley Kincaid; Finddlin' John Carson and Blue Sky Boys; **DATE:** 1892; **RECORDING INFO:** Vernon Balhart; Bradley Kincaid; Fiddlin' John Carson; Blue Sky Boys; John Fahey; **OTHER NAMES:** After the Ball is Over; Life On the Ocean Wave; Over the Ocean Waves; After the Roundup **NOTES:** Tin Pan Alley was established in the 1880s achieving national prominence with the first million selling song hit in American music history- "After the Ball." Eventually selling over five million copies of sheet music, "After the Ball" was the biggest hit in Tin Pan Alley's long history. Typical of most popular 1890s tunes, the song was a tearjerker, a melodramatic evocation of lost love.

Chorus: After the ball is over, After the break of morn,
After the dancers' leaving, After the stars are gone:
Manny a heart is aching, If you could read them all
Many the hopes that have vanished, After the ball.

Bright lights were flashing in the grand ballroom,

Softly the music playing sweet tunes;

There came my sweetheart, my love, my own,

"I wish some water, leave me alone."

When I returned, dear, there stood a man
Kissing my sweetheart, as lovers can.
Down fell the glass, pet, broken, that's all
Just as my heart was, after the ball.

Long years have passed, child, I've never wed
True to my lost love, thought she is dead.
She tried to tell me, tried to explain
I would not listen, pleadings were vain.

One day a letter came from that man,
He was her brother the letter ran;
That's why I'm lonely, no home at all
I broke her heart, pet, after the ball.

Ain't Gonna Lay My Armor

Traditional old-time gospel song. Not well heard of; **DATE**: Early 1900's (recorded 1928); **OTHER NAMES**: Ain't Going To Lay My Armor Down; **RECORDED BY**: McVay and Johnson 1928; Kentucky Coon Hunters 1931; West Maryland Highballers, 1963; **NOTES**: This little known old-time gospel song was first recorded in 1928 by Ancil McVay and Roland Johnson as a vocal duet with fiddle, guitar and banjo.

CHORUS: I ain't gonna lay my armor down, I ain't gonna lay my armor down

I ain't gonna lay my armor down, Till He comes.

I ain't gonna lay my armor down, I ain't gonna lay my armor down,

I ain't gonna lay my armor down, Till He comes.

VERSE: I'm gonna stand on the word of God
I'm gonna stand on the word God
I'm gonna stand on the word God
Till He comes (Repeat)

CHORUS

I'm gonna sing and shout and pray
I'm gonna sing and shout and pray
I'm gonna sing and shout and pray
Till He comes (Repeat)

I ain't gonna run when the battle gets hot
I ain't gonna run when the battle gets hot
I ain't gonna run when the battle gets hot
Till He comes (Repeat)

Ain't Nobody's Business

Old-time song and jazz tune; Widely known and recorded. **DATE**: 1882. "Nobody's Business But Out Own" by C. T. Dockstader; 1911 "Nobody's Bizness But Mine" and "Tain't Nobody's Bizness buy my Own" in JOAFL collected by Howard Odum. **RECORDING INFO**: Earliest recordings: Bert Williams 1919; Sara Martin December 1, 1922 on OK 8043. Billie Holiday; Jimmy Witherspoon; Earl Johnson; Frank Stokes; Ike And Tina Turner Mississippi John Hurt; Billie Holiday: Ella Fitzgerald; Uncle Dave Macon; Bessie Smith; Riley Puckett; **RELATED TO**: Cocaine Done Killed My Baby; Chanpagne Don't Hurt Me Baby; **OTHER NAMES**: Nobody's Buiness If I Do; It Ain't Nobody's Business; Tennessee Jubilee; I' Ain't Nobody's Bizness If I Do; Ain't Nobody's Business; **NOTES**: Gus Meade in 'Country Music Sources' p. 499 attributes the source of this song incorrectly to Will Skidmore's 1919 version but it was clearly published earlier and appears in JOAFL in 1911. Two of the early recordins are based on the arrangement by Porter Grainger and Everett Robbins, which was copyrighted in 1922; Sara Martin-December 1, 1922 [OK 8043] and Bessie Smith-April 11, 1923 [Co A3898]. Porter Grainger and Everett Robbins "'Tain't Nobody's Biz-ness If I Do" is clearly a rewrite of traditional material. Since the spelling is the same as the published in 1911, lyrics from the JOAFL, it is quite possible they took that title and slightly changed the lyrics. A more likely source is "Nobody's Business But Out Own" by C.R. Dockstader in 1882 (see Version 3). It was performed by the Dockstaders in blackface. The last two lines are: "If we don't hang the cranks, put an end to their pranks/Why it's nobody's business ut our own." Published by J.W. Pepper, Philadelphia in 1882, Dockstader's song (although in a longer song form) is very close to the 1911 Odum version and the classic 1922 Porter Grainger and Everett Robbins versions.

C
Sometimes I ramble

F
Get drunk and gamble

C   G
Nobody's business if I do.

CHORUS: It's nobody's business,
              C

F
Nobody's business

C   G   C
Nobody's business if I do.

Some of these mornings I'll wake up crazy
Kill my wife and save my baby
Nobody's business if I do.
CHORUS:

Morphine's gonna run me crazy
Cocaine's gonna kill my baby
Pretty girls gonna cause me to loose my mind.
CHORUS:

When she rides in a Ford machine
I buy the gasoline
Nobody's business it I do.

That's where my money goes
To buy my baby clothes
Nobody's business if I do.

She rides in a Cadillac
Oh boy she makes the jack
Nobody's business if I do.

Alabama Bound

Traditional Old-time Song and Blues; Widely known; US south; **DATE:** First collected version 1908; First published in 1909 Hoffman; First Recording Papa Charlie Jackson May 1925; **RECORDING INFO:** Jelly Roll Morton; Big Joe Williams; Henry Thomas (Ragtime Texas Henry); Dave Von Ronk; Washboard Sam; **RELATED TO:** Baby Please Don't Go (form); Alabama Blues; Elder Green Blues; **OTHER NAMES:** I'm Alabama Bound; Don't You Leave Me Here; Elder Green's in Town; Preacher Got Drunk; Boat's Up the River; Don't Ease Me In; I'm Alabamy Bound; **NOTES:** The sentiment of the song lyrics seems to come from the Minstrel stage. On possible source is I Hab Left Alabama by Marchall S. Pike published in 1849: Alabama agen/ Alabama agen And if I ever lib 'till the sunrise tomorrow/ I's-goin' back to Alabama agen. In an interview with Alan Lomax, Jelly Roll Morton (1890-1941) claimed to have written the song Alabama Bound in 1905 which he recorded it for Bluebird in 1939 as Don't You Leave Me Here. Morton was told to change the name from Alabama Bound to avoid possible copyright conflicts; [Morton: "but I am getting Alabama Bound in (the session with Bluebird) and the title must be changed to Don't You Leave Me Here."] Morton apparently left the Alabama Bond lyric that he knew off his recording which features his vocals on only two verses. The Don't You Leave Me Here/Don't Leave Me Here songs were also known as Elder Brown's in Town in Texas and a similar version to Morton's was recorded by Laura Smith in 1927. From Songsters and Saints by Paul Oliver p. 116: "In Texas W.H. Thomas of College Station included "Don't You Leave Me Here" in some current folk songs which he presented as a paper in 1912 to the Texas Folk Lore Society. Some years later Gates Thomas published his own, fuller version that included Alabama Boun' with Elder Green verses, which he dated at 1908. Its widespread distribtion suggests its early date as a folk song. Though it was described as a dance, a song with the title Alabama bound was published as early as 1910 by Ed Rogers and Saul Aaronson which shows a clear link to the chorus of the folk song." In 1909 a white New Orleans theatre pianist named Robert Hoffman published Im Alabama Bound subtitled The Alabama Blues. Though not a blues in the strict 12-bar form it did feature enough characteristics to be considered one of the first published "blues."

VERSE: Says the preacher in the pulpit, bible in his hand.
Sister's way back in the Amen corner hollerin' that's my man.

CHORUS: I'm Alabama bound, I'm Alabama bound,
                    C   F

And if the train don't stop and turn around, I'm Alabama bound.
           C   G   C

Now the boats up the river, And it's rollin' down.
If you need to go South darlin' babe, Alabama bound.

Elder Green's in town And he turned around,
And he tell all the brothers and sisters he meets, I'm Alabama bound.

Don't you leave this town, Don't you leave this town,
And if you leave me here, leave a dime for beer.

Alabama Jubilee

Traditional Old-Time Bluegrass Jazz tune & Song. George L. Cobb, music; Jack Yellen, lyrics; **DATE:** 1915; **CATAGORY:** Instrumental Tuens; **RECORDIG INFO:** Tweedy Brothers; Roy Clark; Clark Kessinger; Clarence White; Wayne Henderson; **NOTES:** Recorded by many bluegrass pickers usually as an instrumental. Jack Yellen also composed the lyrics to "Happy Days are Here Again." Usually the Chorus is the only part sung by bluegrass pickers.

CHORUS: You ought to see Deacon Jones
$\overset{A7}{}$

When he rattles them bones

Old Parson Brown, foolin' 'round like a clown
$\overset{D}{}$

Aunt Jemima, who is past eighty three
$\overset{G}{}$

Shoutin' I'm full o' pep!
$\overset{C}{}$

(Spoken) Watch yo' step! Watch yo' step!

One legged Joe danced aroun' on his toe,
$\overset{A7}{}$

Threw away his crutch and hollered, "Let 'er go!"

Oh, honey, hail! Hail! The gang's all here,
$\overset{C}{} \overset{E7}{} \overset{F}{} \overset{C}{}$

For the Alabama Jubilee!
$\overset{D}{} \overset{G}{} \overset{C}{}$

Alexander's Ragtime Band

Words and music by Ivring Berlin; Wdely known, **DATE:** 1911; **RECORDING INFO:** Al Johnson, Billy Murray, Louis Armstrong, George Formby, Bing Crosby, Ella Fitzgerald and Ray Charles. **NOTES:** Born in 1888 (died in 1989) Berlin was one of the most famous American songwriters in history. He was on of the few Tin Pan Ally songwriters who wrot both lyrics and music for his songs. Alexander's Ragtime Band was his first hit in 1911. Alexander's Ragtime Band is also the title of a 1938 film that takes off from the song to tell a story of a society boy who scandalizers his family by pursuing a career in ragtime instead of in "serious" music. Many versions like Louis Armstrong's use only the chorus.

CHORUS: Come on and hear...come on and hear

Alexander's Ragtime Band

Come on and hear...come on and hear

It's the best band in the land

They can play a bugle call like you never heard before

So natural that you wanna go to war

That's just the bestest band what am...oh honey lamb.

Come on along, come on along

Let me take you by the hand

Up to the man...I said the man

Who's the leader of the band

If you care to hear that Swanee River

played in ragtime

Come on and hear...come on and hear

Alexander's Ragtime Band.

14

All My Trials, Lord

Traditional African-American spiritual; Southeast and West Indies; **DATE:** discovered in 1950's from Bahamas; **RECORDING INFO**: Bob Gibson 1956; Joan Baez; Kingston Trio; Seekers: Pete Seeger. **NOTES**: From Joan Beaz Songbook: "This spiritual-lullaby is probably originated in the antebellum South, from where it was transpoted to the West Indies. It appears to have died out in this country, only to be discovered in the Bahamas. From there it was reintroduced to us, eventually becoming one of the standards of the popular folk song movement."

VERSE: If religion were a thing that (D)
money could buy (D7)
The rich would live and the poor (D)
would die (G)
All my trials, Lord, soon be over (D) (A7) (D)

CHORUS: Too late, my brothers (D)
Too late, but never mind (G)
All my trials, Lord, soon be over (D) (A7) (D)

Hush little baby, don't you cry
You know you daddy was
born to die
All my trials, Lord, soon be over

I've got a little book that was
given to me
And every page spells liberty
All my trials, Lord, soon be over

There is a tree in Paradise
And the pilgrims call it the
Tree of Life
All my trials, Lord, soon be over

All Night Long/Richmond Blues

Old-time, Bluegrass, Blues/Jazz Song. Widely known; **DATE:** Song by Shelton Brooks 1912; Earliest recording by Roba & Bob Stanley 1924. **EOCRDING INFO**: [Clarence] Ashley & [Gwen] Foster; Burnett & Rutherford; Earl Johnson & his Dixie Entertainers; **RELATED TO:** Paul and Silas; Mary Wore Three Links of Chain; Tupelo Blues; Oh My Lawd; **OTHER NAMES:** Baby, All Night Long; Richmond Blues; Let Your Shack Burn Down; Oh Sweet Mama; It's All Night Long; **NOTES:** The All Night Long songs are a group of songs ending with "all night long/ baby all night long" etc. Paul and Silas is an example of traditional All Night Long song. Most of the bluegrass/old-time songs originated from All Night Long written by the African American composer Shelton Brooks. The verse of Brooks song, which can be viewed online, is the basis for versions by the 1927 versions by Burnett & Rutherford and also Earl Johnson. Later versions sometimes called Richmond Blues were recorded by Doc Watson and Ralph Stanley.

CHORUS: Baby, all night long C

Baby, all night long G

Got the Richmond Blues D

Baby, all night long G.

VERSE: Well I left this depot
Looked up on the board.
This train ain't here
But it's somewhere on the road.

When I left the country
And moved to town.
That's when my baby
Started running around.

I'd rather be dead;
And in my grave
Than be in this old town
Treated this way.

So if I live
And don't get killed
Gonna make my home
In Louisville.

All the Pretty Little Horses

Traditional lullaby and folk song. Widely known. **DATE:** 1926 (Seventy Negro Spirituals); 1927 (Sandburg) Collected by Alan Lomax on his 1939 field recording trip.
RECORDING INFO: Odetta; Texas Gladden; Pete Seeger; Alan Lomax. **OTHER NAMES:** Hush-a-bye Don't You Cry; Black Sheep Lullaby: Poor Little Lamby; Honey Song; Whole Heap a Little Horses. **NOTES:** In the liner notes to "At the Gate of Horn," Odetta says of this song, "A woman crooning a lullaby to a baby while she leaves her own unattended in order to earn money for bread. In the song she refers to her own child as the lamby in the meadow. This lullaby comes from the South, post Civil War." The song first appears in print in 1926 as "Black Sheep" in W.A. Fisher's "Seventy Negro Spirituals." Oliver Ditson Co., Boston, pp. 4–7, with music Called a Kentucky melody from the c collection of Miss M. Crudup Vesey. "...as sung by various black mammies who have hushed to sleep five generations of babies in one old Kentucky family."

Hush-a-bye, don't you cry,

Go to sleepy little baby,

When you wake, you'll have cake,

And all the pretty little horses.

Black and bay, dapple and gray,

Coach and six little horses,

Hush-a-bye, don't you cry,

Go to sleepy little baby.

Way down yonder, down in the meadow,
There's a poor wee little lamby.
The bees and the butterflies pickin' at its eyes,
The poor wee thing cried for her mammy.
(Repeat First Verse)

Amazing Grace

Traditional Tune. First Three Stanzas by John Newton (1715-1807) Stanza 4 Traditional; **DATE:** Lyrics appear in 1779; Lyrics and tune are combined in Southern Harmony-1855; **CATEGORY:** American Folk Hymn: **RECORDED BY:** Clarence Ashley; Buell Kazee; Seldom Scene; Stanley Brothers; Doc Watson; Osbourne Brothers; Don Reno; **SOURCES:** American Melody from Carrol's and Clayton's original Harmony (1831); **OTHER NAMES:** Called "New Britain" in Sacred Harp. **NOTES:** One of the favorite hymns.

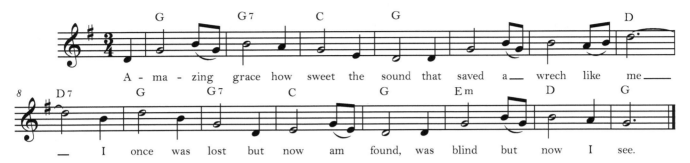

A - ma - zing grace how sweet the sound that saved a wrech like me
I once was lost but now am found, was blind but now I see.

Amazing grace, how sweet the sound
(G) (G7) (C) (G)

That saved a wretch like me
(D) (D7)

I once was lost, but now am found
(G) (G7) (C) (G)

Was blind, but now I see.
(Em) (D) (G)

Twas grace that taught my heart to fear
And grace my fears relieved
How precious did that grace appear
The hour I first believed.

Through many dangers, toils and snares
I have already come
Tis grace hath brought me safe thus far
And grace will lead me home.

When we've been there ten thousand years
Bright shining as the sun
We've no less days to sing God's praise
Than when we first begun.

Angel Band

By William Bradbury and Jefferson Hascal; **DATE**: First appears in J.D. Dadmun's "Melodian" in 1860. **CATEGORY**: American Hymn; **RECORDING INFO**: Stanley Brothers; Flat & Scruggs; Doyle Lawson and Quicksilver; Johnny Cash; Emmylou Harns; Hedy West and Bill Clifton; **NOTES**: Popularized by being included in the "O, Brother" soundtrack.

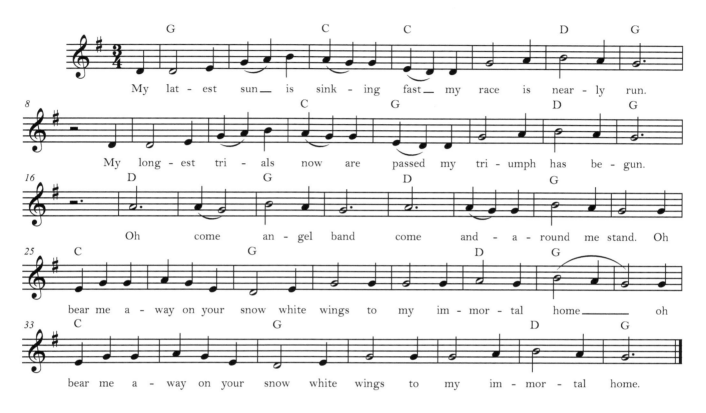

My latest sun is sinking fast

My race is nearly run

My longest trials now are passed

My triumph has begun

CHORUS: Oh, come angel band

Come and around me stand

Oh bear me away on your snow white wings

To my immortal home

Oh bear me away on your snow white wings

To my immortal home.

Oh, bear my loving heart to Him
Who bled and died for me
Whose blood now cleanses from all sins
And gives me victory. CHORUS

I've almost reached my heavenly home
My spirit loudly sings
The holy ones, behold they come
I hear the noise of wings. CHORUS

19

Angeline, The Baker

Old-Time song and Breakdown based on Angeline Baker by Stephen Foster; **DATE:** 1850; **RECORDING INFO:** Uncle Eck Dunford; Kenny Hall and the Sweet Mills String Band; Stuart Duncan; Norman Edmonds; Descret String Band; **OTHER NAMES:** Angeline; Angelina Baker; Rocky Road (NC) Coon Dog (VA) Georgie Row Walk up Georgia Road; Julie Ann Flan; Einstein the Genius; Julie Ann Johnson (tune); **RELATED TO:** Sailing On the Ocean; Little Nell; **NOTES:** This old time song and tune was derived from a sentimental song by Stephen Foster, called Angelina Baker, whose lyrics tell about a slave who is parted from her lover when sold. Foster's original song can be heard played by the Criston Hollow Stringband on their album Sweet Home (Yodel-Ay-hee 002).

Angeline the baker, lives in our village green,

The way I always loved her beats all you ever seen.

CHORUS: Angeline the Baker, her age is twenty-three,

I feed her candy by the peck but she won't marry me.

The last time I saw her, it was at the county fair,
Her father chased me halfway home and told me to stay there.

Angeline is handsome, and Angeline is tall,
She broke her little ankle bone from dancing in the hall.

She won't do the baking because she is too stout.
She makes cookies by the peck, throws the coffee out.

Angeline the Baker, her age is twenty-three,
Little children round her feet and a banjo on her knee.

As I Went Down to the Valley/River to Pray

Traditional Bluegrass, Gospel Tune; **DATE:** Mid 1800's; **CATEGORY:** Gospel Tunes. **RECORDING INFO:** Alison Kraus "O Brother Where Art Thou?" Soundtrack; Tim and Molly O'Brien; Doc Watson; **OTHER NAMES:** The Good Old Way; Down to the River To Pray; NOTES: A gospel song from both black and white sources. L.L. McDowell's Middle Tennessee "Songs of the Old Camp Ground;" White's Fisk "Jubilee Songs". 1872.

1. As I went down in the valley to pray, Studyin' about that good old way.
G C G

And who shall wear the starry crown, Good Lord show me the way.
C G

Oh brothers let's go down, Come on down, don't you want to go down.
D G C G

Oh brothers let's go down, Down in the valley to pray.
D G C G

2. Oh sisters let's go down...
3. Oh fathers let's go down...
4. Oh mothers let's go down...
5. Oh sinners let's go down...

At a Georgia Camp Meeting

Old-Time, Cake-Walk. Words and music by Kerry Mills. **DATE:** Published in 1897. **RECORDING INFO:** WV fiddler Henry Reed; Leake County Revelers; Double Decker String Band; Arthur Smith; Dave Van Ronk. **RELATED TO:** Peaches Down in Georgia. **OTHER NAMES:** Georgia Camp Meeting; Milwaukee Here I Come; Georgia Cake Walk. **NOTES:** The cakewalk was an eccentric, syncopated dance of the 1890's. This song was one of the greatest cakewalk tunes of the time. Some of the lyrics have been edited for content.

A camp meeting took place by the river trace Way down in Georgia. There were folks large and small, lanky lean fat and tall, At this Georgia camp meeting. When church was out, how the Sisters did shout They were so happy but the young folks were tired And wished to be inspired and hired a big brass band. When that big brass band began to play pretty music so gay hats were the thrown away. Thought them foolish people their necks would break when they quit laughing and talking and went to walking for a big chocolate cake.

A camp meeting took place, by the river trace; way down in Georgia.
$\overset{G}{}$ $\overset{C}{}$ $\overset{G}{}$

There were folks large and small, lanky, lean, fat and tall at this Georgia camp meeting.
$\overset{A7}{}$ $\overset{D}{}$

When church was out, how the "sisters" did shout, they were so happy.
$\overset{G}{}$ $\overset{C}{}$ $\overset{G}{}$

But the young folks were tired and wished to be inspired, and hired a big brass band.
$\overset{Em}{}$ $\overset{G}{}$ $\overset{D}{}$ $\overset{G}{}$

CHOURS: When the big brass band began to play pretty music so gay, hats were thrown away.
$\overset{D}{}$ $\overset{G}{}$ $\overset{D}{}$ $\overset{G\#Dim7}{}$ $\overset{G}{}$

Thought them foolish people their necks would break,
$\overset{D}{}$ $\overset{G}{}$

When they quit their laughing and talking and went to walking for a big chocolate cake.
$\overset{C}{}$ $\overset{G}{}$ $\overset{A7}{}$ $\overset{D}{}$ $\overset{G}{}$

The old "sisters" raised sand, when they first heard the band; way down in Georgia.
The preacher did glare and the deacons did stare, at the young people prancing.
The band played so sweet that nobody could eat, 'twas so entrancing.
So the church folks agreed it was not sinful deed, and they joined in with the rest.

Aunt Nancy/Rhody

Traditional song and breakdown, originally from old France. **DATE:** Part of an opera in 1750; Recorded in US in 1925. **RECORDING INFO:** Carolina Tar Hells; Burl Ives; Almeda Riddle; Jean Ritchie; Weaver; Pickart Family; Pete Seeger. **OTHER NAMES:** The Old Gray Goose is Dad; Gray Goose (Not to be confused with the minstrel song-"Gray Goose" which is part of the "My Wife Died on a Saturday Night" family of songs); Go Tell Aunt Rhody/Rhodie; Go Tell Aunt Nancy; **RELATED TO**: Chiny/Chiney/China Doll; Down Came an Angel. **NOTES:** Randolph quotes Chase to the effect that tis tune was used in an opera by jean Jacques Rousseau in 1750.The situation is rather more complex than this would imply. The most recent, and most significant, work on this subject is Murl Sickbert, Jr.'s 'Go Tell Aunt Rhody She's Rousseau's Dream" (published 2000). Norm Cohen reports the following: "In 1752, Rousseau composed 'Le Devin de village,' a pastoral opera bouffe...[The Aunt Rhody tune appears] as a gavotte in the pantomime no. 8 (divertissement or ballet). It is danced by 'la villageoise,' a shepherdess or country girl, to music without words." Sickebert observes that the Rousseau composition is more elaborate than the folk tune, with "two additional parts or reprises, not one as Lomax gives it."

Go tell Aunt Rhody, go tell Aunt Rhody,

Go tell Aunt Rhody The old gray goose is dead.

The one she's been saving, the one she's been saving,
The one she's been saving to make a feather bed.

The old gander's weeping, the old gander's weeping,
The old gander's weeping because his wife is dead.

The goslings are mourning, the goslings are mourning,
The goslings are mourning because their mothers dead.

She died in the mill pond, she died in the mill pond,
She died in the mill pond from standing on her head.

Go tell Aunt Rhody, go tell Aunt Rhody,
Go tell Aunt Rhody the old gray goose is dead.

Back Up and Push

Bluegrass and Old-time Breakdown. Widely known. **DATE:** Early 1900's; My Creole Belle by Lampe 1900; Rubber Dolly late 1800's; **RECORDING INFO:**Skillet Lickers; Flatt & Scruggs & the Foggy Mountain Boys; Bill Monroe; McLain Family; **OTHER NAMES:** Rubber Doll;.Dolly (Rag); My Creole Belle/Belles; **NOTES:** Back Up and Push and Rubber Dolly evolved from the melody of Jens Bodewalt Lampe's piano rag with song lyrics, "My Creole Belles" whichwas published in Detroit, Michigan by Whitney-Warner in 1900. It was the melody to the second strain by J.B Lampe (1869-1929)) that became popular during the early 1900's. "My Creole Belle" by Mississippi John Hurt is a reworking of Lampe's melody and lyrics.

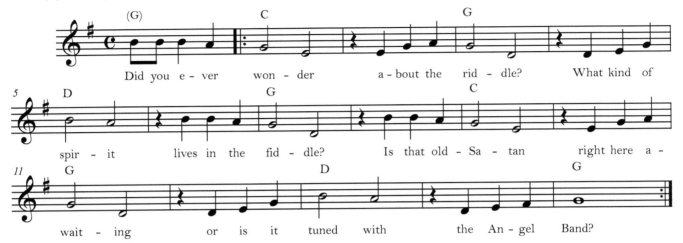

(G)   C   G
Did you ever wonder about the riddle

          D   G
What kind of spirit lives in the fiddle?

      C   G
Is that old Satan, right here a waitin'

     D   G
Or is it tuned with the Angel Band?

Back up and push, Back up and push,
Back off from sin, let glory in.
You can't go wrong, singing this song,
Back up and push away.

If you let the Devil play on your senses,
Prepare to suffer the consequences
The fullest measure of wordly pleasure,
Can only send you into the roaring fire.

Back up and push, Back up and push,
Back off from sin, let glory in.
You can't go wrong, singing this song,
Back up and push away.

Baldheaded End of a Broom

Old-time song, Harry Bennett words and music; **DATE:** 1877; **OTHER NAMES:** Look Before You Leap; Boys Keep Away From the Girls; Love is a Funny Thing; Lines of Love;
RECORDING INFO: George Reneau 1924; Dry City Scar Band; Charlie Poole (as Look Before You Leap); Walter Smith (as Love is a Funny Thing); Mike Seeger; **NOTES:** This oft recorded ditty about marriage was written by Harry Bennett circa 1877 first appearing in Harry Woodson's "Gwine Back To Dixie Songster" published in 1877.

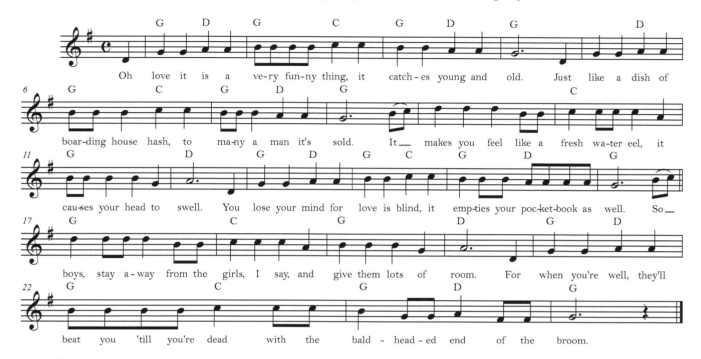

Oh love it is a very funny thing

It catches young and old.

Just like a dish of boardinghouse hash

To many a man it's sold

It makes you feel like a fresh water eel

Causes your head to swell

You'll lose your mind for love is blind

It empties your pocket book as well.

So boys, stay away from the girls I say

And give them lots of room.

For when you're wed

They'll beat you 'till you're dead

With the baldheaded end of a broom.

When a man is going out with pretty little girl
His love is firm and strong.
But when he has to feed them on hash
His love won't last so long.

With a wife and seven half starved kids
Boys I'll tell you it is no fun
When the butcher comes around to collect his debts
With a dog and a double barreled gun.

When your money is gone and your clothing in hock
You'll find the old saying it is true
That a mole on the arm's worth two on the legs
But what is he going to do.

Band Played On, The

Old-time Song by Charles B. Ward, with lyrics by John F. Palmer; **DATE:** 1895**; RECORDING INFO**: Dan Quinn in 1895; Tony Pastor; Gary Lombardo; **NOTES:** This popular song was dedicated to a newspaper, the New York Sunday World, a publicity-minded stunt common in the late 1800's. "The Band Played On' was popularized by a variety of artist and vaudeville inventor Tony Pastor. Many prominent singers performed this sentimental favorite over the years, and it inspried the 1936 Warner Brothers film "The Strawberry Blond" starring James Cagney. This is the lyric as it appears is the 1895 sheet music edition published by the New York Music Company. The verses are in cut time, but the refrain is a ¾ waltz.

Matt Ca-sey formed a so-cial club that beat the town for style, and hire-d for a meet-ing place a hall._____ When pay day came a-round each week they greased the floor with wax And danced with noise and vig-or at the ball._____ Each Sat-ur-day you'd see them dressed up in Sun-day .clothes. Each lad would have his sweet-heart by his side._____ When Ca-sey had the first grand march they all would fall in line be-hind the man who was their joy and pride._____ For_____ Ca-sey would waltz with a straw-ber-ry blonde, and the band played on_____ He'd glide 'cross the floor with the girl he a-dor'ed and the band played on_____ But his brain was so load-ed it near-ly ex-lod-ed the poor girl would shake with a-larm._____

59

He'd ne'er leave the girl with the straw-ber-ry curls and the band played on. ____

VERSE: Matt Casey formed a social club (G)

That beat the town for style, (Am)

And hired for a meeting place a hall. (D) (G)

When pay day came around each week

They greased the floor with wax. (Am)

And danced with noise and vigor at the ball. (D) (G)

Each Saturday you'd see them (Em) (Am)

Dressed up in Sunday clothes, (D) (Em)

Each lad would have his sweetheart by his side. (D)

When Casey led the first grand march (G)

They all would fall in line. (Am)

Behind the man who was their joy and pride. For... (D) (G)

CHORUS: Casey would waltz with a strawberry blond, (G)

And the band played on. (D7)

He'd glide 'cross the floor with the girl he adored,

And the band played on. (G)

But his brain was so loaded it nearly exploded,

The poor girl would shake with alarm (D) (G7) (C)

He'd ne'er leave the girl with the strawberry curls, (Am) (C#Dim) (G) (Em)

And the band played on. (A7) (D) (G)

VERSE 2: Such kissing in the corner
And such whisp'ring in the hall,
And telling tales of love behind the stairs.
As Casey was the favorite and he that ran the ball,
Of kissing and lovemaking did his share,
At twelve o'clock exactly they all would fall in line,
Then march down to the dining hall to eat.
But Casey would not join them
        although everything was fine,
But he stayed upstairs and exercised his feet. For...

VERSE 3: Now when the dance was over
        and the band played home sweet home,
They played a tune at Casey's own request.
He thank'd them very kindly
        for the favors they had shown,
Then he'd waltz once with
        the girl that he loved best.
Most all the friends are married
        that Casey used to know,
And Casey too has taken him a wife.
The blond he used to waltz and glide
        with on the ballroom floor,
Is happy misses Casey now for life. For...

27

Banjo Pickin' Girl/Going 'Round this World, Baby Mine

Old-time Bluegrass song, widely known; **DATE:** First Published as "Baby Mine" Words Charles Mackay; Music Achibald Johnson in 1874; **RECORDING INFO:** Lily May Ledford (Coon Creek Girls); Hazel Dickens and Alice Gerrard; Skirtlifters; Pete Steele; **RELATED TO:** Crawdad (Sugar Babe); New River Train; I'm Going Back to Jordan; Mole in the Ground; **OTHER NAMES:** B aby Mine; Going Round the World Baby Mine; Banjo Pickin' Girl; Going Round This World; Living on the Mountain Baby Mine; Going Away From Home; **NOTES:** The song, Banjo Pickin' Girl originated from a 1847 popular song Baby Mine with words by Charles Mackay and music by Achibald Johnson. The song form used is similar to the Captain Kidd/Froggy Went A-Courtin' family of songs. There are several bluegrass/folk songs that have evolved from Baby Mine with the "baby mine" tag: Banjo-Pickin' Girl and Crawdad Song. The Coon Creek Girls, who popularized the song, were organized around Lily May Ledford of Powell County, Kentucky, in the mid-1930's. Between 1937 and 1939 the quartet (the fourth member was Daisy Lagne, fiddler) was very popular on the Renfro Vally Barn Dance radio program, broadcasting out of Cincinnati. The career of this foursome culminated in a June 1939 performance (they were the only professional country group to be invited) at the White House for President and Mrs. Franklin D. Roosevelt and their guests, King George VI and Queen Elizabeth.

Oh, I'm going 'round the world, baby mine (baby mine),
      G

I'm going 'round the world, baby mine;
  C   **G**

I'm going 'round this world, I'll be a banjo-pickin' girl,
  C   **G** **Em**

I'm going 'round this world, baby mine.
G   **D**   **G**

Oh, I'm going to Tennessee, baby mine (baby mine),
I'm going to Tennessee, baby mine;
I'm going (to) Tennessee, don't you try to foller me,
I'm going (to) Tennessee, baby mine.

Oh, I'm going to Arkansas, baby mine (baby mine),
Oh, I'm going to Arkansas, baby mine;
I'm going to Arkansas, you stay here with maw and paw,
I'm going to Arkansas, baby mine.

Oh, I'm going 'cross the ocean, baby mine (baby mine),
I'm going 'cross the ocean, baby mine;
I'm going 'cross the ocean if I don't change my notion,
I'm going 'cross the ocean, baby mine.

Banks of the Ohio

Traditional Folk Song; **DATE**: First appears around 1913; **CATEGORY**: Early Country; **RECORDING INFO**: Monroe Brothers; Blue Sky Boys; Country Gentlemen; Tony Rice; Joan Baez; Doc Watson; **NOTES**: Was a hit for Blue Sky Boys in 1933.

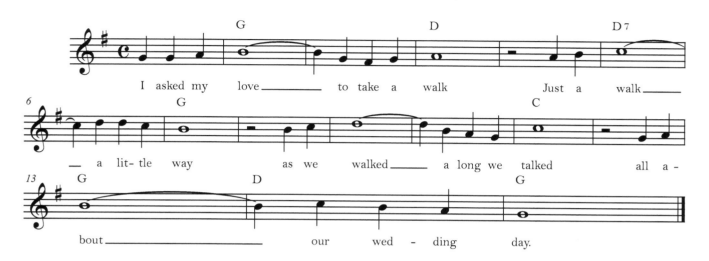

I asked my love ___ to take a walk   Just a walk ___

___ a lit- tle way   as we walked ___ a long we talked   all a-

bout ___   our wed - ding day.

I asked my love to take a walk
       G   D
Just a walk a little way
     D7   G
As we walked along we talked
                C
All about our wedding day.
    G   D   G

And only say that you'll be mine
And our home will happy be
Down beside, where the waters flow
Down on the banks of the Ohio.

I held a knife close to her breast
As into my arms she pressed
She cried, "Oh, Willie, don't murder me,
I'm not prepared for eternity."

I took her by her lily white hand
Led her down where the waters stand
There I pushed her in to drown
And watched her as she floated down.

I started home tween twelve and one
I cried, "My God, what have I done."
I murdered the only woman I loved
Because she would not be my bride.

The very next morning about half-past four
The sheriff came knocking at my door
He said, "Young man, come with me and go
Down to the banks of the Ohio."

Barbara Allen

Traditional Appalachian Folksong, Scottish origin; **DATE:** 1666; **RECORDING INFO:** Everly Brothers; Dolly Parton; Art Garfunkel; Joan Baez; Burl Ives; The King's Singers; Jean Redpath; Mac Wiseman; Vernon Dalhart and The New Lost City Ramblers; **OTHER NAMES:** Barbary/Barbra Allen/Ellen; **NOTES**: The song was first mentioned by Samuel Pepys in 1666. Printed version appears in the McFarlane MS., 1740, in drawing room stle. Bertran Bronson's "Traditional Tunes of the Child Ballads" gives nearly two hundred tunes for the song. Sung by ballad singers, this song has a firm place in bluegrass and country music having been recorded by Dolly Parton, Max Wiseman, The Hillmen and Glen Neaves.

All in the mer-cy month of May, when flow-ers were a-bloom-in', sweet
Will-iam on his death-bed lay, for love of Bar-bara Alen.

D
All in the merry month of may

             A
When flowers were a-bloomin'
     G   D
Sweet William on his deathbed lay
A   D
For love of Barbara Allen.

He sent his servant to the town,
To the place where she was dwellin',
Saying, "Master dear has sent me here
If your name be Barbara Allen."

Then slowly, slowly she got up,
And slowly went she nigh him,
And all she said when she got there,
"Young men, I think you're dyin'."

He turned his face unto the wall
And death was with him dealin',
"Adieu, adieu, my dear friends all;
Be kind to Barbara Allen."

She looked to the east, she look to the west,
She saw his corpse a-comin';
"O set him down for me," she cried,
"That I might gaze upon him."

"O mother, go, and make my bed;
O make it long and narrow;
Sweet William did for me this day,
And I shall die tomorrow."

They buried Willie in the old church yard;
They buried Barbara by him.
From his grave grew a red, red rose,
And out of hers a briar.

They grew and grew in the old church yard
Till they could grow no higher.
And there thy formed a true love knot,
The red rose and the briar.

Battleship of Maine

Old-time Song; **DATE:** 1927; **RECORDING INFO:** Red Patterson's Piedmont Log Rollers; New Lost City Ramblers; **NOTES:** Categorized by Meade as Bloody War, it was recorded as That Crazy War by Lula Belle and Scotty.

McKinley called for volunteers, (C)

I went and got my gun,

First Spaniard I saw coming, (F)

I dropped my gun and run, (C)

It was all about that Battleship of Maine. (G ... C)

CHORUS: At war with that great nation Spain (C)

When I get back to Spain I want to honor my name,

It was all about that Battleship of Maine. (G ... C)

What are you running,
Are you afraid to die?
The reason that I'm running
Is because I cannot fly
It was all about that Battleship of Maine.

The blood was a-running
And I was running too,
I give my feet good exercise
I had nothing else to do,
It was all about that Battleship of Maine.

When they were a-chasing me,
I fell down on my knees,
First thing I cast my eyes upon
Was a great big pot of pea,
It was all about that Battleship of Maine

The peas they were greasy,
The rest it was fat.
The boys was fighting that,
While I was fighting that,
It was all about that Battleship of Maine.

31

Beautiful Dreamer

Old-time Song by Stephen Foster; **DATE:** 1864; **RECORDING INFO:** Bing Crosby with John Scott Trotter & his Orchestra; **NOTES:** "Beautiful Dreamer" is a popular American song, with words and music written by Stephen Collin Foster in 1864. Foster wrote the song near the end of his life and it was published after his death.

C   Dm
Beautiful dreamer, wake unto me,

G7   C
Starlight and dewdrops are waiting for thee.

          Dm
Sounds of the rude world heard in the day,

G7   C
Lulled by the moonlight have all passed away.

G7   C
Beautiful dreamer, queen of my song,

Am   D7 G7
List while I woo thee with soft melody.

C   Dm
Gone are the cares of life's busy throng,

G7   C E7 Am
Beautiful dreamer awake unto me.

F   C G7   C
Beautiful dreamer, awake unto me.

Beautiful dreamer, out on the sea,
Mermaids are chaunting the wild lorelie.
Over the streamlet vapors are home,
Waiting to fade at the bright coming morn.

Beautiful dreamer, bean of my heart,
E'en as the morn on the streamlet and see.
Then will the clouds of sorrow depart.
Beautiful dreamer awake unto me.
Beautiful dreamer, awake unto me.

Been to the East, Been to the West

Old-Time, Breakdown. Traditional music and words; **DATE:** 1927-1928; **RECORDING INFO:** Lesk County Revelers 1928; Dave Winston; Bubba Hutch; **OTHER NAMES:** "Great Big Yam Potatoes.: A similar tune is "Going to Chattanooga," in the 'A' part; **NOTES:** The song appears as Breack-Eyed Susianna (sic) by the Nightingale Serenaders around 1846. It is traditional fiddle and clawhammer banjo tune, the high strain is similar to "Shoot That Turkey Buzzard."

Been to the east and_ been to the west. Been to Al - a - bam - a.

    G
Been to the east and been to the west

    D   G
Been to Alabama.

I'm gonna get me something for to eat
Gonna 'light on the Yellowhammer.

Prettiest little girl I ever did see
Lives in Alabama.

Wanna know her name, I'll tell you what it would be
Her name is Susiana.

Been to the east and been to the west
Been to Alabama.

Prettiest little girl I ever did see
Lives in Alabama.

Big Rock Candy Mountain

Old-time Country Song, Marshall Locke words and music; **DATE:** 1906; **RECORDING INFO:** Harry McClintock, 1928; Frank Luther, 1928; Vernon Dalhart; **NOTES:** Harry McClintock accompanied Borothy Ellen Cole by recorded "The Big Rock Candy Mountain" for Victor on Sept. 6, 1928. According to Meade, the song, words and music, is attributed to Marshall P. Locke, 1906. The song is probably best remembered for its inclusion in the "O Brother Where Art Thou" movie and soundtrack but was a hit for Burl Ives in 1949, but it has been recorded by many artists throughout the world. Another popular version, recorded in 1960 by Dorsey Burnette, reached the Billboard top ten. In an interview with Sam Eskin, folklorist, on a Folkways LP, McClintock tells how and when he wrote Big Rock Candy Mountain. According to Haywire Mac, he composed the song when he was a brakeman on the Denver & Rio Grande Railroad, which parallels the Sevier River across the road from Big Rock Candy Mountain Resort. He sings the song on that Folkways recording but says that the original he'd first written was pretty "adult." Sterilized versions have been popular, especially with children's musicians; in these, the "cigarette trees" become peppermint trees, and the "streams of alcohol" trickling down the rocks become streams of lemonade. The lake of gin is not mentioned and the lake of whiskey becomes a lake of soda pop.

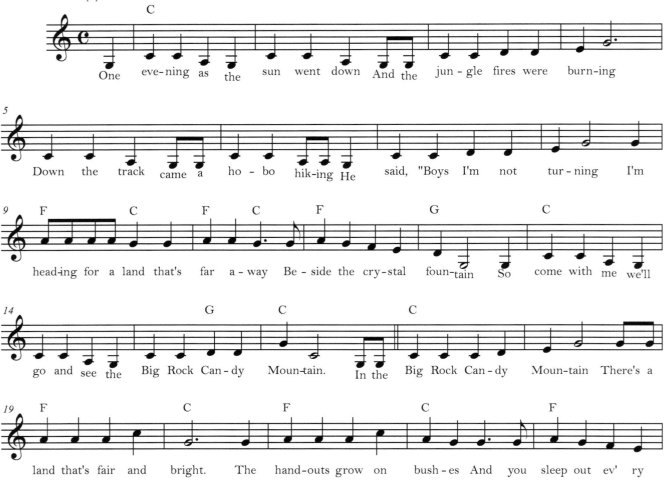

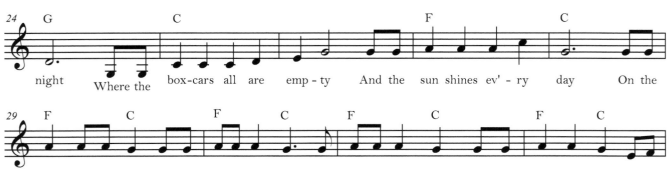

     Big   Rock   Can -   -   dy   Moun -   tain.

C
One evening as the sun went down And the jungle fires were burning,

Down the track came a hobo hiking, He said, "Boys, I'm not turning

    F   C   F   C   F   G
I'm heading for a land that's far away Beside the crystal fountain

        C   G   C
So come with me we'll go and see The Big Rock Candy Mountain"

                   C   F   C
CHORUS: In the Big Rock Candy Mountain, There's a land that's fair and bright,

     F   C   F   G
The handouts grow on bushes And you sleep out every night,

        C   F   C
Where the boxcars all are empty And the sun shines every day

   F   C   F   C   F   C   F   C
On birds and the bees and the cigarette trees, The lemonade springs where the bluebird sings

        G   C
In the Big Rock Candy Mountain.

In the Big Rock Candy Mountain All the cops have wooden legs
And the bulldogs all have rubber teeth And the hens lay soft-boiled eggs
The farmer's tree are full of fruit And the barns are full of hay.
Oh I'm bound to go where there ain't no snow Where there ain't no fog, and the winds don't blow
In the Big Rock Candy Mountain.

In the Big Rock Candy Mountain You never change your socks
And the little streams of alcohol Come a-trickling down the rocks
Oh the brakemen have to tip their hats And the railway bulls are blind
There's a lake of stew and whiskey too You can paddle all around 'em in a big canoe
In the Big Rock Candy Mountain.

In the Big Rock Candy Mountain The jails are made of tin
You can walk right out again As soon as you are in
There ain't no short-handled shovels No axes, saws or picks
I'm bound to stay where you sleep all day Where they hung the jerk that invented work
In the Big Rock Candy Mountain.

Bile Them Cabbage Down

Traditional Old-Time, Breakdown: **DATE:** Early 1900's; **CATEGORY:** Fiddle and Instrumental Tune; **RECORDING INFO:** Charlie Monroe and the Kentucky Pardners; Gid Tanner and the Skillet Lickers; Flatt & Scruggs; **OTHER NAMES**: Boil Them Cabbage Down; Bake Them Hoecakes Brown; Raccoon and the Possum; **NOTES:** On Bluegrass Messengers' CD "Bluegrass Boogie."

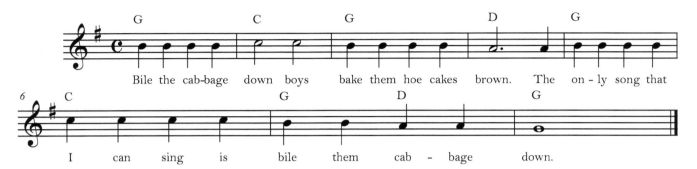

G   C
Raccoon has a bushy tail

G   D
Possum's tail is bare

G   C
Rabbit's got no tail at all

G D G
But a little bunch of hair.

CHORUS: Bile them cabbage down boys
Bake them hoe cakes brown.
The only song I can sing is
Bile them cabbage down.

Raccoon and the possum
Coming cross the prairie
Raccoon said to the possum
Did she want to marry. CHORUS

Raccoon up a 'simmon tree
Possum on the ground
Possum say to the raccoon
"Won't you shake them 'simmons down?" CHORUS

Jaybird died with the whooping cough
Sparrow died with the colic
Along came the frog with a fiddle on his back
Inquiring his way to the frolic. CHORUS

Bill Bailey, Won't You Please Come Home?

American Song Tune by Hughie Cannon, DATE: Published in 1902; **CATEGORY:** Tin-Pan Alley and Jazz Song; **RECORDING INFO:** Louis Armstrong; Ella Fitzgerald; Big Bill Broonzy; Buddy Pendleton; Weavers; Johnny Whisnant; **NOTES:** This song was an instant hit when first introduced by John Queen, a minstrel. Often recorded and often associated with the great Louis Armstrong, Bobby Dain's version was a million seller. Most bluegrass groups play chorus only,

CHORUS: Won't you come home, Bill Bailey, Won't you come home?

She moans the whole day long.

I'll do the cookin', darling, I'll pay the rent,

I know I've done you wrong;

'Member that rainy evening that

I threw you out, With nothing but a fine-tooth comb?

I know I'm to blame, Well, ain't that a shame

Billy Bailey won't you please come home.

Billy Boy

Traditional English Ballad; US version; **DATE:** 1776 (Heard, according to Opie-Oxford2); **OTHER NAMES:** Willie Boy; **RECORDING INFO:** Frank Crummit 1925; Bradley Kincaid; Frank Luther; **NOTES:** The tune is from 18th century England and was eiginally called Willie Lad and Charming William. It is a variant of Lord Randall. The lyrics are typical of those found and recorded in the US.

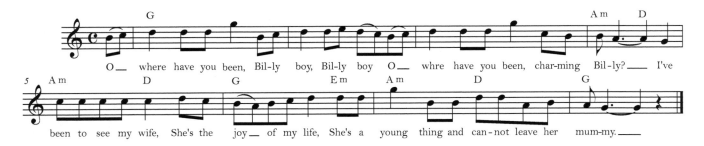

O_ where have you been, Bil-ly boy, Bil-ly boy O_ whre have you been, char-ming Bil-ly?___ I've been to see my wife, She's the joy_ of my life, She's a young thing and can-not leave her mum-my.___

O, where have you been, Billy Boy, Billy Boy? *(G)*

O, where have you been, Charming Billy? *(Am D)*

I have been to seek a wife, She's the joy of my life. *(Am D G)*

She's a young thing, And cannot leave her mummy. *(Em, Am D G)*

Where does she live, Billy Boy, Billy Boy?
O, where does she live? Charming Billy?
She lives on the hill, Forty miles from the mill.
She's a young thing, And cannot leave her mummy.

Did she bid you to come in, Billy Boy, Billy Boy?
Did she bid you to come in, Charming Billy?
Yes, she bade me to come in, And to kiss her on the chin.
She's a young thing, And cannot leave her mummy.

Did she set for you a chair, Billy Boy, Billy Boy?
Did she set for you a chair, Charming Billy?
Yes she set for me a chair, But the bottom wasn't there.
She's a young thing, And cannot leave her mummy.

Can she bake a cherry pie, Billy Boy, Billy Boy?
Can she bake a cherry pie, Charming Billy?
She can bake a cherry pie, Quick's a cat can wink her eye.
She's a young thing, And cannot leave her mummy.

Billy Grimes

American Ballad and old-time song; Words by Richard Coe; Music by W.H. Oakley 1850; **RECORDING INFO**: Shelor Family 1927; New Lost City Ramblers; **OTHER NAMES**: Billy Grimes; the Drover; **NOTES**: There were three published account of this song in the 1850's with N.C. Morse claiming authorship with his version in 1852. The original title was Billy Grimes the Drover. This version is from English Folk Songs in the Southern Appalachian by Cecil Sharp. Collected from Mrs. Margaret Jack Dodd, VA in 1918.

To-mor-row morn-ing I'm sweet six-teen and Bil-ly Grimes, a dro-ver, has popped the ques-tion to me, ma, and wants to be my lo-ver.

G
Tomorrow morning I'm sweet sixteen

D   G
And Billy Grimes, a drover,

Has popped the question to me, ma,

D   G
And wants to be my lover.

He says he's coming here, mama,
Tomorrow morning quite early.
To take a pleasant walk with me
Across the field of barley.

You must not go, my daughter dear,
It's no use now in talking.
You must not go across the field
With Billy Grimes a-walking.

To think of his presumption too,
The ugly, dirty drover.
I wonder where your pride has gone
To think of such a lover.

Old Grimes is dead, you know, mama,
And Billy he's so lonely.
Besides of Grime's whole estate
Billy is the owner.

Surviving heir to all that's left,
That they say is nearly
A good ten thousand dollars, mama,
About six thousand yearly.

I did not hear, my daughter dear,
Your last remark quite clearly,
But Billy he's a clever lad,
And no doubt loves you dearly.

Remember then tomorrow morn
To be up bright and early
To take a pleasant walk with him
Across the field of barley.

Bird in a Cage

Traditional Appalachian song; **DATE**: Early 1900's; 1934 Lomax; **RECORDING INFO**: Terry Duggins and the Zither Band; Jean Ritchie; **NOTES:** The lyrics are first found in the Brown collection and later in a Kentucky version collected by Lomax in 1934 (American Ballads and Folk Songs). The song lyrics are closely related to the Down In the Valley/Birmingham Jail songs.

C
Bird in a cage, love

Am
Bird in a cage,

C
Begging for freedom,

Am   C   G   C
Dying a slave, dying a slave.

High on the mountain,
Valley so low;
All you can feel, dear,
Is the cold rain and snow, cold rain and snow.

Turn your back on me,
Court whom you please;
I can't forget you,
Darlin', I can't get free, I can't get free.

Build up your walls, Love,
Build them so high.
Only let me see you,
Darlin', as you pass by, as you pass by.

Bird In a Gilded Cage, A

Old-time and Tin Pan Alley song by Arthur J. Lamb and Harry Von Tilzer; **DATE:** 1900; **OTHER NAMES:** She's only a Bird in a Gilded Cage; **RECORDING INFO:** North Carolina Ramblers 1927; Arthur Fields; Shirley Temple; Rutherford and Foster; **NOTES:** One of the most popular songs by Lamb and Von Tilzer from 1900.

The ballroom was filed with fashion's throng,

It shone with a thousand lights;

And there was a woman who passed along,

The fairest of all the sights.

A girl to her lover then softly sighed,

"There's riches at her command."

"But she married for wealth, not for love," he cried! "Though she lives in a mansion grand."

CHORUS: She's only a bird in a gilded cage, A beautiful sight to see.

You may think she's happy and free from care, She's not, though she seems to be.

'Tis sad when you think of her wasted life For youth cannot mate with age;

And her beauty was sold for an old man's gold, She's a bird in a gilded cage.

I stood in a churchyard just at eve,
When sunset adorned the west;
And looked at the people who'd come to grieve
For loved ones now laid at rest.
A tall marble monument marked the grave
Of one who'd been fashion's queen;
And I thought, "She is happier here at rest,
Than to have people say when seen:"

Black Dog Blues

Old-time Song and Blues; **DATE:** Early 1900's; **RECORDING INFO:** Dick Justice 1929 (Old Black Dog); Bayless Rose 1930; Stoneman Family; **NOTES:** Black Dog Blues is a white blues that is closely aligned to Don't Let Your Deal Go Down, Salty Dog (chords) and Honey Where You Been So Long (Tempy)? I learned it as a bluegrass breakdown starting on Em and going through the cycle Em/A/ D7/G etc.

CHORUS: You call me your dog when I'm gone, honey babe,

Yes it's black dog when I'm gone.

When I come back with a hundred dollar bill,

It's "Honey where you been so long?"

I've been all around Kentucky,
The state of old Tennessee.
Any old place I hang my hat,
It's home sweet home to me. CHORUS:

My daddy learned me how to gamble,
Told me play that deuce, ace and trey,
Every time when that deal would go down,
I would leave on that deuce, ace and trey. CHORUS:

I shot my dice in Cuba,
Played my cards in Spain,
When I get ready to leave this town,
I'm gonna ride that fast mail train. CHORUS:

Boatman Dance

Old-time song; Widely known. Words and music attributed to Daniel Decatur Emmett, 1815-1904, Leader of the Virginia Minstrels; **DATE:** 1839 tune; 1843 song; **RECORDING INFO:** Cole and Byrd 1930; Elizabeth Cotton; Arkansas Sheiks; Hollow Rock String Band; Mike Seeger; **OTHER NAMES:** Boatman; Boatman; Dance, Come Love Come; Sailing Down the River on the O-hi-o; Ohio River; **RELATED TO:** Little Rabbit; Johnny Booger; Old Aunt Adkin; **NOTES:** Emmett published the song in 1843, advertising it as "An Original Banjo Melody." The tune appears in many American and even English songsters of the 19th and early 20th centuries. The tune was in print (as "Ohio River") in George P Knaudf's Virginia Reels, volume IV (Baltimore, 1839) associated with Ohio River boatmen, before it was played on the minstrel stage. "Little Rabbit" is a related old-time version. The lyrics have been slight changed from Emmett's original.

The $\overset{G}{\text{boatman}}$ $\overset{D}{\text{dance}}$, the $\overset{G}{\text{boatman}}$ $\overset{D}{\text{sing}}$

The $\overset{G}{\text{boatman}}$ $\overset{D}{\text{do}}$ most $\overset{A}{\text{any}}\overset{D}{\text{thing}}$.

And $\overset{G}{\text{when}}$ the $\overset{D}{\text{boatman}}$ $\overset{G}{\text{get}}$ on $\overset{D}{\text{shore}}$,

He $\overset{G}{\text{spends}}$ his $\overset{D}{\text{money}}$, and he $\overset{A}{\text{works}}$ for $\overset{D}{\text{more}}$.

CHORUS: $\overset{D}{\text{Dance}}$, boatman dance! Dance, $\overset{A7}{\text{boat}}$man $\overset{D}{\text{dance}}$.

O Dance all $\overset{A7}{\text{night}}$ till $\overset{D}{\text{broad}}$ daylight

And go home with the $\overset{A7}{\text{gals}}$ in $\overset{D}{\text{de}}$ morning.

$\overset{D}{\text{Hi}}$, ho, the $\overset{G}{\text{boat}}$man $\overset{D}{\text{row}}$, sailin' on the river on the $\overset{A}{\text{Oh}}\overset{D}{\text{io}}$!

$\overset{D}{\text{Hi}}$, ho, the $\overset{G}{\text{boat}}$man $\overset{D}{\text{row}}$, sailin' on the river on the $\overset{A}{\text{Oh}}\overset{D}{\text{io}}$!

I've never seen a pretty girl in my life
But that she'd be some boatman's wife.
When the boatman blows his horn,
Look out, old man, your daughter's gone; CHORUS:

When you go to the boatman's ball,
Dance with my wife or not at all;
Sky-blue jacket and tarpaulin hat,
Look out, my boys, for the nine tail cat. CHORUS:

Bringing in the Sheaves

Old-time Gospel song Rev. Knowles Shaw (1834-1878) words and George Minor music; **DATE:** 1874; **RECORDING INFO:** Eva Quartette 1927; Earl Johnson and his Dixie Entertainers; **OTHER NAMES:** Sowing and Reaping; **NOTES:** Based on Psalm 126: 6, translated in the King James version as "He that goeth forth and weepeth, bearing precious seed, shall doubtless come again with rejoicing, bringing his sheaves with him."

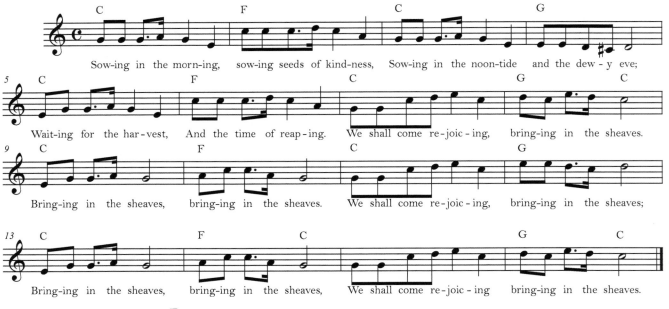

       C   F
Sowing in the morning, sowing seeds of kindness

   C   G
Sowing in the noontide and the dewy eve

   C   F
Waiting for the harvest and the time of reaping

   C   G   C
We shall come rejoicing, bringing in the sheaves

                C   F   C
CHORUS: Bringing in the sheaves, bringing in the sheaves

   C   G
We shall come rejoicing, bringing in the sheaves

   C   F   C
Bringing in the sheaves, bringing in the sheaves

   C   G   C
We shall come rejoicing bringing in the sheaves.

Sowing in the sunshine, sowing in the shadows
Fearing neither clouds nor winter's chilling breeze
By and by the harvest and the labored end
We shall come rejoicing bring in the sheaves

Going forth with weeping, sowing for the master
Tho' the loss sustains our spirit often grieves
When our weeping's over, He will bid us welcome
We shall come rejoicing, bringing in the sheaves

44

Buffalo Gals

Old-time song widely disseminated both in the US and Internationally. Traditional Tune and lyrics "composed" by Cool White; **DATE:** 1844. Used in the 1850's at minstrel shows; **OTHER NAMES:** Alabama Gals; (The name can be changed to any city's name, and was used as New York Gals, etc.; Buffalo Girls; Roundtown Girls/Gals; Won't You Come Out Tonight; I Danced with the Girl with the Hole in Her Stocking; **RELATED MELODY:** Bear Creek Hop; **RECORDING INFO:** Bruce Springsteen; Woody Guthrie; Clark Kessinger; Ernest Stoneman; Fields and Wade Ward; **NORES:** The name Buffalo for the New York town derives from the name of a Native American and was first called Buffalo Creek, becoming simply Buffalo as the town grew. The tune is widespread in American tradition and as Samuel Bayard (1944) points out, the song is widely disseminated and is now an "international melody."

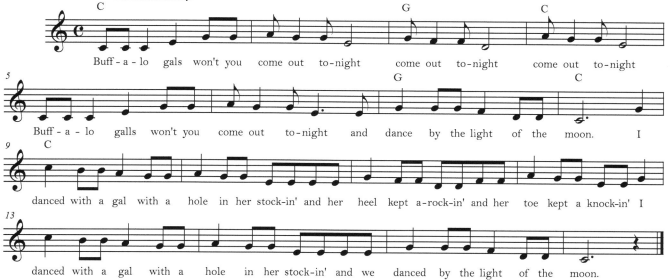

Buff-a-lo gals won't you come out to-night come out to-night come out to-night
Buff-a-lo galls won't you come out to-night and dance by the light of the moon. I
danced with a gal with a hole in her stock-in' and her heel kept a-rock-in' and her toe kept a knock-in' I
danced with a gal with a hole in her stock-in' and we danced by the light of the moon.

C   G
Buffalo gals, won't you come out tonight,

C
Come out tonight, come out tonight?

Buffalo gals, won't you come out tonight,

       G   C
And dance by the light of the moon?

    C
I danced with a gal with a hole in her stockin'
And her heel kept a-rockin' and her toe kept a-knockin'
I danced with a gal with a hole in her stockin',
And we danced by the light of the moon.

As I was walking down the street, Down the street, down the street,
A pretty girl I chanced to meet, Under the silvery moon.

I asked her if she'd stop and talk, Stop and talk, stop and talk,
Her feet covered up the whole sidewalk, She was fair to view.

I asked her if she'd stop and dance, Have a dance, care to dance
I thought that I might get a chance, to shake a foot with her.

I asked her if she'd be my wife, She'd be my wife, she'd be my wife,
Then I'd be happy all my life, If she'd marry me.

Camptown Races

American Old-time song; Words and Music by Stephen Foster; **DATE:** 1850; **RECORDING INFO:** Kanashaw Singers 1929; Pete Seeger; Chet Atkins; John Farley; **OTHER NAMES:** Hoodah Day; Banks of Sacramento; Gwine to Run All Night; Sacramento; Lincoln Hoss and Stephen A; Ho! For Californ-I-O; Bobtail Hoss/Horse; **NOTES:** The melody was collected as a sea shanty called "Banks of Sacramento," whose origins were in the California Gold Rush of 1849. This seems to predate the Stephen Foster copyright, but the relation between the two is unclear. Spaeth in a History of Popular Music in America, p. 107 notes that a "folk-song" called "Hoodah Day" is very similar to this song, and speculates that it or "Banks of Sacramento" could have been the original of the Foster song.

De Camptown ladies sing dis song, Doo-da, Doo-da. / De Camptown race-track two miles long, O de doo-da day. / Gwine to run all night; Gwine to run all day. / I bet my mo-ney on a bob-tailed nag, Some-bo-dy bet on the gray.

De Camptown ladies sing dis song, Doo-da, Doo-da.
(C)   (G)

De Camptown racetrack two miles long, O de doo-da day.
(C)   (G)   (C)

I come down dah wid my hat caved in, Doo-da, Doo-da.
(C)   (G)

I go back home wid a pocket full of tin, O de doo-da day.
(C)   (G)   (C)

CHORUS: Gwine to run all night, Gwine to run all day.
               (C)   (F)

I'll bet my money on de bobtail nag, Somebody bet on de gray.
                               (G)   (C)

De long tail filly and de big black hoss, Doo-da, Doo-da.
De fly de track and dey both cut across, O de doo-da day.
De blind hoss sticken in a big mud hole, Doo-da, Doo-da.
Can't tough bottom wid a ten foot pole, O de doo-da day! CHORUS:

Old muley cow come on to de track, Doo-da, Doo-da.
De bob-tail fling her ober his back, O de doo-da day.
Den fly along like a rail-road car, Doo-da, Doo-da.
Runnin' a race wid a shootin' star, O de doo-da day. CHORUS:

See dem flyin' on a ten mile heat, Doo-da, Doo-da.
Round de race track, den repeat, O de doo-da day.
I win my money on de bob-tail nag, Doo-da, Doo-da.
I keep my money in an old tow-bag, O de doo-da day. CHORUS:

Cannonball Blues/Solid Gone

Old-time song and Blues; **DATE:** Early 1900's; **OTHER NAMES:** The Cannonball; Solid Gone; Hobo Blues; **RECORDING INFO:** Carter Family 1924; Seldom Scene; Jean Ritchie and Doc Watson; Flatt and Scruggs; Furry Lewis; Tom Rush; **NOTES:** Recorded by the Carter Family on May 20th 1924. They had heard the song performed by an itinerant singer/guitarist Lesley Riddle, who played it fingerstyle (now called Travis picking). The song is closely related to White House Blues and has evolved with a chorus was added to the instrumental part.

Oh listen to the train coming down the line (C)

Trying to make up all their lost time (F) (C)

From Buffalo to Washington. (G) (C)

CHORUS:

Now I'm down here crying cause she's gone (F) (C)

Feel like I'm dying cause she's gone (F) (C)

She's solid gone. (G) (C)

You can wash my jumper, starch my overalls
Catch a train they call Cannonball
From Buffalo to Washington

My baby's left me he even took my shoes
Enough t give a man these
          dog gone worried blues
She's gone, she's solid gone.

Yonder comes the train coming down the track
Carrying my away but it ain't gonna carry m back
My honey babe, my blue eyed babe.

I'm going up north, I'm going up north this fall
If luck don't change, I won't be back at all.
My honey babe I'm leaving you.

47

Careless Love

Traditional Old-time Song; **DATE:** Early 1900's; **RECORDING INFO:** Boyd Moore 1930; Dock Boggy; Riley Puckett; Bill Monroe; Joan Baez; Big Bill Broonzy; Flatt & Scruggs with Doc Watson; Brownie McGhee; **CATEGORY:** Early Country & Bluegrass; **NOTES:** This is an early white and black "blues" hat has become a bluegrass standard. This version is the "male" lyrics.

Love, oh love, oh care-less love._____ Love, oh love, oh care-less love._____ Love, oh love, oh care - less love. See what care - less love has done to me._____

G   D   G
Love, oh love, oh careless love

                            D
Love, oh love, oh careless love

G   C
Love, oh love, oh careless love

          G   D   G
See what careless love has done to me.

How I wish that train would come
How I wish that train would come
How I wish that train would come
And take me back where I came from.

Sorrow, sorrow to my heart,
Sorrow, sorrow to my heart,
Sorrow, sorrow to my heart,
Since I and my true love did part.

Casey Jones

Old-time Song; Original text by Wallace Sanders; "Official" text copyrighted 1909 by Newton & Siebert; **DATE:** Early 1900's' **OTHER NAMES:** Jimmy Jones; Kasie Jones (Blues by Furry Lewis); **RELATED TO:** Steamboat Bill (tune); The Big Combine (tune); Peggy Howatt (tune); Old Zeke Perkins; **RECORDING INFO:** Wilmer Watts & the Lonely Eagles; Vernon Dalhart; Elizabeth Cotton; Furry Lewis; J.E. Mainer; **NOTES:** On April 30, 1900 railroad engineer John Luther "Casey" Jones, of the Illinois Central Railroad, died in a train crash near Vaughan, Mississippi. A most well-known and respected driver, he was driving No. 382, possibly for a sick friend. The switching station at Vaughan did not have enough room to accommodate the length of trains there. Flagmen were sent to warn Jones, but for unknown reasons, he was unaware of the problem until it was too late. Jones was killed in the accident. He left a wife and three children. The first Casey Jones ballad was written by Wallace Saunders, Casey's African-American engine wiper. It was sung to the tune Jimmy Jones, which was popular at the time. Engineer William Leighton heard the song. His brothers Frank and Bert, Vaudeville performers, polished the song, added a chorus, and began to perform it in their act. When the ballad was published in 1902 the words were credited to T. Lawrence Siebert, and Eddie Newton was credited with the music.

Come __ all you roun-ers that __ want to hear the sto-ry __ of a brave __ en-gin-eer, Ca-sey Jones was the round-ers name, __ On a six eight wheel-er boys he won his fame. Ca-sey Jones mount-ed to his ca-bin, Ca-sey Jones with his or-ders in his hand, Ca-sey Jones mount-ed to his cab-in and he took his fare-well trip __ to that prom-ised land.

C
Come all you rounders that want to hear

      D   G
The story of a brave engineer.

C
Casey Jones was the rounder's name,

                      G   C
On a six eight wheeler, boys, he won his fame.

               C
CHORUS: Casey Jones mounted to his cabin,

                          G
Casey Jones with his orders in his hand.

C
Casey Jones mounted to his cabin,

                              G   C
And he took his farewell trip to that promised land.

The caller call Casey at half past four,
He kissed his wife at the station door,
He mounted to the cabin with the orders in his hand,
And he took his farewell trip to that promised land.

When he pulled up that Reno bill,
He whistled for the crossing with an awful shrill.
The switchman knew by the engine's moan,
That the man at the throttle was Casey Jones.

He looked at his water and his water was low,
He looked at his watch and his watch was slow,
He turned to his fireman and this is what he said,
"Boy, we're going to reach Frisco, but we'll all be dead."

"So turn on your water and shovel in your coal,
Stick you head out the window, watch those rivers roll;
I'll drive her till she leaves the rail,
For I'm eight hours late by that Western Mail."

When he was within six miles of the place,
There number four stared him straight in the face,
He turned to his fireman, said "Jim you'd better ump,
For there're two locomotives that are going to bump."

Casey said just before he died,
"There're two more roads I would like to ride."
The fireman said, "Which ones can they be?"
"Oh the Northern Pacific and the Santa Fe."

Mrs. Jones sat at her bed a-sighing,
Just to hear the news that her Casey was dying.
"Hush up children, and quit your crying',
For you've got another poppa on the Salt Lake Line."

Cat Came Back, The

Old-time Song; Words and music by Harry S. Miller with later folk additions; **DATE:** 1893; **RECORDING INFO:** Fiddlin' John Carson 1924; Riley Puckett; Fiddlin' Doc Roberts; **OTHER NAMES:** And The Cat Came Back; Cat; **NOTES:** Some say that the minstrel show circuit of the late 1800's was the first pop-song movement in American history. Henry S. Miller, a Chicagoan, was a very popular composer during this time, specializing in comical and novelty songs. Just like the cat in the song. The Cat Came Back endures to this day because of and despite many changes and adaptations. The chords and melody used today (and in this arrangement) are quite different than the original.

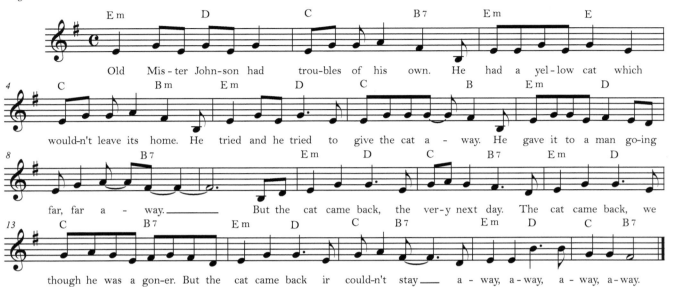

Em D C B7
Old Mister Johnson had troubles of his own

Em E C Bm
He had a yellow cat which wouldn't leave its home;

Em D C B
He tried and he tried to give the cat away,

Em D B7
He gave it to a man goin' far, far away.

Em D C B7
CHORUS: But the cat cam back the very next day,

Em D C B7
The cat came back, we thought he was a goner

Em D C B7
But the cat came back; it just couldn't stay away,

Em D C B7
Away, away, away, away.

The man around the corner swore he'd kill the cat on sight,
He loaded up his shotgun with nails and dynamite;
He waited and he waited for the cat to come around,
Ninety-seven pieces of the man is all they found. CHORUS:

He gave it to a little boy with a dollar note,
Told him for to take it up the river in a boat;
They tied a rope around its neck,
　　　　it must have weighted a pound
Now they drag the river for a little boy that's drowned.

He gave it to a man going up in a balloon,
He told him or to take it to the man in the moon;
The balloon came down about ninety miles away,
Where he is now, well I dare not say.

He gave it to a man going way out West,
Told him for to take it to the one he loved the best;
First the train hit the curve, then it jumped the rail,
Not a soul was left behind to tell the gruesome tale.

The cat it had some company one night out in the yard,
Someone threw a boot-jack, and they threw it mighty hard;
It caught the cat behind the ear, she thought it rather slight,
When along came a brick-bat and knocked the cat out of sight.

Away across the ocean they did send the cat at last,
Vessel only out a day and making water fast;
People all began to pray, the boat began to toss
A great big gust of wind came by and every soul was lost.

On a telegraph wire, sparrows sitting in a bunch,
The cat was feeling hungry, thought she'd like 'em for a lunch;
Climbing softly up the pole, and when she reached the top,
Put her foot upon the electric ire, which tied her in a knot.

They gave the cat to a man in a balloon
And old him to give him to the man in the moon;
But the balloon it busted and everybody said
Ten miles away they picked the man up dead.

The atom bomb fell just the other day,
The H-bomb fell in the very same way;
Russia went, England went, and then the U/S/A.
The human race was finished without a chance to pray.

Cat's Got the Measles (And The Dog's Got The Whooping Cough), The

Old-Time Breakdown and Song; Appalachian Region; **DATE:** Early 1900's (1924 by Papa Charlie Jackson); **RECORDING INFO:** Jerry Jordan, Papa Charlie Jackson 1924; Walter Smith and Friends; Alabama Shieks (Lawdy, Lawdy, Blues); Cousin Emmy; New Lost City Ramblers; **OTHER NAMES:** Cat's Got the Measles; Lawdy, Lawdy, Blues (Alabama Shieks-1931); **NOTES**: The early version of Cat's Got he Measles is jazz banjoist Papa Charlie Jackson's, who recorded the song in Jan. 1924. This version is from Walter "Kid" Smith, vocal, with Posey Rorer on fiddle and Norman Woodlieff on guitar. It was recorded in Richmond, IN, March 20, 1929 and released on Gennett 6825 plus a couple of pseudonymous cheap label reissues on Champion and Supertone, the latter credited Jerry Jordan, one of Smith's recording names, on Supertone (Sears 9407).

CHORUS: The cat's got the measles and the dog's got the whooping cough doggone

The cat's got the measles and the dog's got the whooping cough,

Doggone a man who'd let a woman be his boss, doggone my time.

Thought I heard a rockin' deep down in the ground, doggone
Thought I heard a rockin' deep down in the ground
It musta been the devil a-chainin' my good gal down.

I ain't good lookin' and my teeth don't shine like pearls, doggone
I ain't good lookin' and my teeth don't shine like pearls
But I got what it takes to cry me through this cock-eyed world

I ain't no devil just born in the lion's den, doggone
I ain't no devil just born in the lion's den
My chief oc-pation takin' women from the monkey men

The men don't like me just because I keep my side doggone
The men don't like me just because I keep my side
But the women cry "papa," they want to be my bride.

Charley, He's a Good ol' Man

Traditional Old-time song and fiddle tune; Widely spread; **DATE:** 1700's as "Over the Water To Charlie" in England; Listed as a Song of the Carolina Charter Colonists, 1663-1763; **RECORDING INFO:** Kelly Harrell 1927; (as "Fly Around," Samantha Bumgarner; 1924; Gid Tanner and His Skillet Lickers; Frank Blevins & His Tar Hell Rattlers); **OTHER NAMES:** "Weevily Wheat; Blue-Eyed Girl; Fly Around My Pretty Little Miss; Susannah Gal; Fly Around My Pretty Little Pink; **NOTES:** Kelly Harrell recorded Charley He's a Good ol' Man on August 12, 1927 in Charlotte, NC and issued in January 1928 as Victor 21069. This is part of the large Western Country family of songs that includes "Fly Around My Pretty Little Miss and "Weevily Wheat." The Charley (refers to Bonnie Prince Charlie in England) lyric places it more in the Weevily Wheat lyric branch. It is widely known play party song that originally expressed Jacobite sentiments from the 1700's in England, but that context is long gone.

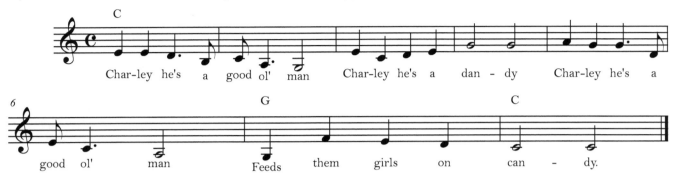

CHORUS: Charley he's a good ol' man

Charley he's a dandy

Charley he's a good ol' man

Feeds them girls on candy.

Single life is a happy life
Single life is lovely.
I am single and no man's wife
And no men control me.

Over the river to feed your sheep
Over the river, Charley
Over the river to feed your sheep
On buckwheat cake and barley.

Don't wan' no more of your weevily wheat
Don't wan' no more of your barley
But I wan' some more of the best ol' flour
To bake a cake for Charley.

Charley he's a nice ol' man
Takes me out a-fishing
I put the bait on Charley's hook
It's nice to see him catch them.

Some folks marry for good looks
Some of them for money
But I'm gonna marry a country boy
Kiss him and call him honey.

53

This page has been left blank
to avoid awkward page turns.

Chicken Reel

Old-time Song and Breakdown; Widely known by Joseph M. Daly words by Sam Marley; **DATE:** 1910; **RECORDING INFO:** Bud Anderson and the Country Ramblers; Falderal String Band; Charlie Monroe; Fiddlin' Doc Roberts; Gid Tanner and the Skillet Lickers; Wade Ward; **RELATED TO:** Bug in the Taters; Sixteen Chickens and a Tambourine; **OTHER NAMES:** Chicken Reel Stomp; Darn Good Girl; **NOTES:** The Chicken Reel was composed by Joseph M. Daly in 1910, and along with Turkey in the Straw, it is probably best known for its use in early animated cartoons as a catchy tune used to represent animal activity. Originally composed as a novelty song, it has since passed into modern folk tradition. Today, the tune is usually played without the words, which would often have been sung in the minstrel style (in stereotyped African-American vernacular).

54

- er board and lost the day that reel. (Chick-en reel chick-en reel) Some reel!

Part I: There is a little tune to sing if you should lonesome feel
A funny little melody they call the chicken reel.
Altho' it's quite simple, everybody hums the tune,
It grows upon you like a wart, you sing it night and noon.

Part II: Grandaddy heard the tune and then forgot his rheumatic,
Threw away his crutch he carried since the Civil War.
Old Hiram Stone who long forgot what smiling is,
Laughed out loud so his teeth fell out on the floor.

Part I: I went into the barn one day a hummin' Chicken Reel,
The mule kicked off the barn door tho' the hinges were made of steel.
The old maid of the town ran to the station out of breath,
She grabbed the first man off the train and hugged him near to death.

Part III: In the general store quite a crowd could be seen,
Reuben Jones had out played the checker champion,
Rube had him cornered and in a bad way
Just then the Chicken Reel started to play.
Up went the checker board and lost the day
That reel (chicken reel chicken reel) some reel!

Sunday mornin' at the meeting something occurred
Folks were prayin' and not one of them stirred
Someone passed by whistlin' Chicken Reel,
Everyone started tapping toe and hell,
Broke up the meeting but it caused great zeal,
That reel (chicken reel chicken reel) some reel!

Part I: Ev'ry chicken has a tale and ev'ry tail has an end,
So here's the end of the Chicken Reel but if you need a friend,
To finish up the evening with and make things complete,
If you're tired of singing you can try it with your feet.
Tag: Roll up the carpet, let's go!

Cindy

Traditional Old-Time Song and Breakdown; **DATE**: Early 1900's; **CATEGORY:** Fiddle and Instrumental Tune; **RECORDING INFO:** The Hill Billies, 1925; J.E. Mainer's Mountaineers; Coon Creek Girls; New Lost City Rambler; **OTHER NAMES**: Cindy in the Summertime; Get Along Home, Cindy; Cindy in the Meadows; Get Along Home (Miss) Cindy; Get Along Cindy; Git Along; Old Time Cindy; Run Along Home, Cindy; Whoop 'Em Up Cindy; Old Time Cindy; **NOTES**: One of the great American folk songs and fiddle tunes.

She told me that she loved me; She called me her Sugar Plum

She threw her arms around me, I thought my time had come.

CHORUS: Get along home Cindy, Cindy. Get along home Cindy, Cindy.

Get along home Cindy, Cindy. I'll marry you someday.

She took me to her parlor, She cooled me with her fan.
She told me I was the prettiest thing, In the shape of mortal man.

Oh where did you get you liquor, Where did you get your dram?
From an old moon shiner, Down in Rockingham.

Cindy got religion, She had it once before.
And when she heard my old guitar, She danced across the floor.

Climbing Up the Golden Stairs

Old-time gospel song, E. Heiser (Monroe Rosenfield) Words and Music; **DATE:** 1884; **RECORDING INFO:** Ernest Thompson 1924; Georgia Crackers; Happy Four; Vernon Dalhart; **NOTES:** This popular gospel song was first recorded in 1924 by Ernest Thompson. Vernon Dalhart and Carson Robison recorded it several times.

They'll put you in the stable

Make you fight with Cain and Abel

Climbing up those golden stairs

Old Adam and his wife

Will be there with drum and fife

Climbing up those golden stairs

CHORUS: Oh hear them bells a ringin'

So sweet I do declare

Oh hear them people singing

While they're climbing up the golden stairs.

Saint Peter looked so wicked
When I asked him for a ticket
Climbing up those golden stairs.

At the sight of half a dollar
He will grab you by the collar
And throw you up those golden stairs.
CHORUS:

Columbus Stockade Blues

Traditional Folk Blues; **DATE:** Early 1900's; **CATEGORY:** Blues; **RECORDING INFO::** Bill Monroe; Doc Watson; **OTHER NAMES**: Go and Leave Me If You Wish To; Way Down in Columbus Stockade; **NOTES**: This version is in a minor key and is similar to the version played by my friend, Doc Watson. I like it best in this key with Capo III.

Way down in Columbus, Georgia wanna to be back in Tennessee
Am ... *E* ... *Am*

Way down in Columbus stockade my friends all turned their backs on me.
E ... *Am*

Go and leave me if you wish to never let it cross your mind
Dm ... *Am* *Dm* ... *E*

If in your heart you love another, leave me, little darling, I don't mind.
Am ... *E* ... *Am*

Last night as I lay sleeping, I dreamt I held you in my arms
When I awoke I was mistaken, I was peering through the bars.

Many a night with you I rambled, many an hour with you I spent
Thought I had your heart forever, now I find it was only lent.

Cotton Mill Blues

Traditional Old-time song; **DATE:** Circa 1900; **OTHER NAMES:** Hard Times in the Mill; **NOTES:** The song was written in the Columbia Duck Mills in Columbia, SC around 1900. First recorded as Cotton Mill Girl by Lester Smallwood in 1927, the popular version by the Lee Brothers Trio (Brunswick 501, re-released on Hard Times in the Country, County CD 3527) was made in 1930. This song concentrates on work in the weave room. The loom tenders were paid by the number of cuts (60 yards) they produced, where "cut" is an old measure for the cloth length.

Work in the cot-ton mill___ all my life I ain't got___ no-thing but a
Bar-low knife. And it's hard times in this old mill it's hard times in here.___

Work in the cotton mill all my life,

I ain't got nothing but a Barlow knife.

CHORUS: And it's hard times in this old mill,

It's hard times in here.

Country folks, they oughta be killed
For leaving their farms and coming to the mill.
 CHORUS

They raised their wages up a half a cent
But the poor old hands
 didn't know what it meant.

They raised our wages up a half a cent more,
But they went up a dime at the company store.

Old man Jones, taking up cloth,
Won't give you half that you take off.

If it lacks one yard of being a two-cart roll
He won't give you but one to save your soul.

Card room kids and the spinning room babies
Can't keep up with the weave shop ladies.

Come downstairs to get a drink of water,
Along come the boss, says,
 "I'll dock you a quarter."

"You can dock me a quarter,
 you can dock me a dime,
I'll go to the office and I'll get my time."

Got to where now you can't show a dime,
You're running on such short time.

If I ever marry, I'll marry a weaver,
And if she won't work, then I won't either.

Working in the cotton mill ain't no harm,
I'd heap rather be down on the farm.

See that train go around the curve,
She's loaded down with cotton mill girls.

See that train go down the track,
Saying "Goodbye, boys,
 we'll never come back."

Crawdad

Traditional Old-Time Breakdown and Song; **DATE:** Early 1900's; **CATEGORY:** Early Country an Bluegrass Song; **RECORDING INFO:** Gus Cannon; Woody Guthrie; Doc Warson; Poplin Family; **OTHER NAMES:** You Get a Line and I'll Get a Pole; The Crow-Fish Man; Sweet Thing; Honey; Honey Babe; The Crawdad Song; **NOTES:** "Crawdad" is a "whine blues" with three repeating lines and one answering line with the tag "honey babe/sweet child of mine." This 16 measure "blues" form is widely known and used in many variants.

Get up old man, you slept too late, honey

Get up old man, you slept too late, babe

Get up old man, you slept too late

Last piece of crawdad's on your plate, Honey, sugar baby, mine.

Whatcha gonna do when the creek runs dry, honey
Whatcha gonna do when the creek runs dry, babe
Whatcha gonna do when the creek runs dry
Sit on the banks and watch the crawdads die, Honey, sugar baby, mine.

Yonder comes a man with a sack on his back, honey
Yonder comes a man with a sack on his back, babe
Yonder comes a man with a sack on his back
He's got more crawdads than he can pack, Honey, sugar baby, mine.

Cripple Creek

Traditional Old-Time; Bluegrass; Breakdown; **DATE:** Early 1900's; **CATEGORY:** Fiddle and Instrumental Tunes; **RECORDING INFO:** The Hill Billies 1925; Doc Roberts 1925; Fiddlin' John Carson; Charlie Poole and the North Carolina Ramblers "Shootin' Creek" 1926; J.E. Mainer & the Mountaineers; Flatt & Scruggs & the Foggy Mountain Boys; Fiddlin' Cowan Powers; Stanley Brothers; Doc Watson; **OTHER NAMES:** Going Up/Down Criple Creek; Going Up/Down Shootin' Creek; Going Up/Down Brushy Fork; Shootin' Creek' Buck Creek Girls (Gals); **NOTES:** The tune had and still has wide currency throughout the South. There have been several suggestions about the origin of the title and tune, although no definitive information has been found. Folklorist Alan Jabbour, of the Library of Congress found that the oldest Appalachian fiddlers he collected from could recall the first time that they had heard "Cripple Creek," leading Jabbour to speculate that the title might have something to do with the Cirpple Creek, Colorado labor troubles. Gold had been discovered there in 1891 and the labor disputes date from 1903-1904. Many think that tune and title older however, and point out a likely candidate for the title origins include the Cripple Creek that flows through Grayson and Carroll Counties in Virginia, emptying into the New River. Below is the Bluegrass Messenger's version from "Live in Mt. Airy."

I got a girl and she loves me, She's as sweet as she can be,
   G   C   G   D   G

She's got eyes of baby blue, Makes my gun shoot straight and true.
                  C   G   D   G

CHORUS: Goin' up Cripple Creek, goin' in a whirl,
              G

Goin' up Cripple Creek to see my girl.
                         D   G

Goin' up Cripple Creek goin' in a run

Goin' up Cripple Creek to have me some fun.
                              D   G

My gal lives at the head of the creek, I go up to see her 'bout twice a week
She's got kisses sweet as any wine,
Wraps herself 'round me like a sweet pertater vine. CHORUS:

Cripple Creek's wide and Cripple Creek's deep,
I'll wade old Cripple Creek before I sleep
Roll my britches to my knees, I'll wade old Cripple Creek when I please. CHORUS:

Crow Black Chicken

Traditional Old-Time Song; **DATE:** 1927; **RECORDING INFO:** Leake County Revelers 1927; New Lost City Ramblers; Sleepy Hollow Hog Stompers; **OTHER NAMES:** Chicken Pie; Finest Chicken in Town; I Love Chicken Pie; **NOTES:** Leake County Revelers was a string band that hailed from Mississippi with Will Gilmer on fiddle and Dallas Jones doing the vocals. They recorded the classic version of Crow Black Chicken in 1927 in New Orleans that The New Lost City Ramblers reworked in 1962. The second verse is a floating verse usually associated with "Boil Dem Cabbage Down."

D
Chicken crow for midnight, chicken crow for day,

Along comes an owl, Oh Lord! Toted that chicken away.
(A7 ... D)

CHORUS: Crow black chicken, crow for day,
(D)

Crow black chicken, fly away,
(A7)

Crow black chicken, crow for day,
(D)

I love chicken pie.
(A ... D)

I went up on the mountain to give my horn a blow,
I thought I heard my true love say, "Yonder goes my beau." CHORUS

Chicken crow for midnight, chicken crow for day,
Along comes a Ford, Oh Lord! Toted that chicken away. CHORUS

The hardest work I ever done was plough a field of rye,
The easiest work I ever done was eating chicken pie.

Oh wish I had a big frame house, fifteen stories high,
Every story in that house was filled with chicken pie.

Crow Jane

Traditional old-time blues song. **DATE:** Early 1900's **OTHER NAMES:** Red River; Dry Land Blues (Furry Lewis) **RECORDED BY:** Joe Williams; Skip James; Sonny Terry Brownie McGee; Reverend Gary Davis **NOTES:** This blues song was known by Big Joe Williams (1903- 1982) in Mississippi in the early 1900s. Early versions were known in the Piedmont area and mainly in SC by Julius Daniels and Reverend Gary Davis.

Crow   Jane   Crow   Jane   Don't you hold your head so   high   Cause

some - day   ba - by   you   know   you're gon - na   die.

CHORUS: Crow Jane, Crow Jane
E   B7
Don't you hold your head so high,
A7   A7
Cause someday baby, you know you're gonna die.
     E   B7   E   B7

Which way, which way,
Does that blood red river run?
From my back door, to the Risin' Sun.

I'm gonna buy me a pistol,
Long as I am tall,
Shoot Crow Jane just to see her fall.

I dug that woman's grave
Eight feet in the ground,
Didn't feel sorry 'til I laid her down

I dug her grave
With a silver spade,
Ain't nobody gonna take my Crow Jane's place.

They laid her down,
With a golden chain
And every link would cry Crow Jane's name.

Daisy Bell/A Bicycle Made for Two

Old-time Song written and composed by Harry Dacre; **DATE**: 1892; **NOTES**: According to David Ewen in American Popular Sangs: "When Dacre, and English popular composer, first came to the United States, he brought with him a bicycle, for which he was charged duty. His friend (the songwriter William Jerome) remarked lightly, "It's lucky you didn't bring a bicycle built for two, otherwise you'd have to pay double duty." Dacre was so taken with the phrase "bicycle built for two") that he decided to use it in a song. That song, Daisy Bell, first came successful in a London music hall, in a performance by Kate Lawrence. Tony Pastor was the first one to sing it in the United States. Its success in America began when Jennie Lindsay brought down the house with it at the Atlantic Gardens on the Bowery early in 1892." Daisy, the nickname for the Countess of Warwick, Frances Evelyn Maynard, one of the wealthiest and most desirable English women of the period is said to have inspired the song. "Daisy Bell" was featured in 2001: A Space Odyssey.

         G   D   G
There is a flower within my heart Daisy, Daisy

                 D
Plated on day by a glancing dart

 G   D   G
Played by Daisy Bell.

 Em   B7   Em
Whether she loves me or loves me not,

 Am   D   G
Sometimes it's hard to tell.

 Em   B7   Em
Yet I am longing to share the lot

     A7   D
Of beautiful Daisy Bell.

             G   C   Am   G
CHORUS: Daisy, Daisy, give me your answer, do!

D   G Em Am   D
I'm half crazy, all for the love of you.

                   G   C   G
It won't be a stylish marriage, I can't afford a carriage.

             C   G   D7   G   D   G
But you'll look sweet on the seat Of a bicycle built for two.

We will go "tandem" as man and wife
Daisy, Daisy.
"Ped'ling" away down the road of life.
I and my Daisy Bell.
When the road's dark we can both despise
P'licemen and lamps as well.
There are "bright lights" in the dazzling eyes,
Of beautiful Daisy Bell.

I will stick by you in "wheel" or woe
Daisy, Daisy
You'll be the bell which I'll ring, you know.
Sweet little Daisy Bell.
You'll take the "lead" in each "trip" we take.
Then if I don't do well,
I will permit you to use the break,
My beautiful Daisy Bell.

Dance All Night With a Bottle in Yer Hand

Traditional Old-Time, Breakdown; **DATE:** 1900's; **CATEGORY:** Fiddle and Instrumental Tune; **RECORDING INFO:** Carter Brothers & Son; Gid Turner and Skillet Lickers; new Lost City Ramblers with Cousin Emmy; Tommy Jarrell; J.E. Mainer's Mountaineers; **OTHER NAMES:** Danced All Night; Danced All Night With a Bootle in My Hand; Give the Fiddler a Dram; Give Me a Bottle of I Don't Care What; **NOTES:** Guthrie Meade thinks the time has some relation to "Buffalo Gals." Rosenbaum (1989) points out that the recording by Gid Tanner and the Skillet Lickers for Columbia was very influential.

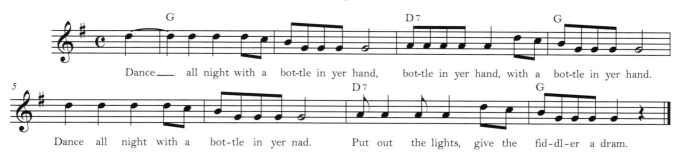

G

Old Aunt Peggy, won't you fill 'em up again,

D7   G
Fill 'em up again, fill 'em up again.

Old Aunt Peggy, won't you fill 'em up again,

D7   G
As we go marching along.

Dance all night with the fiddler's girl,
Swing her round the corner all around the world.
Swing that calico Sally Ann,
For we don't give a damn, gonna catch her if we can.

I left my jawbone sittin' on a fence,
I ain't seen nothin' of my jawbone since.
Walked on home and didn't get along,
In come Sally with her blue dress on.

Who's been here since I been gone?
Pretty little girl with the red dress on.
She took it off and I put it on,
In come Sally with her big boots on.

Danny Boy (Londonderry Air)

Traditional Irish Air with lyrics by Fred F. Weatherby; **DATE:** Tune published in 1855; Lyrics 1913; **RECORDING INFO:** Bill Monroe; Chubby Wise; Sons of Erin; **OTHER NAMES:** Danny Boy is one of over 180 songs composed to the tune, Derry Air or Londonderry Air. Other songs O, Jeanie Dear, and The Young Man's Dream. **NOTES:** Derry Air is one of the most famous Irish airs, known popularly as the tune for the song Danny Boy by Fred F. Weatherby (1848-1929), an Englishman, a lawyer and author of the words of about 1500 songs including The Holy City, also known as Jerusalem. Th Danny Boy lyrics proved particularly popular in the Untied States, where they were recorded by a variety of singers from pop (Bing Crosby) to bluegrass (Bill Monroe).

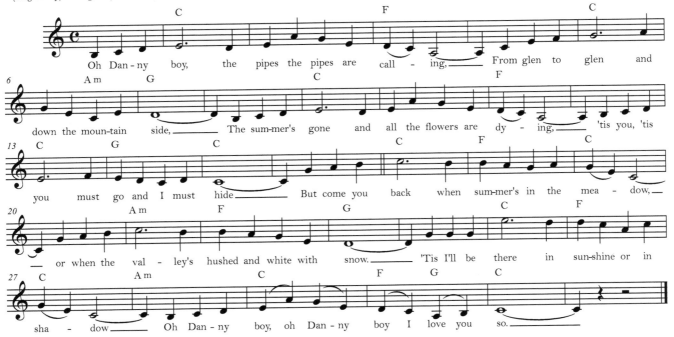

Oh Danny boy, the pipes, the pipes are calling From glen to glen, and down the mountain side
$\quad$ C $\qquad$ F $\qquad$ C $\qquad$ Am $\quad$ G

The summer's gone, and all the flowers are dying 'Tis you, 'tis you must go and I must hide.
$\quad$ C $\qquad$ F $\qquad$ C $\quad$ G $\quad$ C

CHORUS: But come you back when summer's in the meadow
$\qquad$ C $\qquad$ F $\qquad$ C

Or when the valley's hushed and white with snow
$\quad$ Am $\quad$ F $\qquad$ G

'Tis I'll be there in sunshine or in shadow
$\qquad$ C $\quad$ F $\qquad$ C

Oh Danny boy, oh Danny boy, I love you so.
Am $\quad$ C $\qquad$ F $\quad$ G $\quad$ C

And if you come, when all the flowers are dying
And I am dead, as dead I well may be
You'll come and find the place where I am lying
And kneel and say an "Ave" there for me.

And I shall hear, tho' soft you tread above me
And all my dreams will warm and sweeter be
If you'll not fail to tell me that you love me
I simply sleep in peace until you come.

Dark Hollow

Traditional Old-time, Bluegrass; **DATE:** Early 1900's (1917 by Cecil Sharp); **CATEGORY:** Early Country and Bluegrass; **OTHER NAMES:** East Virginia Blues; Dark Looer Blues; Greenback Dollar; I Don't Want Your Millions; Mister-tine; **RECORDING INFO:** Buell Kazer; Stanley Brothers; Seldom Scene; Grateful Dead; Clarence "Tom" Ashley; **NOTES:** Dark Hollow is a variant of "East Virginia Blues." Later in the 1930's the song developed into the very popular "Greenback Dollar."

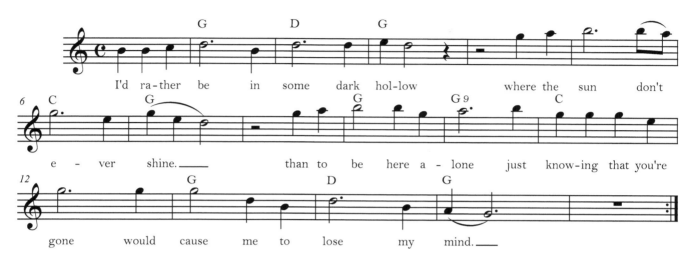

I'd rather be in some dark hollow, where the sun don't ever shine

Than to be here alone just knowing that you're gone,Would cause me to lose my mind.

So blow your whistle freight train, carry me further on down the track
I'm gong away, I'm leaving today,I'm going but I ain't coming back.

I'd rather be in some dark hollow, where the sun don't ever shine
Than to be in some big city, in a small room with your love on my mind.

Darling Nelly Gray

Old-time Song by Benjamin Russell Hanby (1833-1867); **DATE**: 1856; **OTHER NAMES**: Darlin' Nelly Gray; Old Nelly Grey; Oh My Darlin' Nelly Gray; Charming Nellie Ray; **RECORDING INFO**: The Carver Boys 1930; Asa Martin; **RELATED TO**: Maggie May; Dear Prairie Home; **NOTES**: Benjamin Russell Hanby was born in the small town of Rushville, Ohio, southeast of Columbus, in 1833. He composed Darling Nelly Gray in 1856 while attending Otter bein College in Westerville, Ohio. A runaway slave named Joseph Shelby died at the Ohio home of Hanby's father. Shelby was hoping to raise money to win the freedom of another slave named Nelly Gray. Weaving together the lamentations of a lover with the evils of slavery, it gained immediate popularity and became his best known song. Hanby had sent his composition to a music publishing house in Boston. When the Melody swept the nation, he asked for royalties. The published reportedly wrote back to Hanby that he had the fame and they had the money and that balanced the account. He also wrote "Santa Claus/Up on the House Top,"

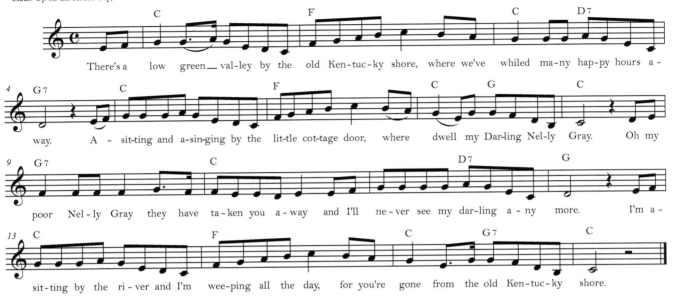

There's a low green valley by the old Kentucky shore
    C   F

Where we've whiled many happy hours away,
   C   D   G

A-sitting and a-singing by the little cottage door,
    C   F

Where lived my darling Nelly Gray.
   C   G   C

CHORUS: Oh my poor Nelly Gray,
            G7

      they have taken you away
           C

And I'll never see my darling any more.
               D7   G

I'm a-sitting by the river and I'm weeping all the day
       C   F

For you're gone from the old Kentucky shore.
      C   G7   C

When the moon had climbed the mountain,
    and the stars were shining too,
Then I'd take my darling Nelly Gray.
We would float down the river in my little red canoe,
While my banjo so sweetly I would play.

One night I went to see her but "she's gone"
    the neighbors say,
The white man bound her with his chain,
They have taken her to Georgie to wear her life away,
As she toils in the cotton and the cane.

My canoe is under water and my banjo is unstrung,
I'm tired of living anymore.
My eyes shall look downward
    and my songs shall be unsung,
While I stay on the old Kentucky shore.

My eyes are getting blinded and I cannot see my way,
Hark! There's someone knocking at my door.
Oh! I hear the angels calling and I see my Nelly Gray,
Farewell to the old Kentucky shore.

FINAL CHORUS: Oh, my darling Nelly Gray,
    up in heaven there they say,
That they'll never take you from me any more.
I'm a-coming, coming, coming,
    as the angels clear the way,
Farewell to the old Kentucky shore.

Days of Forty-Nine

Traditional Old-time Ballad; **DATE**: Earliest report 1872. The Great Emerson's New Popular Songster 1874; **RECORDING INFO**: Jules Allen, "The Days of Forty-Nine" (Victor 21627, 1928; Montgomery Ward M-4463, 1913) Logan English; Bob Dylan; **NOTES**: A song about the California gold rush which began in 1849. It was popularized in part by Bob Dylan's 1970 recording.

Dm   C
I'm old Tom Moore from the bummer's shore

A7   Dm
In the good old golden days.

             C
They call me a bummer and a gin sot, too

  A7   Dm
But what care I for praise.

             C   Dm   A7
I wander around from town to town Just like a roving sign,

     Dm   C
And the people all say "There goes Tom Moore

     A7   Dm
Of the days of forty-nine."

         Dm   F
CHORUS: In the days of old, in the days of gold,

    Dm A7
How often I repine

     Dm   C
For the days of old when we dug up the gold

    A7   Dm
In the days of forty-nine.

There was Nantuck Bill, I knew him well,
A feller that was found of tricks.
At a poker game he was always there
And heavy with his bricks.
He would ante up and draw his cards
And go in a hatfull blind
In a game of bluff, Bill lost his breath
In the days of forty-nine.

There was New York Jake, a butcher boy
He was always getting tight.
And every time that he got full,
He was always hunting a fight.
One night he run up against a knife
In the hands of old Bob Kline
And over Jake they held a wake
In the days of forty-nine.

There was poor old Jess, the old lame cuss
he never would relent.
He never was known to miss a drink
Or ever spend a cent.
At length old Jess like all the rest
Who never would decline,
In all his bloom went up in flame
In the days of forty-nine.

There was roaring Bill from Buffalo
I never will forget.
He would roar all day and he'd roar all night
And I guess he's roaring yet.
One night he fell in a prospector's hole
In a roaring bad design,
In that hole roared out his soul
In the days of forty-nine.

Delia's Gone

Old-time Ballad and Blues song; **DATE:** Mose "Cooney" Houston shot and killed Delia Green on Christmas Eve in 1900. The murder entered oral tradition by the early 1900's; **RECORDING INFO:** Blind Blake; Johnny Cash; Bob Dylan; **OTHR NAMES:** Delia; Delia Holmes; One More Rounder's Gone; **NOTES:** According to Will Win, Delia originated following a murder in Georgie having been composed about 1900 by a white minstrel of Dallas, Texas known as Whistlin' Bill Ruff [John Gurst: "Delia" gained national prominence as "Delia's Gone" after the Bahaman Blind Blake Blake Alphonso Higgs) recorded it in the 1950's. Almost every pop group of the "great folk scare" recorded it. Further, it crossed over into country and rock. Johnny Cash recorded it twice, once in about 1960 and once in 1993. Bob Dylan recorded it in 1992. In field recordings, it goes well back into the '20s and '30s, and it was recorded by jazz band leader Jimmy Bordon at that time.] The song is closely related to Whitehouse Blues and Cannonball Blues.

```
D              G           D           D7        G
To-ny shot his De-lia___ 'twas on a Christ-mas night,  First thing she did, was

A7                 D                        A7            D
hung her head and die.  De-lia's gone, one more round, De-lia's gone.___
```

      D   G
Tony shot his Delia,

        D   D7
'Twas on a Christmas night;

G
First thing she did

      A7   D
Was hung her head and die.

                           A7   D
CHORUS: Delia's gone, one more round, Delia's gone.

Send for the doctor,
The doctor came too late.
Sent for the minister
To lay out Delia straight. CHORUS:

Delia, oh Delia,
Where you been so long?
Everybody's talkin' about
Poor Delia's dead and gone. CHORUS:

Rubber-tired buggy,
Rubber-tired back.
Took Delia to the graveyard,
Ain't gonna bring her back. CHORUS:

Devilish Mary

Traditional Old-Time Ballad and Breakdown; widely known; **DATE:** 1897; **OTHER NAMES:** I'm Going to Take the Train to Charlotte; **RECORING INFO:** Gid Tanner and His Skiller Lickers; Pete Seeger; Beers Family; Kenny Hall and the Sweets Mill String Band; Bob Wills and the Texas Playboys; **NOTES**: I combined several versions to get the lyrics of this version, the chorus is similar to the Skillet Lickers version.

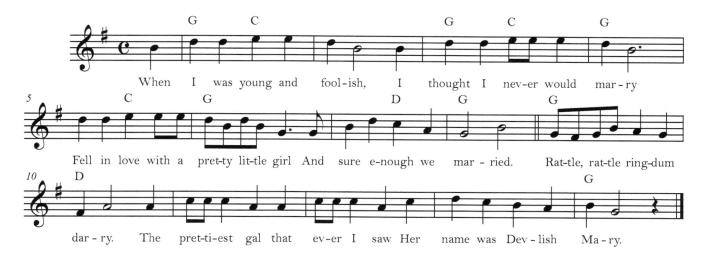

VERSE: When I was young and foolish,
            G   C

I thought I never would marry
   G   C   G

Fell in love with a pretty little gal
       C   G

And sure enough we married.
           D   G

CHORUS: Rattle, rattle ring-dum darry
           G   D

The prettiest little gal that ever I saw

Her name was Devilish Mary.
                 G

We both were young and foolish
Both in a powerful hurry
We both agreed upon one thing
Our wedding day was Thursday CHORUS

We hadn't been married but about three weeks
She got mean as a devil
Every time I look cross-eyed
She knocked me in the head with a shovel. CHORUS

She washed my clothes with ol' soap suds,
 Filled my back with stiches,
She let me know right at the start
She's gonna wear the britches.

We hadn't been married but about three months
We both agreed to be parted
So she up with her leather goods
And down the road she started.

If I marry another time,
Gonna be for love and not riches
Marry a little gal about four feet tall
So she can't wear my britches.

71

Diamond Joe

Traditional Old-time Breakdown; **DATE:** Early 1900's; **RECORDING INFO:** The Georgia Crackers (a cover name for the Cofer Brothers 1927); Desert String Band; New Lost City Ramblers; Tom Rush; **OTHER NAMES:** Willie's Diamond Joe; **NOTES:** The title Diamond Joe, has been used for various folksongs and old-time songs. The song here is the bluegrass/old-time breakdown version similar to the Cofer Brothers version. The song Bob Dylan recorded on "Good As I Been To You" is a different song. Lomax has collected different versions with the same title.

CHORUS: Diamond Joe, come and get me.
                      G

My wife died and left me,
   C

Diamond Joe come and get me,
         G   D

Diamond Joe.
         G

I'm gonna buy me a sack of flour
Cook a hoecake every hour,
Diamond Joe better come and get me,
Diamond Joe.

I'm gonna buy me a piece of meat,
Cook me a slice but once a week,
Diamond Joe you better come get me,
Diamond Joe.

I'm gonna buy me a sack of meal,
Take a hoecake to the field,
Diamond Joe come and get me,
Diamond Joe.

I'm gonna buy me a jug of whiskey,
I'm gonna make my baby frisky,
Diamond Joe come and get me,
Diamond Joe.

I'm gonna buy me a jug of rum,
I'm gonna give my Ida some,
Diamond Joe come and get me,
Diamond Joe.

Didn't He Ramble

Old-time Song based on Darby's Ram (Derby Ram); Widely known; **DATE:** 1902 copyright by Will Handy; **OTHER NAMES:** Oh, Didn't He Ramble; Darby Ram; Darby's Ram; **RECORDING INFO**: Al Hopkins, Uncle Dave Macon; Fiddlin' John Carson; Scotty Wiseman; **NOTES:** This is not a WC Handy song. According to James Weldon Johnson (1921): We took it, re-wrote the version, telling antirely different story from the original, left the chorus as it was, and published the song, at first under the name of Will Handy. It became very popular with college boys, especially at football games. The song was, "Oh Didn't He Ramble!"

Mother raised thee grown songs, Buster, Bil and me;

Buster was the black sheep of our little family.

Mother tried to break him of his rough and rowdy ways;

Finally had to get the judge to give him ninety days.

CHORUS: And didn't he ramble, ramble,

He rambled all around, in and out of town,

And didn't he ramble, ramble,

He rambled till the butchers cut him down.

He rambled in a gambling game, he gambled on the green,
The gamblers there showed him a trick that he had never seen.
He lost his roll and jewelry, he like to lost his life,
He lost the car that carried him there and someone stole his wife.

He rambled in a swell hotel, his appetite was stout,
But when he refused to pay the bill the landlord kicked him out.
He reached a brick to smack him with and when he went to stop,
The landlord kicked him over the fence into a barrel of slop.

Don't Get Trouble In Your Mind

Old-time Bluegrass Breakdown; **DATE:** 1927; **RECORDING INFO**: Frank Blevins and His Tarheel Rattlers; Original Bogtrotters; J.E. Mainer's Mountaineers; Crockett Ward & his Boys; **RELATED TO**: Mollie/Molly and Tenbrooks; Quit that Ticklin' Me; Ain't That Skippin and Flyin'; **OTHER NAMES**: Ain't That Trouble In Mind; **NOTES**: Recorded first by Crockett Ward in 1927, "Ain't That Trouble In Mind" is part of the Mollie and Tenbrooks family of songs that includes "Quit that Tickin' Me" and "Ain't That Skippin' and Flyin'." The song is not related to the blues song, "Trouble in Mind" credited to Richard Jones.

Trouble, oh trouble, it's trouble all the time

If trouble don't kill me, I'll live a long time

CHORUS: Don't get trouble in your mind,

Don't get trouble in your mind.

My Mammy told me something, my Daddy told me more
That if ever I married, it'll bring trouble in the door. CHORUS:

Went to see my baby, thought I'd do some sleepin'
Kissed her right in back of her mouth and her dog gone nose was leakin' CHORUS:

When you see that gal of mine, tell her if you can,
When she goes to bake the bread wash her nasty hands.

Now she gone and left me, sure do wish her well.
Hope she got another man and she can go to ----

Went to see Miss Suzy she's standing in the door
Shoes and stockings in her hand, bare feet all over the floor.

Don't Let Your Deal Go Down

Traditional Old-time Breakdown; **DATE**: Early 1900's; **CATEGORY:** Fiddle and Instrumental Tune; **RELATED SONGS**: Last Gold Dollar; High Top Shoes; Don't Let My Deal Go Down; No Low Down Hanging Around; Lynchburg Town (tune); Black Dog Blues; **RECORING INFO:** Charlie Poole and the North Carolina Ramblers; Bob Wills & his Texas Playboys; Flatt & Scruggs; Wade Ward; Doc Warson; **NOTES**: One of the standard "white blues" from the Piedmont region. "Don't Let Your Deal Go Don" was performed initially by Charlie Poole and Fiddlin' John Carson. It was also adapted by black Piedmont blues artists like Eta Baker and John Jackson. There are many great fiddle versions including those by Bob Wills, Benny Thomason and later Mark O'Coner.

CHORUS: Don't let your deal go down, boys.
$\qquad$ D $\qquad$ G

Don't let your deal go down
C $\qquad$ F

Don't let your deal go down
D $\qquad$ G

'Till your last gold dollar is gone.
$\qquad$ C $\qquad$ F

Now I've been all around this whole wide world
Down to Memphis, Tennessee
Any old place I hang my hat
Looks like home to me.

Now I left my little girl crying
Standing in the door
Throw'd her arms around my neck
Saying "Honey, don't you go."

Now where did you get them high top shoes?
Dress you wear so fine?
Got my shes from a railroad man
And my dress from a driver in the mine.

Down By the Riverside (Ain't Gonna Study War No More)

Traditional Dixieland Jazz Song; **DATE:** 1913; **RECORDING INFO:** Fisk University Jubilee Singers 1920; Vaughn Quartet 1924; Charlie Monroe 1944; Pete Seeger; **OTHER NAMES**: Ain't Going to Study War No More; I Ain't Going to Study War No More; Lay Down My Sword and Shield; **NOTES:** In 1913, Carl Diton collected an African-American version on Frogmore (Island), near Beaufort, South Carolina. I suspect it is much older. It has become a Dixieland Jazz Band standard and was often sung during the Civil Rights and anti-Vietnam War movements of the 1960s.

Gonna lay down my sword and shield Down by the riverside, (G)

(D) Down by the riverside, (G) Down by the riverside,

Gonna lay down my sword and shield Down by the riverside,

I'll (D) study war no (G) more.

CHORUS: I ain't gonna (C) study war no more,

I ain't (G) gonna study war no more,

I ain't gonna (D) study war no (G) more. (Repeat Chorus)

Gonna join hands with ev'ryone...

Gonna put on my long white robe...

Gonna put on my starry crown...

Gonna put on my golden shoes...

Gonna walk with the Prince of Peace...

Down in the Valley/Birmingham Jail

Traditional Old-time Song; Widely Known; **DATE:** Lyrics- 1910; Melody- Circa 1850; **RECORDING INFO:** Marion Underwood 1927; Frank Luther and Carson Robison; Bradley Kincaid; Callahan Brothers; **OTHER NAMES:** Birmingham Jail; Angels in Heaven; **NOTES:** This popular waltz was first recorded in 1927 under both common titles. The tune appeared as the first part of "The Happy Home Waltz'" by Julien around 1850.

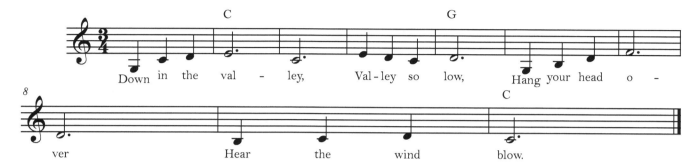

Down in the valley, the valley so low

Hang your head over, hear the wind blow

Hear the wind blow, dear, hear the wind blow

Hang your head over, hear the wind blow.

Writing this letter, containing three lines
Answer my question, will you be mine?
Will you be mine, dear, will you be mine?
Answer my question, will you be mine?

Write me a letter, send it by mail
Send it in care of the Birmingham jail,
Birmingham jail, dear, Birmingham jail
Send it in care of the Birmingham jail.

Roses love sunshine, violets love dew
Angels in Heaven know I love you
Know I love you, dear, know I love you
Angels in Heaven know I love you.

Down on Penny's Farm

Traditional Old-time Song; **DATE**: Early 1900's; **RECORDING INFO**: Bescom Lamar Lunsford; Bently Boys; Bob Dylan; **OTHER NAMES:** Out on Penny's Farm; On Tanner's Farm (Skillet Lickers); Penny's Farm; Down on Robert's Farm; **NOTES:** Bascom Lamar Lunsford says he learned the song from a Claude Reeves of North Carolina, who claims he wrote it as personal experience around 1935. Curiously, on the 1929 classic version the Bently Boys sing "Out on Penny's farm" but the song is titled "Down on Penny's Farm."

Come you ladies and you gentlemen
And listen to my song,
I'll sing it to you right, but you might think it's wrong,
May make you mad, but I mean no harm
It's all about the renters on Penny's farm.

CHORUS: It's a hard time in the country,
Down on Penny's farm.

Now you move out on Penny's farm,
Plant a little crop of 'bacco and a little crop of corn,
He'll come around to plan and plot,
Till he gets himself a mortgage
On everything you got.

You go the fields
And you work all day,
Till way after dark, but you get no pay,
Promise you meat or a little lard,
It's hard to be a renter on Penny's farm.

Now here's George Penny come into town,
With his wagon-load of peaches,
    not one of them sound,
He's got to have his money or somebody's check,
You pay him for a bushel,
And you don't get a peck.

Then George Penny's renters, they come into town,
With their hands in their pockets,
    and their heads hanging down,
Go in the store and the merchant will say:
"Your mortgage is due
And I'm looking for my pay."

Goes down in his pocket with a trembling hand-
"Can't pay you all but I'll pay you what I can."
Then to the telephone the merchant makes a call,
"They'll put you on the chain gang
If you don't pay it all."

Down Yonder

Bluegrass and Old-time song by L. Wolfe Gilbert; **DATE:** 1921; **RECORDING INFO:** Happy Siz 1921; Peerless Quartet 1921; Clayton McMichen 1926; Skillet Lickers; Roy Clark; Fiddlin' Doc Roberts; Clark Kessinger; **NOTES:** One of the most popular old-time song tunes ever recorded. The 1934 Skillet Lickers recording was kept in print by RCA until 1960 and sold over a million copies all told, it was the third best-selling country music record in the initial release year (backed with "Back Up and Push"). Many performers of this bluegrass standard don't realize it was a hit song before it became as instrumental favorite. Only the chorus is included here.

CHORUS: Down yonder, someone beckons to me,
C   G

Down yonder, someone reckons on me.
F

I seem to see a race in memory
C

Between the Natchez and the Robert E. lee.

Swanee shore, I miss you more and more;
D

Ev'ryday, my mammy land, you're simply grand.
G

Down yonder, when the folks get the news,
C

Don't wonder at the hullabaloo.
F

There's Daddy and mammy, there's Ephram and Sammy,
C

Waitin' down yonder for me.
D   G   C

Downhearted Blues

Blues song by Alberta Hunter **DATE:** 1921; **RECORDING INFO:** Bessie Smith 1923; Charlie Walker; Bob Wills; Janis Joplin; **NOTES**: Alberta Hunter (1895-1984) was one of the most popular blues singers in the 1920's. Her song Downhearted Blues became Bessie Smith's first hit record in 1923. Sing "she" also, "woman, sister and mother" when singing the male version.

Gee, but it's hard to love someone when that someone don't love you
I'm so disgusted, heartbroken, too I've got those downhearted blues
Once I was crazy 'bout a man, He mistreated me all the time
The next man I get he's got to promise to be mine, all mine

If I could only find the man oh how happy I would be
To the good Lord ev'ry night I pray, Please send my man back to me
I've almost worried myself to death wond'ring why he went away
But just wait and see he's gonna want me back some sweet day

             C   F   C   C7
CHORUS: Trouble, trouble, I've had it all my days

F
Trouble, trouble, I've had it all my days
                                  C

     G
It seems that trouble's going to follow me to my grave.   C F C G

Got the world in a jug, the stopper's in my hand
Got the world in a jug, the stopper's in my hand
Going to hold it, baby, till you come under my command

Say, I ain't never loved but three men in my life
No, I ain't never loved but three men in my life
T'was my father, brother and the man who wrecked my life.

'Cause he mistreated me and he drove me from his door
Yeah, he mistreated me and he drove me from his door
But the good book says you'll reap just what you sow.

Oh, it may be a week and it my be a month or two
Yes, it may be a week and it may be a month or two
But the day you quit me honey, it's coming home to you.

Oh, I walked the floor and I wrung my hands and cried
Yes, I walked the floor and I wrung my hands and cried
Had the down hearted blues and couldn't be satisfied.

Drunken Sailor/Early in the Morning

Traditional Shanty; **DATE**: Tune early 1800's; Lyrics 1900's; **OTHER NAMES:** Early in the Morning; What Shall We Do with a Drunken Sailor?; Kate Lay Sleeping; **RECORDING INFO**: John Baltzell, 1923; Kingston Trio; Cadgwith Fishermen; Richard Maitland; Pete Seeger; **NOTES:** The Irish air is known as Oro se do bheatha bhaile. According to Bayard (1981) there are more vocal than instrumental versions of this air which was often used for play-party and shanty ditties.

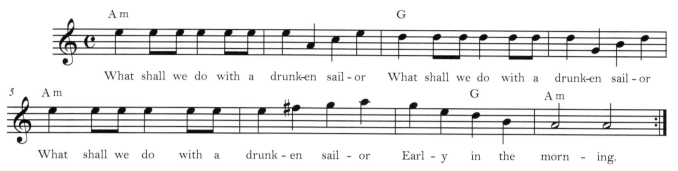

Am
What shall we do with a drunken sailor

G
What shall we do with a drunken sailor

Am
What shall we do with a drunken sailor

Early* in the morning?
     G   Am

CHORUS: Way hay and up she rises
Way hay and up she rises
Way hay and up she rises
Early in the morning

Put him a long-boat till he's sober

Keep him there and make him bale her.

Take him and shake him and try an' wake him.

Give him a dose of salt and water.

Give him a taste of the bosun's rope-end.

Stick on his back and mustard plaster.

Soak him in oil till he sprouts a flipper.

Shave his belly with a rusty razor.

*Early is pronounced "earl-i"

Easy Rider/ C.C. Rider/ See See Rider

Traditional blues song; **DATE:** Early 1900's-1924 recorded, 1926 in print; **OTHER NAMES:** C.C. Rider; See See Rider, Easy Rider Blues; **RECORDING INFO:** Ma Rainey, 1924; Big Bill Broonzy; Texas Alexander; Blind Lemon Jefferson; Sam McGee; **NOTES:** Easy Rider is a slang name for a romantic counterpart usually with loose morals. Two classic version are See See Rider by Ma Rainey and C.C. Rider by Bill Broonzy. Some versions repeat the first line three times and others (like Leadbelly's) have a tag on the end.

CHORUS: Easy Rider, see what you done, done

Easy Rider, you see what you done, done

You made me love you

And now your man done come.

My home is on the water, I don't like no land at all
Home's on the water and I don't like no land at all
I'd rather be dead than to
Stay here and be your dog.

I'm goin' away baby, sure don't wanna go
Goin' away baby, but I sure don't wanna go
When I leave this time
You'll never see me no more.

I'm goin' away now baby, I won't be back till fall
I'm goin' away now baby, I won't be back till fall,
Just might find me a good girl,
Might not come back at all.

Fall On My Knees

Traditional Old-Time Breakdown and Song; **DATE:** Late 1800's; **RECORDING INFO:** Ace Weems and His Far Meat Boys; Camp Creek Boys; Tommy Jarrell; Iron Mountain String Band; **OTHER NAMES:** Fred Cockerham's tune; Lonesome Road; **NOTES:** Tommy Jarrell said, "he knew a hundred verses" and remembered the tune in the Round Peak area around 1915. It has been known in neighboring Grayson County, Va., for a generation before that, testifying perhaps to the isolation of that mountainous region.

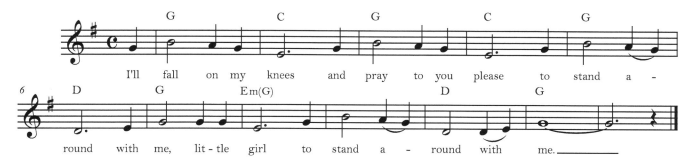

I'll fall on my knees and I pray you please,

To stand around with me little girl, To stand around with me.

I looked up, I looked down, that lonesome old road,
It's hang down you pretty head and cry little girl,
Hand down your pretty head and cry.

Well my suitcase is packed and I'm never comin' back,
Goodbye little woman I'm gone, I'm gone,
Goodbye little woman I'm gone.

Well I wish to the Lord that I'd never been born,
Or died when I was young, little girl,
Or died when I was young.

Then I'd never have kissed your red rosy cheek,
Or heard your lying tongue, little girl,
Or heard your lying tongue.

You've told me more lies than there's stars in the sky,
And you'll never get to heaven when you die, little girl,
Never get to heaven when you die.

My suitcase is packed and my trunk key's done gone,
And it's goodbye little woman I'm long gone,
Goodbye little woman I'm gone.

I pawned you my watch and I pawned you my chain,
And I pawned you my gold diamond ring, little girl,
I pawned you my gold diamond ring.

Fishing Blues (I'm A-Goin' Fishin')

Old-time Rag; **DATE:** Early 1900's; 1928 recording by Henry Thomas; **RECORDING INFO:** Henry "Ragtime Texas" Thomas in 1928 Vocalion 1249; Taj Mahal; Doc Watson; **NOTES:** Born in 1874, Henry Thomas was an African-American "songster," tracing his musical style back to pre-blues tradition, including playing a rack of quills (a folk instrument made from cane reeds). Thought not a regular blues, "Fishing Blues" is a popular fingerstyle guitar piece and has been successfully reworked by Taj Mahal and others.

Bet you're goin' fishin' all the time Baby's goin' fishin' too.

Bet your life that your sweet wife Gonna catch more fish than you.

CHORUS: Many fish bite if you got good bait. Here's a little tip that I'd like to relate:

Many fish bite if you got good bait. I'm a-goin' fishin',

Cause everybody's fishin', And my baby's goin' fishin' too.

Went on down to my favorite fishin' hole.
Baby, grab me a pole and line.
Threw my line in, caught a nine-pound catfish.
Brought him home for suppertime, provin' CHORUS:

I lean right back against an old pine tree
Then a big old bass took a look at me
He took my bait when I threw my line
When I got him to the bank, Lord, he sure looked fine CHORUS:

You put him in a pot or you put him in a pan,
Cook him till he's nice and brown.
Make a batch of buttermilk hoecakes,
Grab your fork and chomp 'em on down. CHORUS:

Footprints in the Snow

Bluegrass and Old-Time Song; Harry Wright, words and music 1880's; GR Jackson words and CW Bennet music 1886; **CATEGORY:** Early Country and Bluegrass Song; **DATE:** 1880's;
RECORDING INFO: Bill Monroe and his Bluegrass Boys, Hylo Brown; Doc Watson; Clint Howard & Fred Price; Don Reno; Bill Harrell and the Tenn. Cutups; Mac Wiseman; **OTHER NAMES:**
I Traced Her Little Footsteps; Only Girl I Ever Loved; Little Foot Prints; **NOTES:** The tune is similar especially in the beginning to "Little Stream of Whiskey."

Some folks like the summer time, When they can walk about ^{G} ^{C}

Strolling through the meadow, There's comfort there no doubt ^{D} ^{G}

But give me the winter time, When snow is on the ground ^{C}

I found her when the snow was on the ground. ^{D} ^{G}

CHORUS: I traced her little footprints in the snow, ^{G} ^{D}

I found her little footprints in the snow ^{G}

Bless that happy day, when my Nellie lost her way, ^{C}

I found her when the snow lay on the ground. ^{D} ^{G}

I went out to see her, there was a big round moon
Her mother said she just stepped out but would be returning soon
I found her little footprints and traced them through the snow
I found her when the snow lay on the ground.

Now she's up in Heaven with that angel band
I know I'm going to meet her in that promised land
Every time the snow falls it brings back memories
I found her when the snow lay on the ground.

Four Cent Cotton

Old-Time Song and Breakdown; **DATE**: 1929; The tune was one of those cited in the Fayette Northwest Alabamian of August 29th, 1929; Recorded by Skillet Lickers and Lowe Stokers Georgia Potlickers in the early 1930's. **RECORDING INFO**: Lowe Stokers Georgia Potlickers; Skillet Lickers; Freight Hoppers; **RELATED TO:** Eleven Cent Cotton; **NOTES**: Four Cent Cotton is a reference to cheap whiskey or moonshine. The relationship to the song Eleven Cent Cotton by Bob Miller (1929) is not documented. It's possible Miller's most famous song, Eleven Cent Cotton, Forty Cent Meat was based on the Four Cent Cotton lyrics he heard somewhere. Miller later recorded a version on his Eleven Cent song entitled, Four Cent Cotton.

C
Old John Davy is dead and rottin'

              G   C
He got drunk on four cent cotton

        Am
Hey, hey four-cent cotton

C   G   C
Hey, hey four-cent cotton

Sleep all night with a hole in your stockin'
Get no more of the four cent cotton
Hey, hey four-cent cotton
Hey, hey four-cent cotton

All year runnin' in cotton
I went broke on four cent cotton
Hey, hey four-cent cotton
Hey, hey four-cent cotton

Billie goat a-runnin' in the holler
We gonna sell some four cent cotton
Hey, hey four-cent cotton
Hey, hey four-cent cotton

Four cent cotton sure as you're born
I'm gonna drink some Georgia corn,
Hey, hey four-cent cotton
Hey, hey four-cent cotton

76

Four Nights Drunk (Our Goodman)

Old-time Song; originally from England; **DATE:** 1776 [Herd}; **OTHER NAMES:** Five Nights Drunk; Seven Nights Drunk; When I Came Home; Last Saturday Night; Three Night's Experience; **RECORDING INFO:** Thomas Ashley, Four Nights' Experience, 1928; Blind Lemon Jefferson, Laboring man Away from Home (Paramount, unissued, rec 1927); Earl Johnson & his Dixie Entertainers, Three Nights Experience (Okeh 45092, 1927); JE Mainer & Band, Three Nights Drunk; Gid Tanner & his Skillet Lickers, Three Nights Drunk (Bluebird B-5748, 1934); Sonny Boy Williamson (pseud. For Rice miller) Wake Up Baby (Checker 894, 1958); **NOTES:** Joseph Hickerson, an archivist at the Archive of American Folk Culture, Library of Congress, who has studied the ballad, says this is the most commonly recovered Child ballad, surpassing even Barbara Allen (Child 84).

Now I came home the other night drunk as I could be;
Found a horse in the stable where my horse ought to be.
Oh, come my wife, my pretty little wife, explain this thing to me,
How come that horse in the stable where my horse ought to be?
You blind fool, you drunken fool, can't you never see?
That's only a milk cow my granny sent to me.
I've traveled this wide world over, a hundred miles or more,
But a saddle on a milk cow I've never seen before.

I came home the very next night, drunk as I could be;
Found a coat on the coat-rack where my coat ought to be.
Oh, come my wife, my pretty little wife, explain this thing to me
How come that coat on the coat-rack where my coat ought to be?
You blind fool, you drunken fool, can't you never see?
That's only a blanket my granny sent me.
I've traveled this wide world over, a hundred miles or more,
But pockets on a blanket I've never seen before.

Now, I came home the late Friday night, drunk as I could be;
Found some pants on the dresser where my pants ought to be.
Oh, come my wife, my pretty little wife, explain this thing to me,
How come those pants on the dresser where my pants ought to be?
You blind fool, you drunken fool, can't you never see?
That's only a dish rag my granny sent to me.
I've traveled this wide world over, a hundred miles or more,
But a zipper on a dish rag I've never seen before.

Now I came home the next night, drunk as I could be
I saw a head a-laying on my bed where my head ought to be.
Oh, come my wife, my pretty little wife, explain this thing to me,
How come there's a head on my bed where my head used to be.
You blind fool, you drunken fool, can't you never see?
That's just a cabbage head your mother gave to me.
I been around this great big world a hundred times or more
But a mustache on a cabbage head, I've never seen before.

Frankie and Johnny

Old-Time Blues Ballad; Widely known; **DATE:** Melody 1904 (Copyright as "He Done Me Wrong" by Hughie Cannon); **OTHER NAMES:** Frankie and Albert; Maggie Was a Lady; Leaving Home; (Charlie Poole); Joking Henry; You're Gonna Miss Me; **RECORDING INFO:** Earnest Thompson 1924; Dukes Magic City Trio 1927; Mississippi John Hurt; Doc Watson; **NOTES:** Various theories have been proposed to explain the origin of the :"Frankie and Johnny" ballad. One theory connects it with the story of Frankie Silvers in 1831. Another basis for the origin is the murder of Allen Britt ("Al Britt"=Albert) by Frankie Baker in St. Louis, MO, on Oct. 15, 1899. "He Done Me Wrong," was written by Hughie Cannon in 1904. In 1912 the Leighton Brothers and Ren Shields collaborated on a first modern version of "Frankie and Johnny."

Frankie and John-nie were lov-ers. Oh, Lor-dy how they could love. They swore to be true to each o-ther, Just as true as the stars a-bove. He was her man, but he done her wrong.

Frankie and Johnny were lovers,

Oh, Lordy how they could love!

They swore to be true to each other,

Just as true as the stars above,

He was her man, but he done her wrong.

Frankie went down to the corner,
Just for a bucket of beer.
She said to the fat bartender,
"Has my lovin' man been here?"
He was her man, but he done her wrong.

"I don't want to cause you no trouble,
I don't want to tell you no lie;
But I saw your man an hour ago
With a gal named Nelly Bly,
And if he's your man, he's a-doing you wrong."

Frankie looked over the transom,
And found, to her great surprise,
That there on the bed sat Johnnie,
A-lovin' up Alice Bly.
He was her man, but he done her wrong.

Frankie drew back her kimono;
She took out her little forty-four;
Root-a-toot-toot, three times she shot.
He fell on that hardwood floor,
She shot her man, 'cause he done her wrong.

Roll me over easy,
Roll me over slow,
Please don't touch my wounded side,
'Cause my blood's gonna overflow,
I was her man, but I done her wrong.

The judge said to the jury
"It's as plain as plain can be
This woman shot her lover
It's murder in the first degree
He was her man, though he done her wrong.

They took Frankie down to the courthouse,
Put her in a big armchair,
She sat right there till that judge and jury
Gave that gal ninety-nine years,

This story has no moral
This story has no end
This story only goes to show to the gals
That there ain't no good in men.
He was her man, though he done her wrong.

88

Froggie Went A-Courtin'

Appalachian and Old English Ballad; **DATE:** First appears in 1549 (Wedderburn's "Complaynt of Scotland"); **CATEGORY:** English Ballad; **OTHER NAMES:** Frog Went A-Courting; A Frog He Would A-Wooing Go; The Frog's Courtship; The Frog and the Mouse; It was a frog in a well; There Was a Puggie in the Well; There Lived a Puddie in a Well; The Frog's Wooing; **RECORDING INFO:** John Jacob Niles; Peggy Seeger; McLain Family; Bluegrass Messengers; Doc Watson; **NOTES:** Horace M. Belden believes this is the most widely known song in the English language. The exchange of lyrics with "Froggie" and many other folk songs and fiddle tunes in the US has caused some confusion. Fiddle tunes often borrow short rhyming lines that make little sense as a narrative. Presumably some of the nonsense rhymes could have traveled from songs like "Froggy" and "Martin Said to His Man," to the related "Kemo Kimo" and the "Kitty Alone" songs. Lyrics from Bluegrass Messengers on "Diggin' Up Roots" CD.

Froggie went a-courtin' and he did ride, Uh-huh,

Froggie went a-courtin' and he did ride, Uh-huh,

Froggie went a-courtin' and he did ride,

A sword and a pistol by his side,

Uh-huh, Uh-huh, Uh-huh.

Well he rode up to Miss Mousey's door, Uh-huh,
Well he rode up to Miss Mousey's door, Uh-huh,
Well he rode up to Miss Mousey's door,
He hit it loud and made it roar,
Uh-huh, Uh-huh, Uh-huh.

He took Miss Mousey on his knee, Uh-huh,
He took Miss Mousey on his knee, Uh-huh,
He took Miss Mousey on his knee,
Said, "Miss Mousey, will you marry me?"
Uh-huh, Uh-huh, Uh-huh

"Without my uncle Rat's consent, Uh-huh,
"Without my uncle Rat's consent, Uh-huh,
"Without my uncle Rat's consent,
I wouldn't marry the president,
Uh-huh, Uh-huh, Uh-huh.

Uncle Rat laughed and he shook his fat sides, Uh-huh,
Uncle Rat laughed and he shook his fat sides, Uh-huh,
Uncle Rat laughed and he shook his fat sides,
To think his niece would be a bride,
Uh-huh, Uh-huh, Uh-huh.

Oh were will the wedding party be? Uh-huh,
Where will the wedding party be? Uh-huh,
Where will the wedding party be? Uh-huh,
Way down yonder in a holler tree,
Uh-huh, Uh-huh, Uh-huh.

The first to come were two little ants, Uh-huh,
First to come were two little ants, Uh-huh.
First to come were two little ants, Uh-huh.
Fixin' around to have a dance,
Uh-huh, Uh-huh, Uh-huh.

Next to come in was a bumble bee, Uh-huh,
Next to come in was a bumble bee, Uh-huh,
Next to come in was a bumble bee, Uh-huh,
Bouncin' a fiddle on his knee,
Uh-huh, Uh-huh, Uh-huh.

Next to come was a big bull-frog, Uh-huh,
Next to come was a big bull-frog, Uh-huh,
Next to come was a big bull-frog, Uh-huh,
He jumped up high and started to clog,
Uh-huh, Uh-huh, Uh-huh.

Mr. Frog went swimmin' across the lake, Uh-huh,
Mr. Frog went swimmin' across the lake, Uh-huh,
Mr. Frog went swimmin' across the lake, Uh-huh,
And he got swallowed up by a big black snake,
Uh-huh, Uh-huh, Uh-huh.

Gambler's Blues/Saint James Infirmary

Traditional Minor Blues Song; **DATE:** 1925 Scarborough 1927 Sandburg; **OTHER NAMES:** Old Time Gambler's Song, St. James Infirmary; Dyin' Crap Shooter's Blues; Those Gambler's Blues; **RELATED TO:** St. James Hospital (Sharp collected 1918); **RECORDING INFO:** Dock Boggs; Martha Copeland (Dyin' Crap Shooter's Blues 1927); **NOTES:** The Gambler's Blues was very popular (usually as St. James Infirmary) in the late 1920's and 30's with recordings by Jimmie Rodgers, Cab Calloway and Louis Armstrong.

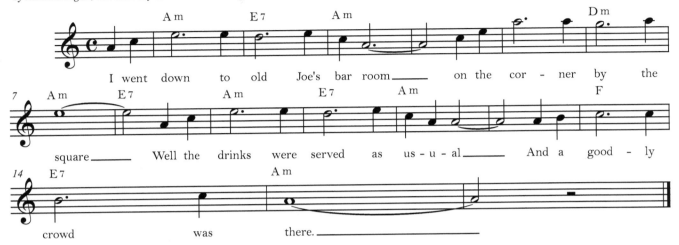

I went down to old Joe's bar room on the cor-ner by the square_____ Well the drinks were served as us-u-al_____ And a good-ly crowd was there._____

I went down to old Joe's bar room, On the corner by the square.
(Am) (E7) (Dm Am E7)

Well, the drinks were served as usual, And a goodly crowd was there.
(Am) (E7) (Am) (F) (E7) (Am)

On my left stood Joe McKenny, And his eyes were bloodshot and red.
Ho gazed at the crowd around him, And there were the words he said:

As I passed St. James Infirmary, I was my baby there.
She was stretched out on a long white table, So pale, so cold, so fair.

Let her go, let her go, God bless her, wherever she may be.
There'll never be another like her, There'll never be another for me.

Sixteen coal-black horses to pull that rubber-tired hack.
Well, it's seven long miles to the graveyard, But my baby's never comin' back.

Well, now you've heard my story. Well, have another round of booze.
And if anyone should ever, ever ask you, I've got the St. James Infirmary blues!

George Collins (Child 85)

Old-time English Ballad; **DATE:** 1810 in the United States; **OTHER NAMES:** Lady Alice; **RECORDING INFO:** Henry Whitter 1926; Roy Harvey and the North Carolina Ramblers; Riley Puckett; **NOTES:** This arrangement is based on a record by Roy Harvey and the North Caroline Ramblers, made in Ashland, KY in 1928.

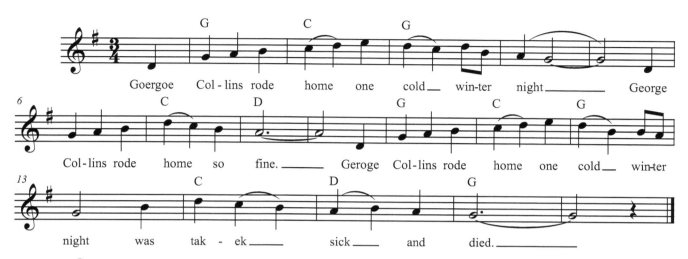

G   C   G
George Collins rode home one cold winter night,

   C   D
George Collins rode home so fine

G   C   G
George Collins rode home one cold winter night,

C D G
Was taken sick and died.

Dear little sweet Nell in younder room
Was sewing her silks so fine,
But when she heard that George was dead,
She laid her silk aside.

She followed him up, she followed him down,
She followed him to the grave;
And there she sat on a cold, cold stone,
She wept, she mourned, she prayed.

"Set down the coffin, take off the lid,
Lay back the linens so fine,
And let me kiss his cold, pale cheeks,
For I know he'll never kiss mine."

"O daughter, dear daughter,
   why do you weep so?
There's more young men than one."
"O mother, O mother, George has my heart,
His day on earth is done."

Look up and down that lonesome road,
Hang down your head and cry;
The best of friend is bound to part,
And why not you and I.

O, don't you see that lonesome dove,
There, flyin' from pine to pine;
He's mournin' for his own true love,
Just like I mourn for mine.

Georgia Railroad (Peter Went Fishing)

Traditional Old-Time; Breakdown & Song; **DATE:** Early 1900's; Gid Tanner recorded 1924; **OTHER NAMES:** Peter Went Fishing; Peter and I Went a Fishing; Gary Dawson's Tune; Georgia Gal; **RECORDING INFO:** Fiddlin' John Carson; Gid Tanner and his Skillet Lickers; Howdy Forrester; Norman and Nancy Blake; Ledford String Band; **NOTES:** The song was recorded in the 1920's by Gid Tanner and the Skillet Lickers. Melody was sung by Tanner to the A part only.

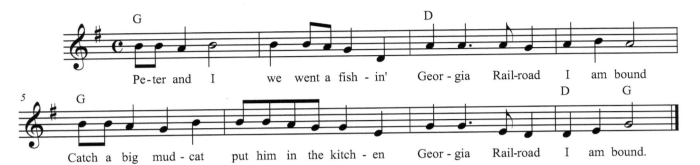

G
Peter and I, we went a-fishin'

D
Georgia Railroad I am bound;

G
Catch a big mud-cat, put him in the kitchen,

Georgia Railroad, I am bound.
            D   G

Walked down the road 'til it got right muddy,
Georgia Railroad, I am bound;
But I'm so drunk I can't stand steady,
Georgia Railroad, Georgia gal.

I got drunk and fell in a gully
Georgia Railroad, I am bound;
I got drunk but I never got muddy.
Georgia Railroad, Georgia gal.

Cow and the sheep put down to the pasture,
Georgia Railroad, I am bound;
The cow said, "Sheep can't you go a little faster,"
Georgia Railroad, Georgia gal.

Girl I Left In Sunny Tennessee

Old-time Song by Harry Baisted and Stanley Carter **DATE**: 1899 **RECORDED BY**: Charlie Poole 1925; Earnest Stoneman; Fiddlin' John Carson **OTHER NAMES**: Sunny Tennessee; **NOTES**: Charlie Poole (and the North Carolina Ramblers) recorded it in his very first session in New York City July 27, 1925. The song was a bit for him and proceeded to sell over 65,000 copies and to enter oral tradition.

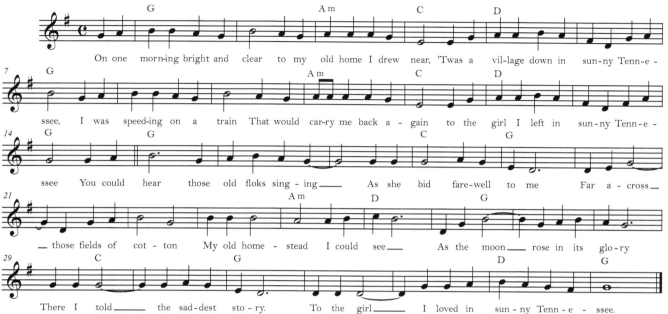

On one morning bright and clear
My old home I drew near,
It's a vintage down in sunny Tennessee.

I was speeding on a train
That would carry me back again
To that girl I left in sunny Tennessee.

CHORUS: You could hear those old folks singing
As she bid farewell to me.
Far across those fields of cotton,
My old homestead I could see.
As the moon rode in its glory,
There I told the saddest story
To the girl I loved in sunny Tennessee.

It has been but quite a few years
Since I kissed away her tears,
As I left her at my dear old mother's side.
And each day we've been apart,
She's grown closer to my heart
As the night I asked of her to be my bride.

As the train run in at last
Those familiar scenes I passed,
When I kissed my mother at the station door.
When the crowd gathered round,
Tears on every face I found,
But I missed the one that I was looking for.

As I whispered, "Mother, dear,
Where is Mary? She's not here,"
All the world seemed lonely, sadness came to me.
She just pointed to a spot
In the little churchyard lot
Where my sweetheart sleeps in sunny Tennessee.

It was spring, I remember well,
When little Tommy slipped and fell
Down into the icy Cherokee
Mary jumped in and saved the lad,
But her heart gave all it had,
And now she sleeps in sunny Tennessee.

Give Back My Fifteen Cents

Old-time Song and Breakdown; **DATE:** Early 1900's Brinkley Brothers' Dixie Clodhoppers 1928; **OTHER NAMES:** Fifteen Cents; **RECORDING INFO:** Dixie Clodhoppers 1928; Doc and Merle Watson; Norman Blake; Carter Brothers and Son; **NOTES:** Earl Johnson, fiddler for the Dixie Clodhoppers, was born on August 24, 1886 in Gwinett County, Georgia. He started his first group with his brother (guitar and banjo). After his brother died in 1923, he played with Fiddlin' John Carson and his band the Virginia Reelers. The next group he formed with brilliant guitarist, Byrd Moore, and banjoist Emmet Bankton was called the Dixie Entertainers. When Lee "Red" Henderson replaced Byrd Moore as the guitar player, the group became known as the Clodhoppers. They recorded some of the wildest and most exciting versions of standard breakdowns that have ever been released.

I left my home in Tennessee,
Thought I'd lean to travel,
But then I met a pretty little girl
And soon we played the devil.

I loved that gal and she loved me
And I thought we'd live together
But then we tied that fatal knot
And now I'm gone forever.

CHORUS: Gimme back my fifteen cents,

Gimme back my money;

Gimme back my fifteen cents

And I'll go home to mammy.

T'was fifteen cents for the preacher man
A dollar for the paper,
Then dear old mother-in-law moved in
And, Lordy, what a caper!

I fiddled a tune for her one day
And she called me a joker
Then that old sow got mad at me
And hit me with a poker.

I worked in town and I worked on the farm,
But there's no way to suit 'em
They're both so dad-burn mean to me
Somebody oughter shoot 'em.

I'm tired of looking at my mother-in-law
I'd like to see my Granny,
Gonna leave the state of Arkansas
And go back home to Mammy!

Going on Down to Lynchburg Town

Old-time Song and Breakdown based on "The Original Lynchburg Town" by Frank Spencer; **DATE: 1848; OTHER NAMES:** Going Down Town; Going Down to Town; Lynchburg; I'm Going Down to Lynchburg Town; The Old Hat; Git Along Down to Town, **RECORDING INFO:** Gid Tanner and Riley Puckett 1924; Grandpa Jones; Wade Mainer; **NOTES:** This song enjoyed a life on the minstrel stage. Appearing as "The Original Lynchburg Town" by Frank Spencer, the songwas published in New York, 1848, by Wm. Vanderheck. It was popularized by the Christy Minstrels. Lynchburg Town is constructed by "floating" verses frommany different songs including "Old Joe Clark," "Cindy" and "Bile Dem Cabbages Down" which are sung usually before each chorus.

G
I went down to town

And went into the sto̲re,
        D

And e̲very pretty girl in that town
     G

Came running t̲o the do̲or.
           D   G

CHORUS 1: Go̲ing down to town,
             G

I'm going down to to̲wn,
                D

G
Going down to the Lynchburg Town,

To take my to̲bacco do̲wn.
        D   G

CHORUS 2: Ti̲mes a-getting hard,
            G

Money getting sca̲'ce,
             D

G
Pa̲y me for them tobacco, boys,

And I will le̲ave this pl̲ace.
          D   G

Last time I saw my girl,
She was standing in the door,
Her shoes and stockings in her hand
And her feet all over the floor.

I went down to town
To get my a jug o' wine,
They tied me up to a whipping post
And give me forty-nine

I went down to town
To get me a jug of gin,
They tied me up to the whipping post
And give me hell again.

Old Man Jones was a rich old man
He was richer than a king
He made me beat the old tin pan
While Sary Jane would sing.

Old Man Jones had an old black hen,
She laid behind the door,
Every day she laid three eggs
And Sunday she laid more.

Grandfather's Clock

Old-Time Breakdown and Song; Words and Music by Henry Clay Work, Dedicated to his Sister Lizzie; **DATE**: 1876; **CATEGORY**: Fiddle and Instrumental Tunes; **RECORDING INFO**; Country Gentlemen; Homer and the Barnstormers; Songs of the Pioneers; Doc Watson; **NOTES**: Famous bluegrass instrumental and song tune by Henry Clay Work, usually in the key of G.

My grandfather's clock was too large for the shelf, So it stood ninety years on the floor,

It was taller by half than the old man himself, Though it weighed not a pennyweight more.

It was bought on the morn of the day that he was born. And was always his treasure and pride.

But it stopp'd short, never to go again, When the old man died.

Green Pastures

Traditional Southern Gospel based on a hymn composed by Isaac Watts; **DATE:** 1709; **CATEGORY**: Fiddle and Instrumental Tunes; **RECORDING INFO**: Emmylou Harris with Gillian Welch and David Rawlings on Down From the Mountain from the movie, O Brother, Where Art Thou?; **NOTES**: This graceful hymn dates back to 1709, being composed by Isaac Watts. Its original title was The Hopes of Heaven Our Support Under Trials on Earth, which was shortened to the title in the hymnal, Saints Delight. Among the folk song community, the song is probably better known as Green Pastures. Congregations in Southern Appalachia have sung this song for well over 200 years, following the melody and harmony in their "shape-note" hymnals.

Troubles and trials often betray those,

Out in the weary body to stray

But we shall walk beside the still waters,

With the Good Shepherd leading the way

Those who have strayed were sought by the Master
He who once gave His life for the sheep
Out on the mountain still He is searching
Bringing them in forever to keep.

Going up home to live in green pastures
Where we shall live and die never more
Even the Lord will be in that number
When we shall reach that heavenly shore.

We will not heed the voice of the stranger
For he would lead us to despair
Following on with Jesus our Savior
We shall all reach that country so fair.
(Repeat 3rd verse)

Gypsy Davy/Black Jack Davy

Old-time English Ballad; **DATE:** circa 1720; **OTHER NAMES:** Black Jack Davy/David; Gypsy Laddie; **RECORDING INFO:** Cliff Carlisle 1939 with slide guitar; Carter Family as Black Jack David; Doc and Richard Watson; **NOTES:** This song is popular in both British Isles and the US (usually titled Black Jack Davy/David).

D
It was late last night when the boss came home

Asking about his lady

And the only answer he received

She's gone with the Gypsy Davy
A7   D

She's gone with the Gypsy Davy.
A7   D

Go saddle for me my buckskin horse
And my hundred dollar saddle
Point out to me their wagon tracks
And after them I'll travel
And after them I'll travel.

Well, he had not rode to the midnight moon
When he saw their campfire gleaming
And he heard the notes of the big guitar
And the voice of the gypsy singing
And the voice of the gypsy singing.

Take off, take off your pigskin gloves
And your boots of Spanish leather
And give to me your lily white hands
We'll ride back home together
We'll ride back home together.

No, I won't take off my pigskin gloves
Nor my boots of Spanish leather
I'll go my way from day to day
And sing with the Gypsy Davy
I'll go with the Gypsy Davy.

Have you forsaken your house and home
Have you forsaken your baby
Have you forsaken your husband dear
To go with the Gypsy Davy
And sing with the Gypsy Davy.

Yes, I've forsaken my house and home
To go with the Gypsy Davy
And I've forsaken my husband dear
But not my blue eyed baby
But not my blue eyed baby.

Handsome Molly

Traditional Old-Time Song; Widely known; **DATE**: Early 1900's; 1927 recording, Grayson & Whitter; **RECORDING INFO:** Grayson & Whitter, 1927; New Lost City Ramblers; Doc Watson; Country Gentlemen; Wade Mainer; Flatt & Scruggs; Stanley Brothers; **RELATED TO**: Black-Eyed Mary; Lovely Molly; Loving Hannah; Irish Girl; Going Across the River to Hear My Banjo Ring; **OTHER NAMES**: Hannah My Love; **NOTES:** Handsome Molly is a version of the Irish Girl/Farewell Ballymoney" branches of tunes with which it shares several verses and the whole plot, as well as melodic similarities.

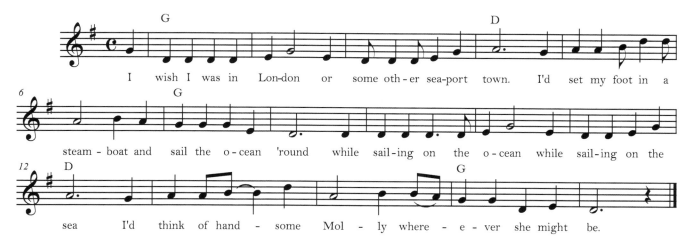

I wish I was in London, Or some other seaport town

I'd set my foot in a steamboat, And sail the ocean 'round.

While sailing around the ocean, While sailing around the sea,

I'd think of handsome Molly, Wherever she might be.

She goes to church a-Sunday, She passed me on by,
I saw her mind was changing, By the roving of her eye.

Don't you remember Molly, When you gave me your right hand?
You said that if you ever married, That I'd be the man.

Now you've broken your promise, Go home with who you please,
My poor heart is aching, You're lyin' at your ease.

Her hair was black as raven, Her eyes was black as coal.
Her cheeks was like lilies, Out in the morning grown.

He's Got the Whole World in His Hand

Traditional Old-time Gospel; **DATE**: 1927; **RECORDING INFO:** Bessie Johnson's Sanctified Singers, "The Whole World in His Hand" (Okeh 8765, 1930; on Babylon) Odetta; Tome Glazer; **NOTES:** This gospel song was popularized during the 1960's and remains a popular campfire song.

He's got the whole world in His hands, (C)

He's got the whole world in His hands, (G)

He's got the whole world in His hands, (C)

He's got the whole world in His hands. (G ... C)

He's got you and me brother, in His hands (3x's)
He's got the whole world in His hands.

He's got the little bitty babies in His hands (3x's)
He's got the whole world in His hands.

He's got the lyin' man in His hands (3x's)
He's got the whole world in His hands.

Hesitation Blues

Traditional Old-Time Blues Song; **DATE**: Early 1900's, W.C. Handy- 1905; **CATEGORY:** Old-Time Blues Songs; **RECORDING INFO:** Jerry Garcia and David Grisman; Kenny Hall and the Sweet Mill String Band; Holy Modal Rounders; Bascam Lamar Lunsford; Charlie Poole and the North Carolina Ramblers; Doc and Merle Watson; Old Crow Medicine Show; **OTHER NAMES:** If the River Was Whiskey; The Hesitation Blues; **NOTES**: There are many different sources and versions of this blues song. The main versions are WC Handy's "Hesitation Blues"; Charlie Poole's "If the River Was Whiskey"; Rev. Gary Davis's "Hesitation Blues." The lyrics from Hesitation Blues are generally floaters from other songs, especially the "Rye Whiskey/ Jack O'Diamonds" group.

1. If the river was whiskey and I was a duck

I'd dive to the bottom and I'd never come up

CHORUS: Oh, tell me how long have I got to wait

Oh, can I get you now, Ot must I hesitate?

2. If the river was whiskey and the branch was wine
You would see me in bathing just any old time. CHORUS:

3. I was born in England, raised in France
I ordered a suit of clothes and they wouldn't send the pants.

4. I was born in Alabama, I's raised in Tennessee
If you don't like my peaches, don't shake on my tree.

5. I ain't no doctor but the doctor's son
I can do the doct'rin' till the doctor comes.

6. Got the hesitation stockings, the hesitation shoes
Believe to my Lord I've got the hesitation blues.

101

Home on the Range

Old-Time Cowboy Song; Widely Known; **DATE**: 1873 (lyrics published in Smith County [KS] Pioneer; **RECORDING INFO**: Vernon Dalhart 1927; Jules Allen 1928; Black Bros. 1952; **NOTES**: No one is sure who wrote this song but Daniel Kelley and Dr. Brewster Higley are two possible candidates. Different adaptations have been published over the years such as "Arizona Home" by William and Mary Goodwin in 1904 and John Lomax's 1910 version which is frequently used today.

Oh, give me a home where the buffalo roam, Where the deer and the antelope play,
    G   C   G   A7   D

Where seldom is heard a discouraging word And the skies are not cloudy all day.
      G   C   G   D   G

CHOURS: Home, home on the range, Where the deer and the antelope play;
        G   C   G   Em   A7   D

Where seldom is heard a discouraging word And the skies are not cloudy all day.
      G   C   G   D   G

Where the air is so pure, the zephyrs so free, The breezes so balmy and light,
That I would not exchange my home on the range, For all of the cities so bright.

The red man was pressed from this part of the west, He's likely no more to return,
To the banks of Red River where seldom if ever, Their flickering camp-fires burn.

How often at night when the heavens are bright, With the light from the glittering stars,
How I stood here amazed and asked as I gazed, If their glory exceeds that of ours.

Oh, I love these wild flowers in this dear land of ours, The curlew I love to hear scream,
And I love the white rocks and the antelope flocks, That graze on the mountain-tops green.

Oh, give me a land where the bright diamond sand, Flow leisurely down the stream;
Where the graceful white swan goes gliding along, Like a maid in a heavenly dream.

Hop Along Peter

Traditional Old-Time Song by Frank Dumont **DATE:** Circa 1875; **RECORDING INFO:** Wade Mainer 1936; Fisher Hendley and the Aristocratic Pigs; Happy Valley Boys; New Lost City Ramblers; **NOTES:** I've been unable to see the original music by Dumont which is referred to by Gun Meade. The song is fairly rare with only three old-time recordings listed above.

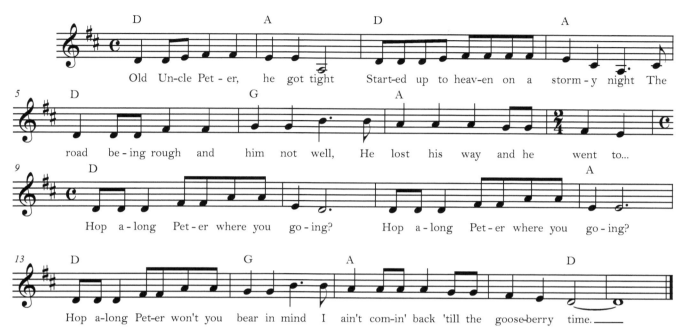

Old Uncle Peter, he got tight, Started up to heaven on a stormy night.
(D) (A) (D) (A)

The road being rough and him not well, He lost his way and he went to ----.
(D) (G) (A)

CHORUS: Hop along, Peter, where you going? Hop along, Peter, where you going?
(D) (A)

Hop along, Peter, won't you bear in mind, I ain't comin' back till the gooseberry time.
(D) (G) (A) (D)

Old mother Hubbard and her dog were Dutch,
A bow-legged rooster and he hobbled on a crutch.
Hen chewed tobacco and the duck drank wine;
The good played the fiddle on the pumpkin pie.

Down in the barnyard playing seven-up,
The old tom cat and the little yellow pup,
The old mother Hubbard, she's a-pickin' out the fleas,
Rooster in the cream jar up to his knees.

I've got a sweet gal in this here town.
If she weights an ounce, she weights seven hundred pounds,
Every time my sweet gal turns once around,
The heel of her shoe makes a hole in the ground.

House of the Rising Sun

Traditional Old-Time Song; **DATE:** Early 1900's; **CATEGORY:** Early Country and Bluegrass Songs; **RECORDING INFO:** Tom Ashley and Gwen Foster recorded Rising Sun Blues on September 6, 1933 on Vocalion 02576; Texas Alexander recorded The Risin' Sun on November 15, 1928 [OK 8673]; Homer Callahan recorded Rounder's Luck on April 11, 1935-issued on ARC in February 1926; Recorded by E. Tubb in 1936 (both he and Acuff where on Grand Old Opry); Roy Acuff recorded Rising Sun on November 3, 1938-issued as Vo/OK 04909 in August 1939; Recorded by Josh White in 1942, copyrighted by Leeds Music Corps., N.Y.; Mike Auldridge; Joan Baez; Bob Dylan; Country Gentlemen; Roscoe Holcomb and Wade Ward (Rising Sun); Leadbully; Doc Watson; Seldom Scene; **OTHER NAMES:** In New Orleans; Rising Sun Blues; **NOTES:** In 1905, House of the Rising Sun is said to have been known by miners. Clarence Ashley said he taught Rising Sun Blues or House of the Rising Sun to Roy Acuff after 1924, when Acuff graduated from high school in Knoxville and joined Dr. Hauers Medicine Show. Ashley has said that he thought he recalled his grandmother, Enoch Ashley, singing it to him when he was a young boy. R. Shelton has in the Josh-White-Songbook the following information "He (J. White) learned Rising Sun from a white hilbilly singer in N.C. His only time in North Carolina was in 1923 and early 1924, when he had been leased out by Arnold to Blind Lemon Jefferson whom he led through the major cities of N.C., the same area Clarence Ashley toured with a medicine show since 1911. Ashley night have been the "White hilbilly singer." In 1937 a "ragged Kentucky Mountain girl sang it to A. Lomax."

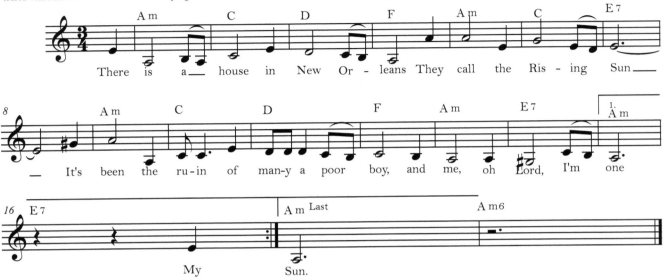

There is a house in New Or- leans They call the Ris- ing Sun ___

It's been the ru-in of man-y a poor boy, and me, oh Lord, I'm one

My Sun.

	Am		C		D		F		Am		C		E7
There is a house in New Orleans, they call the Rising Sun.

| | Am | | C | | D | | F | | Am | | E7 | | Am | | Am6 |

It's been the ruin of many a poor boy, and me, oh Lord, I'm one.

My mother, she's a tailor; she sewed those new blue jeans.
My father was a gamblin' man way down in New Orleans.

The only thing a drunkard needs is a suitcase and a trunk.
The only time he's satisfied is when he's on a drunk.

Fills his glasses to the brim, pass them around.
Only pleasure he gets out of life is hoboin' from town to town.

One foot is on the platform and the other one on the train,
I'm going back to New Orleans to wear that ball and chain.

Going back to New Orleans, my race is almost run.
Going to spend the rest of my days beneath that Rising Sun.

How Long Blues

Traditional Eight-Bar Blues; **DATE:** 1921; **OTHER NAMES:** How Long, How Long Blues; How Long, Papa, How Long?; **RECORDING INFO:** Daisy Martin 1921; Ida Cox/Papa Charlie Jackson in 1925 as "How Long, Papa, How Long?" Recorded in 1928. Tampa Red's Hokum Jazz Band; Gladys Bentley; Leroy Carr and Scrapper Blackwell; **NOTES:** The classic version is Leroy Carr and Scrappy Blackwell's "How Long, How Long Blues" on Vocalion 1191 which was recorded in Indianapolis, Indiana, circa June 1928.

How long, how long, has that evenin' trail been gone?

How long, how long, baby how long.

Heard the whistle blowin', couldn't see the train
Way down in my heart I had an achin' pain.
TAG: How long, how long, baby how long.

If I could holler like a mountain jack
I'd go up on the mountain and call my baby back. TAG:

I went up on the mountain, looked as far as I could see
The man had my woman and the blues had poor me. TAG:

I can see the green grass growin' on the hill
But I ain't seen the green grass on a dollar bill. TAG:

I'm goin' down to Georgia, been up in Tennessee
So look me over baby, last you'll see of me. TAG:

The brook runs into the river, river runs into the sea
If I don't run into my baby, a train is goin' to run into me. TAG:

I Am A Pilgrim

Traditional Gospel Song; **DATE:** 1862; CATEGORY: Early Southern Gospel; **RECORDING INFO:** Merle Travis on Capitol "Folk Songs of the Hills," 1947; Country Gentlemen; Bill Monroe; Stanley Brothers; Doc Watson; **RELATED TO:** Wayfaring Stranger; Going Over Jordan; **NOTES:** The origin of this song are entwined with Poor Wayfaring Stranger which appears in the Sacred Harp 1844, I'm a Pilgrim appears in The Southern Zion's Songster printed in Raleigh, NC in 1864 and in Hymns For the Camp in 1862 and begins: "I'm a pilgrim and I'm a stranger/I can tarry but a night." This hymn seems to have been a favorite in the South during the Civil War. The current song is similar to Merle Travis's version, who first heard a version of this song from Lyman Rager, who learned it while he was in the Elkton, Kentucky jail.

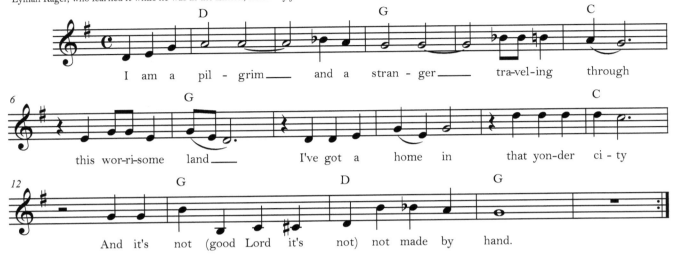

I am a pilgrim and a stranger

Traveling through this worrisome land

I've got a home in that yonder city

And it's not (Good Lord it's not), not made by hand.

I've got a mother, and a brother
Who have gone on before
And I'm determined to go and meet them, Good Lord
Over on that other shore. CHORUS

I'm going down to the river of Jordan
Just to cleanse my weary soul
If I could touch but the hem of his garment, Good Lord
I do believe it would make me whole. CHORUS

Now when I'm dead, layin' in my coffin
All my friends gathered 'round.
They can say that he's just layin' there sleepin', Good Lord
Sweet peace his soul has found. CHORUS

I Don't Love Nobody

Old-time Song By Lew Sully; **DATE**: 1896; **OTHER NAMES**: I Love a Nobody; Nobody Loves Me; I Don't Want to Get Married; Duplin County Blues; I Ain't Got Nobody; **RELATED TO**: Sam McGee Stomp; Santa Claus; **RECORDING INFO**: Gid Tanner and his Skillet Lickers; Tweedy Brothers; Elizabeth Cotton; Dickel Brothers; **NOTES**: This popular ragtime and Tin Pan Ally song by Lew Sully been covered by many old-time fiddlers; The sheet music cover features a photo of Sully in black-face. Paul Stamler points out that this was a "popular string ragtime song in the 1920's." Charlie Wolfe (1983) remark that it was issued by no less than six labels in the early 1930's. These are the original lyrics (edited).

Am   E   Am   E   Am
Met Miss Martha Johnson at a fancy ball,
C   D   G7 E
Tried her best to shake me, wouldn't work at all.
Am   E Am   E7   Am
Told her that I loved her, marry quick as a wink,
C   G7   C   G   D   G
She said look here fella, I'm gwine to talk distinct!

               C   F   C
CHORUS: "I don't love a nobody, nobody loves me,
                        D   G
You're after my money, you don't care for me.
C   F   C
I'm gonna live single, always a be free,
F   D7   C A D G   C
I don't love a nobody, nobody loves me."

Born in Kentucky, lived there all of my life
I've been very lucky, never had a wife
Mighty near it Sunday, I asked a girl to wed
Met the lady Monday, and this is what she said,

Went out Tuesday evening, 'long with Carter Bryce,
Broke that Kansas gambler shootin' poker dice;
Made love to his lady, kissed her right away,
Pulled a razor on me, then I heard her say,

Went out promenading down on Thompson St.
Met a good lookin' lady, smiled on her so sweet,
Said, "Ah there my honey, I thought I had her dead,
When I tried to kiss her this is what she said,

107

I Got A Bulldog

Old-time Song and Breakdown; **DATE:** Early 1900's; 1916 Collected by Cecil Sharp; **RELATED TO:** Take This Hammer; Roll On, Buddy; Swannanoa Tunnel; Don't You Hear My Hammer Ringing; **OTHER NAMES:** I've Got a Bulldog; **RECORDING INFO:** Sweet Brothers 1928; Famous Pyle Brothers; SkirtLifters; Roundtown Boys; **NOTES:** I got a Bulldog is related to the John Henry/Nine Pound Hammer songs which have a variety of names. Swannanoa Tunnel/Asheville Junction variants are based on tunnel made for the The Western Carolina Railway in North Carolina. Sharp collected two version of Swannanoa Tunnel with the Bulldog verse. From Sarah Buckner and Mrs. Ford 1916, Swannanoa Tunnel No. 91 A; When you hear my bull-dog barking, Somebody 'round, baby somebody round. The same lyrics appear in My Old Hammah from Carl Sandburg's book. Some suggest that bull-dog symbolizes a hand gun.

I've got a bulldog, he cost five hundred (C)

I've got a bulldog, he cost five hundred (F) (C)

I've got a bulldog, he cost five hundred (Am)

In my back yard babe, in my back yard. (C) (G) (C)

When he barks he roars like thunder
When he barks he roars like thunder
When he barks he roars like thunder
He barks at you baby, he barks at you babe.

Take this hammer and give it to the captain
Take this hammer and give it to the captain
Take this hammer and give it to the captain
Tell him I'm gone babe, tell him I'm gone.

When you pass by oh say good morning
When you pass by oh say good morning
When you pass by oh say good morning
Tell him I'm gone babe, tell him I'm gone.

When you see my long haired buddy
When you see my long haired buddy
When you see my long haired buddy
Tell him I'm gone babe, tell him I'm gone

I Never Will Marry

Traditional Old-Time Song; **DATE**: 1906 (Belden); **OTHER NAMES**: The Shells of the Ocean; Down by the Sea Shore; **RECORDING INFO**: Carter Family 1933; Texas Gladden with Hobart Smith, 1940s; Country Gentlemen; **NOTES:** The classic recording is the Carter Family recording done in Camden, NJ in 1933.

One morning I rambled down by the sea shore

The wind it did whistle and the waters did roar.
I heard some fair maiden give a pitiful cry
It sounded so lonesome, it swept off on high.

CHORUS: I never will marry, I'll be no man's wife
I expect to live single all the days of my life.

The shells in the ocean shall be my death-bed
While the fish in deep water swim over my head.
She cast her fair body in the water so deep
And closed her pretty blue eyes forever to sleep. CHORUS

I Ride an Old Paint

Old-time Cowboy Song; **DATE:** Early 1900's; **OTHER NAMES:** Old Paint; **RECORDING INFO:** Almanac Singers; Woody Guthrie; Harry Jackson; Tex Ritter 1933; **NOTES:** Pete Seeger says this was first published in Margaret Larkin's book of cowboy songs, but gives no date.

G
I ride an old Paint, I'm leadin' old Dan

    D   G
I'm goin' to Montana just to throw the hou li han,

        D   G
They feed in the coulées, they water in the draw

       D   G
Their tails are all matted, their backs are all raw.

               D   G
CHORUS: Ride around, little doggies, ride around them slow,

           D   G
For they're fiery and snuffy and rarin' to go.

Old Bill Jones had two daughters and a song,
One went to Denver, the other went wrong.
His wife, she died in a poolroom fight
But still he keeps singing from morning to night:

When I die, take my saddle from the wall
And put it on my pony, and lead him from his stall;
Tie my bones to his back, turn our faces to the west
And we'll ride the prairies that we love the best.

I Truly Understand You Love Another Man

Old-time Song; **DATE:** Early 1900's; **RECORDING INFO:** George (Shortbuckle) Roark 1928; New Lost City Ramblers; **NOTES:** The classic version was recorded in 1928 by George (Shortbuckle) Roark, of Pineville, Kentucky, who played clawhammer banjo and sang the verses, while other members of his family sang along on the chorus. The song is related to the family of song classified under the Lass of Loch Royal (Lochroyan); Little Red Shoes; Storms Are on the Ocean; Blue Eyed Boy; Single Girl; Married Girl; True Lover's Farewell; Who's Gonna Be Your Man?; He's Gone Away; Green Valley Waltz; Oh Have You Seen the Turtle Dove.

I wish to the Lord I never been born,

Nor died when I was young,

I never would've seen them two brown eyes,

Nor heard that flattering tongue, my love,

Or heard that flattering tongue.

CHORUS: I truly understand that you love another man,

And your heart shall no longer be mine.

I truly understand that you love another man,

And your heart shall no longer be mine.

Who will shoe your little feet,
Who will glove your hand,
Who will kiss your red rosy cheeks,
When I'm in the foreign land, my love,
When I'm in the foreign land?

Remember what you told me, dear,
As we stood side by side,
You promised that you'd marry me,
And be no other man's bride, my love,
And be no other man's bride.

I never will listen what another woman says,
Let her hair be black or brown,
For I'd rather be on the top of some hill,
And the rain a-pouring down, down,
The rain a-pouring down.

My father will shoe my little feet,
My mother will glove my hand,
And you will kiss my red rosy cheeks,
When I'm in the foreign land, O love,
When I'm in the foreign land.

I Want A Girl

Tin Pan Alley Song; music by Harry Von Tilzer lyrics by Will Dillon **DATE:** 1911; **NOTES:** Harry Von Tilzer altered the sound of his pianos by jamming bits of paper between the strings making a tinny tone. While visiting Von Tilzer's office Journalist Monroe Rosenfield heard the sound o many pianos echoing around the music publishing district on West 28th Street in NYC. In his newspaper Rosenfield's repeated use of the area as Tin Pan Alley in his articles, the name caught on.

When I was a boy my mother often said to me, Get married boy and see How happy you will be.

I have looked all over, but no girlie can I find, Who seems to be just like the little girl I have in mind.

I will have to look around Until the right one I have found.

CHORUS: I want a girl, Just like the girl who married dear old Dad.

She was a pearl, And the only girl that Daddy ever had;

A good old fashioned girl with heart so true, One who loves nobody else but you,

Oh I want a girl, Just like the girl that married dear old Dad.

By the old mill stream there sits a couple old and gray
Though years have rolled away Their hearts are young today.
Mother Dear looks up at Dad with love light in her eye
He steals a kiss, a fond embrace While evening breezes sigh,
They're as happy as can be, So that's the kind of love for me.

I'll Rise When the Rooster Crows

Traditional Old-time Song; **DATE:** 1880's; **OTHER NAMES:** Rise When the Rooster Crows; **RECORDING INFO:** Uncle Dave Macon 1926; Binkley Brothers' Dixie Clodhoppers 1928; Feldmann, Peter & the Pea Patch Quintet; J.E. Mainer; Doc Watson; **NOTES:** According to Meade, this song is in the style of an 1880's song but no record of it has been found.

CHORUS: I'll rise when the rooster crows I'll rise when the rooster crows
I'm going back south where the sun shines hot Oh down where the sugar cane grows.

VERSE: If the golden shoes you bear so much about Was worn down here you'd soon wear 'em out

We're gonna take up 'em yonder for to put on my robes Gonna put on my golden shoes.

Don't let old Satan try to fool you For the gates'll be closed and you can't get through
With a long white robe and the white socks too Gonna put on my golden shoes.

When Gabriel comes for to blow his horn Well you needn't pull back for you gotta go on
So prepare yourself for the judgment day For you can't take money and buy your way.

We'll have cider all the fall For I said I's going to the ball
Where the duck chews tobacco and the goose drinks wine The old hen cackles while the rooster keeps time.

Whatcha gonna do when the women all dead? Gonna sit in the corner with a hung down head
Well if I had to marry I wouldn't marry for the riches I'd marry a big fat gal who couldn't wear the britches.

I've Always Been a Rambler

Old-time Song; Found in British Isles and America; **DATE:** before 1852 (broadside; Bodleian Firth); **OTHER NAMES:** The Gal/Girl I Left Behind (not the Civil War tune The Girl I Left Behind Me); Maggie Walker Blues; **RECORDING INFO:** Jules Allen (The Gal I Left Behind), 1929; Clint Howard with Watson and Ashley (Maggie Walker Blues); Dock Boggs (Peggy Walker); G.B. Grayson & Whitter in 1928. **NOTES:** The singer goes from Marion, Virginia, and then on to Johnson City, Tennessee, a distance of about 100 miles.

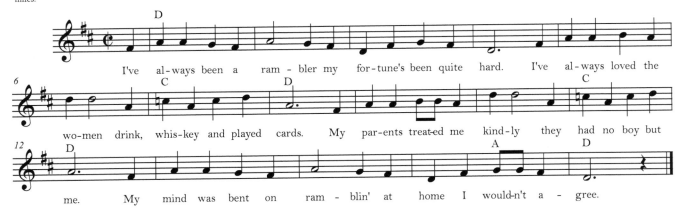

I've always been a rambler, my fortune's been quite hard.

I've always loved the women, drink whiskey and played cards.

My parents treated me kindly, they had no boy but me,

My mind was bent on rambling, at home I wouldn't agree.

There was a wealthy farmer who lived in the country by,
Had one handsome daughter on who I cast an eye.
She was so tall and handsome, so pretty and so fair.
There ain't one girl in the wide world with her I could compare.

So I asked if it made any difference if I crossed o'er the plain.
She says it'll make no difference so you return again.
She said that she'd prove true to me until I proved unkind.
Kissed, shook hands and parted with the one I left behind.

I left old North Caroliner, to Marion I did go,
Then on to Johnson City, gonna see this wide world o'er.
Where money and work was plentiful and the girls treated me kind.
The only object of my heart weather one I left behind.

I rambled out one evening down on the public square,
The mail had just arriven when the post-boy met me there.
He handed me a letter which give me to understand
The girl I'd left in Caroliner had married another man.

I read a few lines further 'til I found that it was true.
My heart was filled with trouble, I didn't know what to do.
My heart was filled with trouble, while trouble's on my mind,
Going to drink and gamble for the one I left behind.

114

Ida Red

Traditional Old-Time Breakdown; **DATE:** Late 1800's-early 1900's; Meade, Spottswood, Meade: Journal of American Folklore XXVIII, 1915. **CATEGORY:** Fiddle and instrumental Tunes**; RECORDINGS:** Fiddlin' Powers & Family 1924; Riley Puckett 1926; Charlie Poole and the North Carolina Ramblers 1928; Bob Wills 1938; Gid Tanner and His Skillet Lickers; Tommy Jarrell**; OTHER NAMES:** Idy Red; Shootin' Creek; Over the Road I'm Bound to Go**; RELATED TO:** Cripple Creek; Shootin' Creek (Charlie Poole); Feather Bed (Cannon's Jug Stompers); Over the Road I'm Bound To Go (Uncle Dace Macon); Down the Road (Uncle Dave Macon & Flatt and Scruggs; **NOTES:** Ida Red was originally supposed to have been an African-American bad man (Lomaz), but the gender of the character in most versions is feminine or androgynous. Riley Pucket's (north Goergia) version of the tune, released in 1926, became the second best-selling country music record for the year. There are two distinct branches of the Ida Red song: 1)The western branch includes Bob Wills's 1938 version which is based on "The Parlor is a Pleasant Place to Sit on Sunday Night," by Albert E. Porter 1886. 2) The southern branch features short clipped floating lyrics (Ida Red/Ida Green) similar to Cripple Creek. The Skillet Lickers and also Charlie Poole's versions are part of this line. Woody Guthrie, a popular radio entertainer in the 40's, sung Ida Red, and its melody was used by rock and roll pioneer Chuck Berry for his 1955 classic (Mabelline." Some versions sing a verse then sing the chorus twice.

VERSE: Ida Red, Ida Green Prettiest gal I ever seen.

CHORUS: Ida Red, Ida Red I'm just crazy 'bout Ida Red.

Ida Red lives in town
Weights three hundred and forty pounds.

Ida Red, Ida Red
I'm plum crazy about Ida Red.

Ida Red, Ida Red
Ida bit a hoecake half in two.

Ida Red. Ida Red
Everybody's crazy 'bout Ida Red.

If I'd 'a listened to what Ida said
I'd 'a been sleepin' in Ida's bed.

If Ida said that she'd be mine
I'd be Ida's all the time.

If Ida said she'd be my wife
I'd be happy all my life.

In the Good Old Summertime

Old-time song by Ren Shields and George Evans **DATE:** 1902 **RECORDING INFO:** William Redmond, Edison record 1902; Walter Peterson 1924; Riley Puckett 1925; Uncle Dave Macon 1926; Leake County Revelers **NOTES:** One of the favorite songs of the early 1900's that has proven the test of time. It was also widely recorded by country music artists in the 20s and 30s.

VERSE: There's a time in each year that we always hold dear, (A) Good old summertime, (D) (A)

With the birds and the trees and sweet scented breezes, (E) Good old (B7) summertime (E)

When your day's work is over then you are in clover, (A) And life is on beautiful rhyme, (D) (A)

No trouble annoying, each one is enjoying, (E) The good old (B7) summertime. (E)

CHORUS: In the good old summertime, (A) In the good old summertime, (D) (A)

Strolling through the shady lanes (F#) (C#) with that baby of (B7) mine (E) You hold (A) her hand ans she hold yours,

And that's a very good sign, (D) That she's your (A) tootsey-wootsey (C#7)

In the good (F#m) old s(B7)ummertime. (A)

Oh to swim in the pool you'd play hooky from school Good old summertime
You would play "ring-a-rosie" with Jim, Kate and Josie Good old summertime
Those are days full of pleasure we now fondly treasure When we never thought it a crime
To go stealing cherries with face brown as berries In the good old summertime.

In the Jailhouse Now

Traditional Old-time and Blues Song; **DATE:** Early 1900's; Whistler's Jug Band "Jailhouse Blues" 1924; **OTHER NAMES**: Jailhouse Blues; He's in the Jailhouse Now; I'm in the Jailhouse Now; **RECORDING INFO:** Whistler's Jug Band "Jailhouse Blues" 1924; Earl MacDonald's Original Louisville Jug Band 1925; Blind Blake 1927; Jimmie Rodgers 1928; Mississippi Sheiks 1930; **NOTES:** Though the song is identified with the great Jimmie Rodgers, it was a traditional jugband and blues song (being recorded Whistler's Jug Band as "Jailhouse Blues" in and by 1924 Blind Blake as "He's in the Jailhouse now" in 1927) before Rodgers recorded it.

C
I had a friend named Ramblin' Bob, Who used to steal, gamble and rob,

He thought he was the smartest guy in to^{F}wn. But I found out last Monday,

That Bob got locked up Sunday, The^{D}y've got him in the jailhouse way down to^{G}wn.

CHORUS: He's in the jailhouse n^{C}ow, he's in the jailhouse n^{F}ow,

I t^{G}old him once or twice, quit playin' cards a shootin' di^{G9}ce, He's in the jailhouse n^{C}ow.

He played a game called poker, pinoccle with Dan Yoker, But shooting dice was his greatest game
Now he's downtown in jail, nobody to go his bail, The judge done said that he refused a fine.
CHORUS:

I went out last Tuesday, met a gal named Susie, Told her I was the swellest guy around,
We started to spend my money, Then she started to call me honey,
We took in every cabaret in town.
CHORUS: We're in the jailhouse now, we're in the jailhouse now,
I told the judge right to his face, We didn't like to see this place, We're in the jailhouse now.

In the Pines

Traditional Old-Time and Bluegrass Song; **DATE:** Early 1900's; **CATEGORY:** Early country and Bluegrass Songs; **RECORDING INFO**; Bascom Lamar Lunsford; Fiddlin' Aruthur Smith and His Dixieliners; Bill Monroe & His Blue Grass Boys; Roscoe Holscomb; Blue Sky Boys; Louvin Brothers; Stanley Brothers; Doc Watson; **OTHER NAMES:** Grave in the Pines; Look Up Look Down that Lonesome Road; The Longest Train; Black Girl; **NOTES:** First recorded by Doc Walsh in 1926, the song is closely related to Long Lonesome Road and Longest Train songs. This song became the basis of Blue Diamond Mines in the 1970's. In the Pines/Longest Train has been traced to black convict coal miners. Sharp collected a version in Kentucky and it is found throughout the southern mountains. This version is similar to the classic Bill Monroe version the the tag after the chorus.

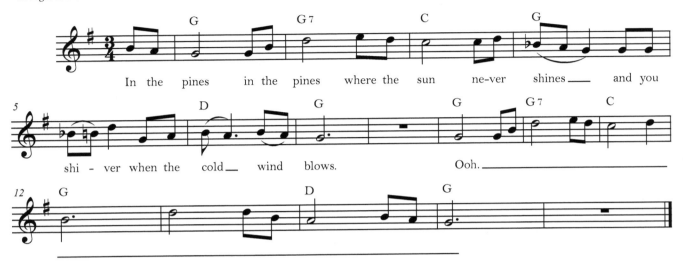

In the pines, in the pines, Where the sun never shines

And you shiver when the cold wind blows,

Ooh, ooh, ooh, ooh, ooh, ooh, Ooh, ooh, ooh, ooh, ooh.

The longest train I ever saw, Went down Georgia Line

The engine passed at six o'clock, And the cab passed by at nine.

Little girl, little girl, what have I done, That makes you treat me so
You've caused me to weep, you've caused me to mourn
You've caused me to leave my home.

I asked my captain for the time of day, He said he throwed his watch away
It's a long steel rail and a short cross tie, I'm on my way back home.

Jawbone

Traditional Old-Time Breakdown and Minstrel song; Widely known; **DATE:** Originated in the minstrel era, 1830-1890; Words and Music by Silas Sexton Steele "Walk, Jaw Bone" 1844; **OTHER NAMES:** Old Jawbone; Jaw Bone; Walk Jawbone; Hung My Jawbone on the Fence; **RECORDING INFO:** Pope's Arkansas Mountaineers June 1928; Carter Brothers and Song (Old Joe Bone-1929); New Lost City Ramblers; Willie Chapman; Hollow Rock String Band; **NOTES:** The Jaw Bone is a dance, an instrument, a stock character in minstrel shows as well as a fiddle tune and song. The instrument is made from the actual jaw-bone of a horse or mule. When the bone is thoroughly dried the teeth become so loose that they rattle and produced a sound as loud as that of a pair of castanets. The earliest printed version is by Silas Sexton Steele "Walk Jaw Bone" in 1844. My arrangement is based on Pope's Arkansas Mountaineers "Jaw Bone" recorded February 6, 1928 in Memphis, Tennessee, and issued as Victor 21577 in October 1928.

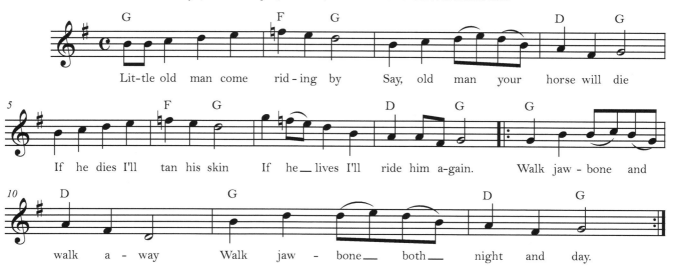

G   F   G
Little old man came riding by

               D   G
Say, Old man, your horse will die

           F   G
If he dies, I'll tan his skin

             D   G
If he lives, I'll ride him again.

              G   D
CHORUS: Walk jawbone and walk away

 G   D   G
Walk jawbone both night and day

 G   D
Walk jawbone and walk away

 G   D   G
Walk jawbone both night and day

Jawbone walk and jawbone talk
Jawbone eat with a knife and fork CHORUS

Jawbone broke and wire flew
Hide my head in the high land too CHORUS

If I die in Tennessee
Send that jawbone back to me CHORUS

Hung my jawbone on the fence
I haven't seen my jawbone since CHORUS

ALTERNATE CHORUS
Hug jawbone both night and day
Hug jawbone and fly away.
Hug jawbone both night and day.

Jesse James

Old-Time Ballad and Bluegrass Song; **DATE:** Circa 1882; **CATEGORY:** Early Country and Bluegrass Songs; **RECORDING INFO:** Bascom Lamar Lunsford 1924; Riley Puckett; Vernon Dalhart; Fiddlin' John Carson; Uncle Dave Macon; Bogtrotters; **NOTES:** Jesse James, living in St. Joseph, Missouri under his pseudonym "Thomas Howard" was shot by Robert Ford on April 4, 1882. Robert Ford was a member of Jesse's gang whom Jesse regarded as a friend. Ford shot Jesse in the back while Jesse was hanging a picture. According to Randolph, the song became popular throughout the Midwest almost immediately after Jesse's death. Ford himself was shot in 1892 by another member of Jesse's gang.

Jesse James was a lad who killed many a man, he robbed the Glendale train.

And the people they did say for many miles away, it was robbed by Frank and Jesse James

CHORUS: Jesse had a wife to mourn for his life, three children they were brave

But that dirty little coward who shot Mr. Howard, has laid poor Jesse in his grave.

It was on a Wednesday night, the moon was shining bright, they robbed the Glendale train
And the people they did say for many miles away, it was robbed by Frank and Jesse James CHORUS

It was on a Saturday night when Jesse was at home, talking with his family brave
Robert Ford came along like a thief in the night and laid poor Jesse in his grave. CHORUS

Robert Ford, that dirty little coward, I wonder how he feels
For he ate of Jesse's bread and he slept in Jesse's bed and he laid poor Jesse in his grave. CHORUS

This song was made by Billy Gashade, as soon as the news did arrive
He said there was no man with the law in his hand, who could take Jesse James when alive. CHORUS

Jim Along Josie

Breakdown and minstrel song, known both here and abroad, Written by Edward Harper; **DATE:** 1838; **RECORDING INFO:** Coon Creek Girls; 2nd South Carolina String Band; Mike Seeger; Lawrence Older; **OTHER NAMES:** Hey Jim Along Josie; Jim Along Josy; Hey Jim Along; **RELATED TO:** The Limber Jim/Buckeye Jim group which is related to Seven Up; Shiloh and the large Liza Jane family has floating lyrics with Jim Along Josey. Floating lyrics from Cotton-eyed Joe, Fire on the Mountain and Granny Will Your Dog Bite; **NOTES:** Jim Along Josey is a minstrel song written by Edward Harper around 1838., It is not clear if the song was in the African-American tradition before 1838 and adapted by Harper or whether it was an original composition. I suspect Harper rewrote (adapted) the song from traditional sources. In the title Jim Along Josey the Josey, is used as a name (could be a man or woman's name). The word Josey is an African-American dance step. The word, Jim, is not really used for a name. Get Along Josey could just as easily be substituted for Jim Along Josey. There is one version entitled Git Along Josie. Beside the minstrel version there is a play party version where the first word in the chorus line is changed: Hey jim along, jim along Josie/Walk jim along, jim along Josie/Hop jim along, jim along Josie, etc.

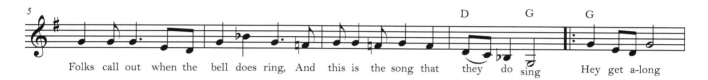

Down in Mississippi as you well know There's a song named Jim Along Joe

Folks call out when the bell does ring And this is the song that they do sing:

CHORUS: Hey get along, Jim along Josie,

Hey get along, Jim along Joe! (Repeat CHORUS)

Sister the other night did dream,
She was floating up and down the stream
When she awoke she began to cry,
And the white cat scratched out the black cat's eye. CHORUS

Barley, barley, buckwheat straw,
Hazelnuts and a crosscut saw,
Any pretty girl that wants a beau
Fall in the arms of a Jim-a-long-Joe. CHORUS

John Hardy

Traditional Old-Time Breakdown and Song; **DATE:** 1916 by Cecil Sharp; **CATEGORY:** Fiddle and Instrumental Tunes; **RECORDING INFO:** Carter Family 1928; Dock Boggs; Buell Kazee; Kingston Trio; Tony Rice; Country Gentlemen; **OTHER NAMES:** John Hardy Was a Desperate Little Man; **NOTES:** John Hardy is popular not only as a song but also as an instrumental solo (banjo, fiddle, or guitar). John Hardy was a black man working in the tunnels of West Virginia. In fact, as Alan Lomax remarks, "the two songs (John Henry and John Hardy) have sometimes been combined by folk singers, and the two characters confused by ballad collectors..." One payday, in a crap game at Shawnee Coal Company's camp (in what is today Eckman, WV), John Hardy killed a fellow worker. His white captors protected him from a lynch mob that came to take him out of jail and hang him. When the lynch fever subsided, Hardy was tried during the July term of the McDowell County Criminal Court, found guilty and sentenced to be hanged. While awaiting execution in jail, he is said to have composed this ballad, which he later sang on the scaffold. He also confessed his sins to a minister, became very religious and advised all young men, as he stood beneath the gallows, to shun n liquor, gambling and bad company. The order for his execution shows that he was hanged near the courthouse in McDowell County, January 19, 1894.

John Har-dy was a des-perate lit-tle man he car-ried two guns ev-ery

day He shot a man on the West Vir-gin-ia line you should have seen John

Har-dy get-ting a-way poor boy you should have seen John Har-dy get-ting a-way.

He went on across to the East Stone bridge, There he thought he'd be free
C   G   C   G

Up steps the sheriff and he takes him by the arm
C   G

Saying, "Johnny, come along with me, poor boy, Johnny, come along with me."
         D   G

He sent for his Mama and his Papa, too, To come and go his bail
But there weren't no bail on a murder charge
So they threw John Hardy back in jail, poor boy, Threw John Hardy back in jail.

John Hardy had a pretty little girl, The dress that she wore was blue
She came into the jailhouse hall
Saying, "Johnny, I'll be true to you, poor boy, Johnny, I'll be true to you."

I've been to the East and I've been to the West, Traveled this wide world around
Been to the river and I've been baptized
And now I'm on my hanging ground. Now I'm on my hanging ground.

John Henry

Traditional Old-Time Breakdown and ballad; **DATE:** Ca. 1900; **CATEGORY:** Early Country and Bluegrass; **RECORDING INFO:** Kenny Baker and Josh Greaves; Big Bill Broonzy; Tommy Jarrell; Lilly Brothers; Gid Teanner and the Skillet Lickers; Ralph Sunley; Flatt and Scruggs; **OTHER NAMES:** John Henry Blues; Death of John Henry; Steel Drivin' Man; **NOTES:** One of the earliest known versions of John Henry was printed as what is now known as the Blankenship Broadside, John Henry, The Steel Driving Man. There is no indication of date of place. Guy Johnson dated it based on information provided by the source of his copy of the broadside, a woman living in Rome, Georgia, as "ca. 1900." One of the most popular of all American folksongs, the raging debate that started in the 1920's about the identity of the real John Henry goes on.

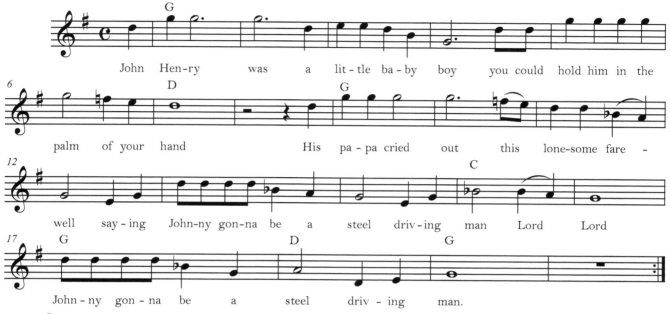

John Henry went upon the mountain, his hammer was striking fire

But the mountain was too tall, John Henry was too small

So he laid down his hammer and he died, Lord, Lord, laid down his hammer and he died.

John Henry went into the tunnel, had his captains by his side
The last words that John Henry said,
"Bring a cool drink of water before I die. Lord, Lord, cool drink of water before I die."

Talk about John Henry as much as you please, say and do all that you can
There never was born in the United States
Never such a steel driving man, Lord, Lord, never such a steel driving man.

John Henry had a little woman and her name was Polly Ann
John Henry took sick and he had to go to bed
Polly drove steel like a man, Lord, Lord, Polly drove steel like a man.

John Henry told his captain, I want to go to bed
Lord, fix me a pallet, I want to lay down
Got a mighty roaring in my head, Lord, Lord, mighty roaring in my head.

Took John Henry to the graveyard and they buried him under the sand
Now every locomotive comes a roaring by
Says, "Yonder lies a steel driving man, Lord, Lord, yonder lies a steel driving man."

Johnny Get Your Gun

Old-time Song and Breakdown; Words and music by F. Belasco (Monroe Rosenfield); **DATE:** 1886; **RECORDING INFO:** Bill Chitwood and Bud Landress 1924; Earl Johnson and his Dixie Entertainers 1927; Fate Norris and the Tanner Boys 1929; **NOTES:** The original song by F. Belasco AKA Monroe Rosenfield is a three part jubilee song which can be viewed on-line at the American Memory site. The folk and country versions use floating verses but keep the "Johnny get your gun, get your gun" tag and use it as the chorus. "Over There" by George M. Cohan written in 1917 used the "Johnny get your gun" line in the opening verse. This arrangement is based on Earl Johnson and his Dixie Entertainers' 1927 version.

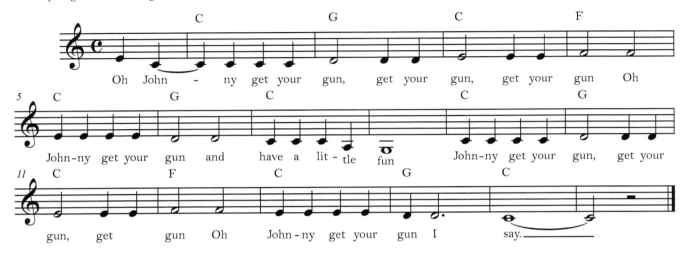

Oh Johnny get your gun, get your gun, get your gun
C   G   C   F

Oh Johnny get your gun and have a little fun.
C   G   C

CHORUS: Johnny get you gun, get your gun, get your gun
C   G   C   F

Oh, Johnny get your gun, I say.
C   G   C

Johnny pulled the trigger and the hammer came down,
Gun kicked Johnny right back on the ground.

Johnny got his gun, the gun was loaded
Johny pulled the trigger and the gun exploded

Johnny got his gun, says turn me loose
Shot at a crow and hit an old goose
Crow went caw, the duck went quack
Ought to seen the goose balling the jack

My ol 'Johnny was a great ol' man
Washed his face in the frying pan
Combed his hair in a wagon wheel
Died with a toothache in his heel

124

June Apple

Old-time Bluegrass banjo and fiddle tune; **DATE:** Earliest recordings of Train: 1927 by JP Nestor and Norman Edmonds of Galax; also 1927 Crockett Ward and his Boys; **RECORDING INFO:** Wade Ward; Riley Baugus Black Mountain Band; Camp Creek Boys; Cockerham, Jarrell and Jenkins; Red Clay Ramblers; Smokey Valley Boys; **RELATED TO:** Wooden Legs; **NOTES**: A June apple is an early ripening variety of apple, maturing in the spring in the southern United States. It tends to be smaller and more tart than later-ripening apples. Tommy Jarrell learned the tune from his father, Ben Jarrell. The lyrics for June Apple are commonly used from Train On The Island with some verses from Cindy and other songs with similar form (like Shady Grove). The 1927 recording of Train On The Island by Crockett Ward is sung to the June Apple tune.

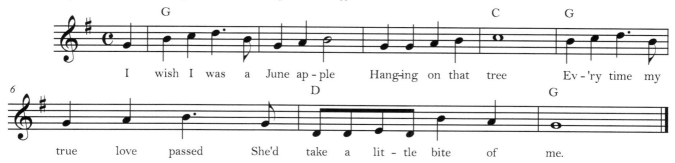

I wish I was a June apple

Hanging on that tree

Every time my true love passed

She'd take a little bite of me

Going across the mountain
I'm going in the spring
It's when I get on the other side
I'm gonna hear my woman sing

Can't you hear that banjo sing
I wish that girl was mine
Don't you hear that banjo sing
I wish that girl was mine

I wish I had some sticks and poles
To build my chimney higher
Cos every time it rains and snows
It puts out all my fire

Just a Closer Walk With Thee

Traditional Gospel Song; **DATE:** Late 1800's; **CATEGORY:** Early Gospel Songs; **RECORDING INFO:** Jethro Burns; Patsy Cline; John Jackson; Red Foley; Mahalia Jackson; **NOTES:** This gospel song has its roots in the African-American tradition. In the 1920's, Thomas Dorsey, a Georgia bluesman who later moved to Chicago, coined the term "Gospel" and was the acknowledged leader of the gospel movement. Just a Closer Walk With Thee is one of the popular Gospel numbers to come from this period, although there is some debate as to its origin.

Just a closer walk with Thee, Grant it, Jesus, is my plea.

Daily walking close to Thee, Let it be, dear Lord, let it be.

I am weak, but Thou art strong Jesus, keep me from all wrong.
I'll be satisfied as long, As I can walk, dear Lord, close to thee.

In this world of toil and snares, If I falter, Lord, who cares?
Who but Thee my burden shares? None but Thee, oh Lord, none but Thee.

When my weary life is o'er, Pain and suff'ring are no more.
Who will lead me safely o'er, Canaan's shore, that sweet Canaan's shore.

Keep on the Sunnyside

Southern Gospel Song; words by Ada Blenkborn; music by J. Howard Entisle; **DATE:** 1899; **NOTES**: Ada Blenkborn's invalid cousin always insisted that she push his wheelchair down the "sunny side of the street." This inspired her to write "Keep on the Sunny Side of Life." It was recorded on a cylinder in 1910 but the Carter family made it famous and used it as their closing (trademark) song. They recorded it on May 9, 1928 and again on May 8, 1935 for the American Record Company.

There's a
G
dark and
C
troubled side of life, There's a bright and sunny side, too.
D

Though we meet with the darkness and
G
strife, The
D
sunny side we also may
G
view.

CHORUS:
G
Keep on the sunny side, always
C
on the
G
sunny side

Keep on the sunny side of
D
life.

It will
G
help us every day, it will
C
brighten all the
G
way.

If
G
we'll
C
keep on the
G
sunny
D
side of
G
life.

The storm and its fury broke today, Crushing hopes that we cherished so dear
Clouds and storm will in time pass away, The sun again will shine bright and clear. CHROUS:

Let us greet with a song of hope each day, Though the moment be cloudy or fair
Let us trust in out Savior always, To keep us every one in his care. CHORUS:

Kentucky Moonshiner

Traditional Old-time Song; **DATE:** Early 1900's; **RELATED TO:** I'm a Rambler and a Gambler; **OTHER NAMES:** Moonshiner; Old Whiskey Bill; The Moonshiner; **RECORDING INFO:** Buell Kazee "Old Whiskey Bill, The Moonshiner," Brunswick E 22500, April 19, 1927; Leonard Rutherford and John Foster as "Kentucky Moonshiner" 1929; The Clancy Brothers and Tommy Makers; Roscoe Holcomb; New Lost City Ramblers; **NOTES:** First appears in Josiah Combs' 1925 dissertation at the University of Paris from Monroe Combs, Hindman, Knott Co., KY and then in Sandburg's American Songbag, 1927.

    G   Am   C   G
I've been a moonshiner for sev'nteen years

              Am   C   G
I've spent all my money on whiskey and beer

      Am   G   Am
In a wild lonesome hollow I'll build me own still

         G   Am   C   G
And I'll make you a gallon for a two-dollar bill.

I'll go to some grocery, I'll drink with my friends
Nobody to follow me to see what I spend
God bless those pretty women, I wish they was mine
Their breath smells as sweet as the dew on the vine.

Well its cornbread when I'm hungry, corn licker when I'm dry
If moonshine don't kill me I'll live till I die.
The world's but a bottle and life's but a dram
When the bottle is empty, it ain't worth a damn.

King Kong Kitchie Kitchie Ki-Me-O

Old-Time Song; **DATE:** Late 1800's; **RELATED TO:** Froggy Went A-Courtin'; **OTHER NAMES:** Sing Song Kitty Wontcha Ki-Me-O; Kemo Kime; **RECORDING INFO:** Chubby Parker; Ed McCarty; Doc Watson; **NOTES:** A modernized traditional version of Froggie Went A-Courting, this arrangement is similar to the hit song recorded by Chubby Parker in 1930.

A froggy went a courting and he did ride

King kong kitchie kitchie ki-me-o

With a sword and a pistol by his side

King kong kitchie kitchie ki-me-o

CHORUS: Ki-mo-ke-mo ki-mo-ke,

Way down yonder in a hollow tree

An owl and a bat and a bumble bee

King kong kitchie kitchie ki-me-o

He rode 'til he came to miss mousie's door,
King kong kitchie kitchie ki-me-o
And there he knelt upon the floor,
King kong kitchie kitchie ki-me-o.

He took miss mouse upon his knee
King kong kitchie kitchie ki-me-o
And he said little mouse will you marry me
King kong kitchie kitchie ki-me-o

Miss mouse had suitors three or four
King kong kitchie kitchie ki-me-o
And there they came right in the door
King kong kitchie kitchie ki-me-o

They grabbed Mr. Frog and began to fight
King kong kitchie kitchie ki-me-o
In the hollowed tree it was a terrible night,
King kong kitchie kitchie ki-me-o

Mr. Frog brought the suitors to the floor
King kong kitchie kitchie ki-me-o
With the sword and the pistol he killed all four
King kong kitchie kitchie ki-me-o

They went to the park on the very next day
King kong kitchie kitchie ki-me-o
And left on their honeymoon right away
King kong kitchie kitchie ki-me-o

Now they live far off in a hollow tree
King kong kitchie kitchie ki-me-o
Where they now have wealth and children three
King kong kitchie kitchie ki-me-o

Kitty Alone

Traditional Song and Dance Tune in the US and British Isles; **DATE**: "Froggie Went A Courting" branch-1549; "Martin Said to His Man" branch-1588; **OTHER NAMES**: Who's the Fool Now?; Old Blind Drunk John/Martin; Fooba-Wooba John; Johnny Foo'; Kitty and I; For in the Well; **RELATED TO**: Martin Said to His Man; Froggie Went A Courting; Limber Jim; Keno Kimo/ Sing Song Kitty; **RECCORDING INFO**: Carter Family; Been Family; Anne Hills and Cindy Mangsen; Mike Seeger; **NOTES**: "Kitty Alone" is a branch of the "Froggie Went A Counting" and "Frog in the Well" songs. It is also related to the "Old Blind Drunk John/Marting Said to His Man" songs and the text is found in the "Limber Jim/Buck-Eye Jim" group of songs.

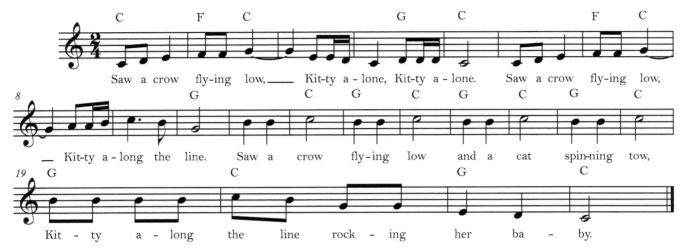

Saw a crow fly-ing low,___ Kit-ty a-lone, Kit-ty a-lone. Saw a crow fly-ing low,
___ Kit-ty a-long the line. Saw a crow fly-ing low and a cat spin-ning tow,
Kit-ty a-long the line rock-ing her ba-by.

Saw a crow flying low,

Kitty alone, Kitty alone,

Saw a crow flying low,

Kitty along the line.

Saw a crow flying low

And a cat spinning tow,

Kitty along the line

Rocking her baby.

Saw a louse chance a mouse,
Kitty alone, Kitty alone,
From the kitchen to the house,
Kitty along the line.

Saw a mule teachin' school,
Kitty alone, Kitty alone,
To the bullfrogs in the pool.
Kitty along the line.

Saw a flea heave a tree,
Kitty alone, Kitty alone,
In the middle of the sea.
Kitty along the line.

Saw a rat catch a cat
Kitty alone, Kitty alone,
Can you tell a lie like that?
Kitty along the line.

Kumbaya

Traditional Gospel Song; **DATE**: 1920 referenced by Pete Seeger; **OTHER NAMES**: Kumbayah; Come By Here; **RECORDING INFO**: Joan Baez; Seekers; Weavers; Pete Seegar; **NOTES**: Kumbaya apparently originated with the Gullah, an African-American people living on the Sea Islands and adjacent coastal regions of South Carolina and Georgia. Sometimes between 1922 and 1931, members of an organization called the Society for the Preservation of Spirituals collected a song from the South Carolina coast. "Come By Yah," as they called it, was sung in Gullah, the dialect spoken by the former slaves living on the Sea Islands. Another version was preserved on a wax cylinder in May 1936 by Robert Winslow Gordon discovered a woman named Ethel Best singing "Come By Here" with a group in Raiford, Florida. Martin V. Frey has long claimed authorship of the song. He wrote his version in 1936 and it was printed in 1939. He taught it to a family of missionaries that was going to Angola and there they changed 'come by here' to Kumbaya, the African pronunciation.

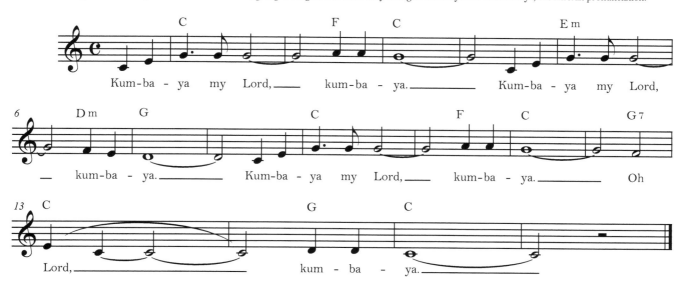

Kumbaya, my Lord, kumbaya
   C   F C

Kumbaya, my Lord, kumbaya
   Em   Dm G

Kumbaya, my Lord, kumbaya
   C   F C

Oh Lord, kumbaya.
G7 C G C

Someone's sleeping, Lord, kumbaya
Someone's sleeping, Lord, kumbaya
Someone's sleeping, Lord, kumbaya
Oh Lord, kumbaya.

Someone's crying, Lord, kumbaya
Someone's crying, Lord, kumbaya
Someone's crying, Lord, kumbaya
Oh Lord, kumbaya.

L'il Liza Jane

Old-Time, Bluegrass, Western Swing-Composed by Countess Ada de Lachas; **DATE:** Published in 1916; **CATEGORY:** Fiddle and Instrumental Tunes; **OTHER NAMES:** Little Liza Jane; Sweet Little Liza Jane; Used for other; Liza Janes songs. **RECORDING INFO**: First recorded L'il Liz Jane by Harry C. Brown in 1918, Co A2622; Bob Wills and his Texas Playboys 1941 on OK 06371; Charlie Monroe and the Kentucky Pardners; **NOTES**: Composed by Countess Ada de Lachas in 1916, L'il Liza Jane Jane was a take off on the earlier minstrel songs and was written in minstrel dialect. It is similar to Camptown Races by Stephen Foster with L'il Liza Jane substituted for "Oh Doo-day day." The L'il Liza Jane song ("I's got a gal an you've got none, L'il Liza Jane") is an entirely different song than Liza Jane. The tag (Chorus) was added making it a unique adaptation: "Oh Liza, L'il Liza Jane; Oh Liza, L'il Liza Jane."

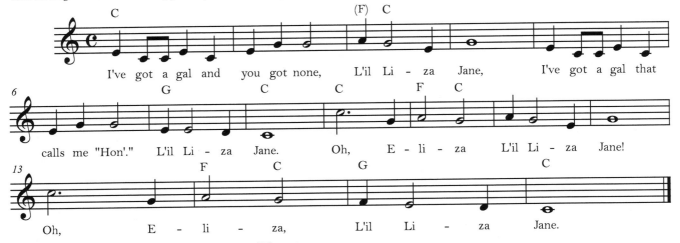

I've got a gal and you've got none, L'il Liza Jane

I've got a gal that calls me hon', L'il Liza Jane

CHORUS: Oh Eliza, L'il Liza Jane; Oh Eliza, L'il Liza Jane.

Come my love and live with me; L'il Liza Jane
I will take good care of thee; L'il Liza Jane CHORUS:

Jimmy John is layin' low, L'il Liza Jane
Come and take me for you beau, L'il Liza Jane. CHORUS:

Gonna throw the dice away, L'il Liza Jane
When you name that happy day, L'il Liza Jane.

Liza Jane done come to me; L'il Liza Jane
Both as happy as can be; L'il Liza Jane.

Ev'ry mornin' when I wakes, L'il Liza Jane
Smell the ham an' buck-wheat cakes; L'il Liza Jane.

House an' lot in Baltimo',
Lots of children roun' the door, L'il Liza Jane.

Never more from you I'll roam; L'il Liza Jane
Best place is home sweet home; L'il Liza Jane.

Letter Edged in Black, The

Old-time Song by Hattie Nevada; **DATE:** 1897; **RECORDING INFO:** Fiddlin' John Carson; Vernon Dalhart; Bradley Kincaid; JE Mainer's Mountaineers; Marty Robbins; **NOTES:** Although The Letter Edged In Black was written by Hattie Nevada, the authorship was forgotten. The song moved into the folk tradition and was popularized in the 1920's and has remained a country music standard.

I was stan-ding at the win-dow yes-ter-day mor-ning, With-out a thought of wor-ry or of care. When I saw the post-man co-ming up the path-way With such a hap-py look and jol-ly air.

I was standing by the window yesterday morning,
Without a thought of worry or of care,
When I saw the postman coming up the pathway,
With such a hapy look and jolly air.

CHORUS: As I heard the postman

whistling yesterday morning,

Coming down the pathway with his pack,

Oh he little knew the sorrow that he brought me

When he handed me that letter edged in black.

Oh, he rand the bell and whistled while he waited,
And the he said, "Good morning to you, Jack."
But he little knew the sorrow that he brought me
When he handed me that letter edged in black.

With trembling hand I took the letter from him,
I broke the seal and this is what it said:
"Come home, my boy, your dear old father wants you!
Come home, my boy, your dear old mother's dead!"

"The last words that your mother ever uttered--
'Tell my boy I want him to come back,'
My eyes are blurred, my poor old heart is breaking,
For I'm writing you this letter edged in black."

I bow my head in sorrow and in silence,
The sunshine of my life it all has fled,
Since the postman brought that letter yesterday morning
Saying, 'Come home, my boy,
          your dear old mother's dead!"

"Those angry words, I wish I'd never spoken,
You know I never meant them, don't you Jack?
May the angels bear me witness, I am asking
Your forgiveness in this letter edged in black."

Listen to the Mockingbird

Old-Time and Bluegrass Song; Melody by Richard Millburn, Written and arranged by Septimus Winner (aka Alice Hawthorne); **DATE**: April 17,1855; **OTHER NAMES:** Mockingbird Schottishe; Mockingbird; **RECORDING INFO:** Arthur Smith; Clark Kessinger; Vasser Clements; Chet Atkins; Chubby Wise; Bradley Kincaid; **NOTES**: A once-popular minstrel song melody by Richard (Whistling Dick) Milburn, a free Philadelphia black composer, arranged with lyrics by Alice Harthorne (really Septimus Winner) that has been extremely popular as a contest tune among fiddlers. Soon after the song was out it became a hit especially in the South where the mockingbird is a common sight. For years afterwards, Southern mothers named their baby girls Kally (or Hallie) after this song. The song became popular all over Eurpoe and it is estimated that by 1905 total sheet copies sold ran approximately twenty million. This song's immense popularity has struck solidly for over a century. It was adapted by Lyle "Spuds" Murphy as the Three Stooges Theme Song-"Listen to the Mockingbird" incorporating "Hickory, Dickory Dock."

I'm dreaming now of Hallie,
D7   G

sweet Hallie, sweet Hallie,
     D7   G

I'm dreaming now of Hallie,
     D7   G

For the thought of her is one that never dies;
        C   D7   G

She's sleeping in the valley, the valley, the valley;
     D7   G   D7   G

She's sleeping in the valley,
     D7   G

And the mockingbird is singing where she lies.
        C   D7   G

CHORUS: Listen to the mockingbird,
                      D7

Listen to the mockingbird,
              G

The mockingbird still singing o'er her grave.
    D7   G

Listen to the mockingbird,
              D7

Listen to the mockingbird,
              G

Still singing where the weeping willows wave.
     C   D7   G

Ah! well I yet remember,
     remember, remember,
Ah! well I yet remember,
When we gather'd in the cotton side by side;
'Twas in mild September, September, September,
'Twas in the mild September,
And the mockingbird was singing far and wide.
CHORUS:

When the charms of spring awaken,
     awaken, awaken;
When the charms of spring awaken,
And the mockingbird is singing on the bough.
I feel like on forsaken, forsaken, forsaken.
I feel like one forsaken,
Since my Hallie is no longer with me now.
CHORUS:

Little Brown Jug

Old-time Minstrel Waltz by Joseph Eastburn Winner, 1837-1918; Widely known **DATE:** 1869; **RECORDING INFO:** Henry Whitter 1924; Ernest Thompson (Co147-D, 1924) NYC; Uncle George Reneau (Vo 12812, 1924) NYC; Dave Macon "Muskrat Medley" (Vo 15101, 1925) NYC; Chubby Parker Gnt Uniss 1927); **OTHER NAMES:** Bring Out the Little Brown Jug; Robinson County; Black River; Wild John; **NOTES:** Originally composed for the minstrel stage by one "Eastburn," believed to be a pseudonym for Joseph E(astburn) Winner (1837-1918). He copyrighted the melody in 1869. Despite its stage origins, the tune quickly entered tradition and has been widely disseminated. Here are the original lyrics.

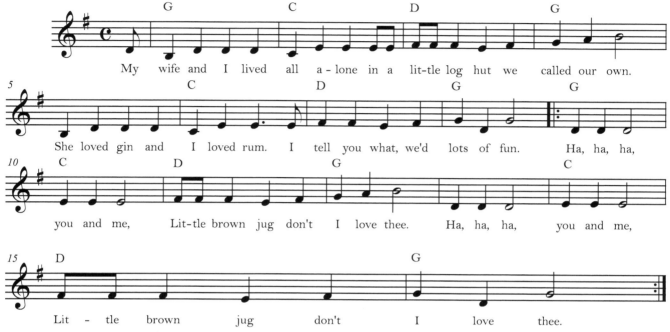

My wife and I lived all alone;
In a little log hut we called our own;
She loved gin, and I loved rum,
I tell you what, we'd lots of fun.

CHORUS: Ha, ha, ha, you and me,
"Little brown jug" don't I love thee;
Ha, ha, ha, you and me,
"Little brown jug" don't I love thee.

'Tis you who makes my friends my foes,
'Tis you who makes me wear old clothes;
Here you are, so near my nose,
So tip her up and down she goes. CHORUS:

When I go toiling to my farm,
I take "Little Brown Jug" under my arm;
I place it under a shady tree,
"Little Brown Jug" 'tis you and me.

If all the folks in Adam's race,
Were gathered together in one place;
Then I'd prepare to shed a tear,
Before I'll part from you, my dear.

If I'd a cow that gave such milk,
I'd clothe her in the finest silk;
I'd feed her on the choicest hay,
And milk her forty times a day.

The rose is red, my nose is too,
The violet's blue, and so are you;
And yet I guess before I stop,
We'd better take another drop.

Little Maggie

Old-Time, Bluegrass; Breakdown and song; **DATE:** late 1800's; **CATEGORY:** Fiddle and instrumental tunes; **RECORDING INFO:** Little Maggie with a dram glass in her hand" was first recorded by Grayson and Whitter in 1928; the Stanley Brothers; Fred Cockerham; Kingston Trio; Ricky Skaggs; **NOTES:** Little Maggie is part of the Darling Cory/Corey family of "white blues" songs that include country blues/hustling gamblers which were found in the Appalachian region in the late 1800's. Barry O'connell suggests that this "lyric and tune family has been around in the southern mountain for over a centruy. The family of tunes probably originates late in the 19th century and belongs to the then developing traditions of white blues ballads." Little Maggie was recorded by the Stanley Brothers in 1946, when their music was more old-time than bluegrass in style. Mt. Airy, North Carolina fiddler Tommy Jarrell remembered the tune "going around" the Round Peak area (where he grew up) around 1915 or 1916, and it became quite popular with the younger folk.

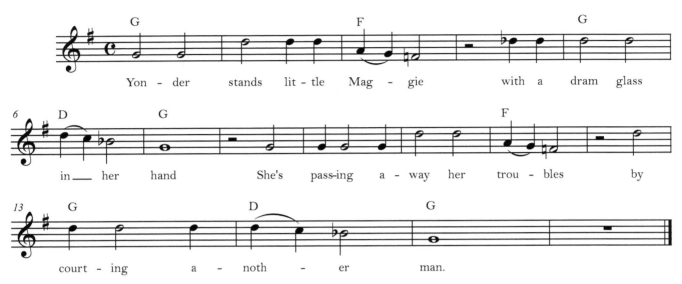

Yonder stands little Maggie with a dram glass in her hand

She's passing away her troubles by courting another man.

Oh how can I ever stand it just to see them two blue eyes
A-shining in the moonlight like two diamonds in the skies.

Pretty flowers were made for blooming, pretty stars were made to shine
Pretty women were made for loving, Little Maggie was made for mine.

Last time I saw little Maggie she was setting on the banks of the sea
With a forty-four around her and a banjo on her knee.

Lay down your last gold dollar, lay down your gold watch and chain
Little Maggie's gonna dance for Daddy, listen to this old banjo ring.

I'm going down to the station with my suitcase in my hand
I'm going away for to leave you, I'm going to some far distant land.

Go away, go away little Maggie, go and do the best you can
I'll get me another woman, you can get you another man.

Little Old Log Cabin in the Lane

Old-Time Song Tune. Words & Music by William S Hays; **DATE**: 1871; **CATEGORY**: Fiddle and Instrumental Tunes; **RECORDING INFO**: Fiddlin' John Carson; Wade Mainer; Tennessee River Boys; Mac Wiseman; **OTHER NAMES**: Little Old Log Cabin Down the Lane; Hungry Hash House (Blues; Fiddle and Bow; Little Joe, the Wrangler; Lily of the Valley; Little Old Sod Shanty (on the Claim); Little Red Caboose Behind the Train; Another Fall of Rain; Beans, Gravy and Bacon, **NOTES**: The song was written and published in 1871 by a Kentucky riverman turned vaudeville songwriter, Will Hayes. The southern gospel hymn, Lily of the Valley, with words by Charles W. Fry (1881) was adapted from Hays' Little Old Log Cabin. The piece was first released in 1923 when Fiddlin' John Carson's (north Georgia) version became the second best-selling country music record for that year. Yet another performance, Ernest Stoneman's, made the charts that decade, in 1926 when his version became the fifth best-selling country music record. Some bluegrass versions are played in the Key of F but immediately change to the Key of G for the solos.

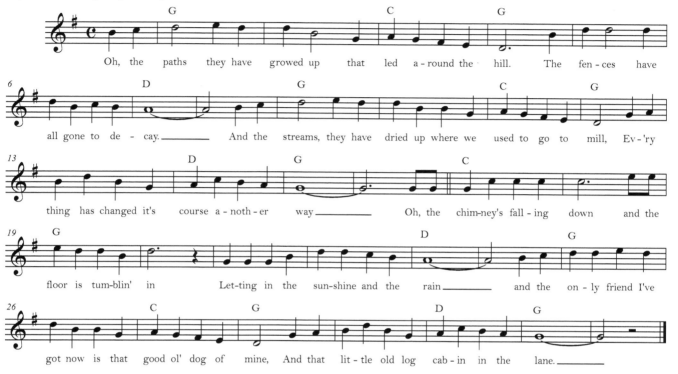

Oh, the paths have all growed up that led around the hill

The fences have all gone to decay

And the streams they have all dried up where we used to go to mill

Ev'ry thing has changed its course another way.

CHORUS: Oh, the chimney's falling down and the roof is all tumblin' in

Letting in the sunshine and the rain

And the only friend I've got now is that good old dog of mine

And that little old log cabin in the lane.

Oh, I ain't got long to stay here, what little time I got, I want to rest content while I remain
Till death shall call this dog and me to find a better home
And that little old log cabin in the lane. CHORUS:

Little Rabbit

Traditional Old-Time, Breakdown; **DATE:** 1800's as "John Brown's Dream" was recorded in 1927 by Da Costa Woltz's Southern Broadcasters (with calls by Ben Jarrell). The first recording was in 1924 by Fiddlin' Powers and Family. First recorded as "Little Rabbit" by Crockett's Kentucky Mountaineers in 1931. **RECORDING INFO:** Tommy Jarrell & Fred Cockerham; New Lost City Ramblers; Kenny Hall and the Sweets Mill String Band; Hobart Smith; **RELATED TO:** Pretty Little Gal, Pretty Little Miss, Johnny Bring the Jug Around the Hill, Little Rabbit, Red Steer, Table Mountain Road, Stillhouse Branch, Rabbit Where's Your Mammy?; **OTHER NAMES:** Brownslow's Dream, Brown's Dream, Brownstream, Herve Brown's Dream, Stillhouse Branch, Jeff Davis Dream; **NOTES:** The song is from a family of tunes that includes Brown's Dream songs, Little Rabbit songs and Pretty Little Gal songs. The tune family is popular one in the Blue Ridge Mountains where it probably originated.

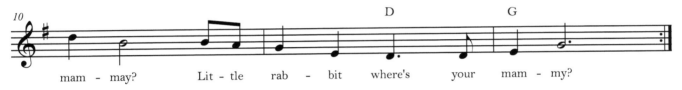

CHORUS: Poor little rabbit, poor little rabbit,
G   C   G

Poor little rabbit, Little rabbit where's yer mammy?
C   C   G

VERSE 1: Little rabbit where's yer mammy? Little rabbit where's yer mammy?
G   D   G

VERSE 2: She's died and gone to glory. She's died and gone to glory.

VERSE 3: Some day I'm gonna join her. Some day I'm gonna join her.

Little Sadie

Old-time Appalachian Blues; **CATEFORY**: Early County and Bluegrass Songs; **DATE**: Early 1900's (1922); **RECORDING INFO**: Clarence Ashley 1930; Freight Hoppers; Tommy Jarrell; Doc Watson; Hedy West; **OTHER NAMES**: Bad Man's Blunder; Bad (Man) Lee Brown; Penitentiary Blues; Bad Man Ballad; Cocaine Blues; Chain Gang Blues; **NOTES**: Little Sadie originated in the Appalachian region but has been found as far west as Arkansas as early as 1939. Bad Man' Blunder by Hays and Cisco Houston is a variant of Little Sadie that was a hit for the Kingston Trio. Penitentiary Blues/Cocaine Blues was released by Johnny Cash in 1960 and redone by George Thorogood many years later. In the song lyrics the reference to Thomasville (North Carolina) and Jericho (South Carolina) could possibly represent a local North Carolina murder ballad.

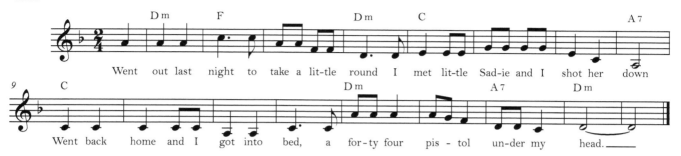

Went out one night to make a little round, I met little Saide and I shot her down.

Went back home, and I got into bed, Forty-four pistol under my head.

Wake up the next morning about half past nine, The hacks and the buggies all standing in line.
Gents and the gamblers all standin' around, Taking Little Sadie to her buryin' ground.

Then I begun to think of what a deed I'd done, I grabbed my hat and away I run.
I made a good run but a little too slow, They overtook me in Jericho.

I was standin' on the corner a readin' the bill, When up stepped the sheriff from Thomasville.
He said young man ain't your name Brown, Remember the night you shot Sadie down.

Well I says, "Yes sir, my name is Lee, And I shot little Sadie in the first degree.
First degree, second degree, If you got any papers won't you read them to me."

They took me down town, dressed me in black, And they put me on a train and started me back
All the way back to that Thomasville jail, And I had no money for to go my bail.

That judge and the jury took their stand, The judge had the papers in his right hand.
Forty-one days, and forty-one nights, Forty-one years to wear the ball and stripes.

Lonesome Road Blues

Traditional Old-Time Breakdown and Song, Widely known; **DATE:** Early 1900's; **OTHER NAMES:** Goin' Down This Road Feelin' Bad; Chilly Winds; Levee Moan; Honey Your Hair Grows Too Long; East Coast Blues; **RECORDING INFO:** Henry Whitter 1923; Tommy Jarrell; Cisco Houston; Wade Ward; Woody Guthrie; **NOTES:** Chilly Winds is a related version of Goin' Down This Road Feelin' Bad. Both are frequently categorized under Lonesome Road Blues. Mt. Airy, North Carolina, fiddler and banjo player Tommy Jarrell learned the tune around 1917 from Carlie Holder. The Skillet Lickers included it in their skit, A Corn Likker Still in Georgia, in about 1930. A bluegrass favorite recorded by Bill Monroe to Doc Watson.

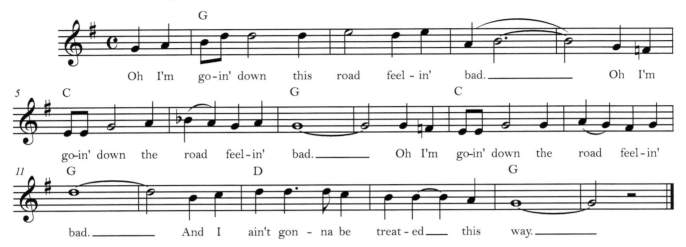

Oh I'm goin' down this road feelin' bad,

Oh I'm goin' down this road feelin' bad,

Oh I'm goin' down this road feelin' bad,

And I ain't gonna be treated this way.

Oh I'm goin' where the chilly wind never blows,
Oh I'm goin' where the chilly wind never blows,
Oh I'm goin' where the chilly wind never blows,
And I ain't gonna be treated this way.

Oh I'm way down in jail on my knees,
Oh I'm way down in jail on my knees,
Oh I'm way down in jail on my knees,
And I ain't gonna be treated this way.

Oh they feed me on cornbread and peas,
Oh they feed me on cornbread and peas,
Oh they feed me on cornbread and peas,
And I ain't gonna be treated this way.

Oh I'm goin' where the climate suits my clothes,
Oh I'm goin' where the climate suits my clothes,
Oh I'm goin' where the climate suits my clothes,
And I ain't gonna be treated this way.

Oh I'm goin' if I never come back,
Oh I'm goin' if I never come back,
Oh I'm goin' if I never come back,
And I ain't gonna be treated this way.

Lovesick Blues

Old-time Tin Pan Alley/Country Song and Blues by Irving Mills and Cliff Friend; **DATE**: 1922; **RECORDING INFO:** Emmett Miller; Bertha "Chippie" Hill; Hank Williams 1948; Slim Whitman 1957; Patsy Cline; Jerry Lee Lewis; Don McLean; Linda Ronstadt; George Strait; **NOTES:** A Tin Pan Alley song written by Cliff Friend and Irving Mills, "I've Got the Lovesick blues" has become a popular country song and pop standard. In 1948, the song was the first of many number one hits for Hank Williams. This version is based on the original music.

142

CHORUS: Got the fellin' called the blue-hoos, (D7) G

Since my baby said good-bye D

Lord I don't know what I'll do-hoo

All I do is sit and sigh and cry G

That last long day we spent alone C

I'm yearning for it yet G E

She thrilled me, filed me A

With a kind of lovin'

I never will forget D

The way she calls me sweet daddy G

Was just a beautiful dream D

I hate to think it's all over

I lost my heart it seems B7

I got so used to her somehow Cm

But I'm nobody's baby now G C E

Gee it's awful when you're lonesome A7

And got those lovesick blues. D G

VERSE: I'm in love, I'm in love, Em B7

I'm in love with a girl

That's what's the matter with me Em

I'm in love, I'm in love with a beautiful gal

But she don't give a darn about me D

To make her love me I tried,

how I sighed and I cried

But she just refused Em

And ever since she'd gone away Am D

I've got those lovesick blues (Repeat CHORUS) A D

143

Lula Walls

Traditional Old-Time and Bluegrass Song; **DATE:** 1888; **CATEGORY:** Early Country and Bluegras Song; **RECORDING INFO:** Bascom Lammar Lunsford, 1927; Carter Family, 1929; Aunt Idy Harper & Coon Creek Girls, 1938; **OTHER NAMES:** Lula Walls; **NOTES:** The Carter Family popularized this old-time love song. It first appears in Wehman's Collection of Songs Jan. of 1888, issue number 17. The lyrics resemble Lunsford, but I've used the Carter family chords.

She's a maid-en bright and fair. She has love-ly gold-en hair. She's as love-ly as an an-gel from on high. She has stole my heart a-way. Has left me in sad dis-may. She's that ag-gra-va-tin' beaut-y, Lu-la Walls. And ev-'ry lit-tle while she greats me with a smile. She'll ask me to her hap-py home to call. If she'd on-ly be my wife, I'd be hap-py all my life with that ag-gra-va-tin' beaut-y, Lu-la Walls.

One evening after dark, I met her in the park (G, C, G)

I knew my time to fall in love had come (D)

I lifted up my hat and we began to chat (G, C, G)

She said that I could see her at her home. CHORUS (D7, G)

One evening it was late and I met her at the gate
She said that she would wed me in the Fall
But no answer would she say and only turned away
She's that aggravating beauty Lula Walls. CHORUS

Oh if she were only mine I'd build a mansion fine
And around it I'd build a fence so tall
And I would so jealous be if any one but me
Could gaze upon the beauty of Lula Walls. CHORUS

CHORUS: And ev'ry little while she greets me with a smile. (C, G)

She'll ask me to her happy home to call. (D)

It she'd only be my wife, I'd be happy all my life (G, C, G)

With that aggravatin' beauty Lula Walls. (D, G)

Mama Don't 'Low

Traditional Old-Time and Bluegrass Song; **DATE:** Early 1900's; **CATEGORY:** Early Country and Bluegrass Songs; **RECORDING INFO:** Riley Puckett 1929 Roots RL-701, LP (1971), cut # 10; Allen Brothers; Shelton Brothers; J.E. Mainer's Mountaineers; Cow Cow Davenport; **OTHER NAMES:** No Low Down Hangin' Around; Mama Won't Allow No Low Down Hangin' Around; Mama Don't Allow; **NOTES:** First recorded by Riley Puckett as "Mama Won't Allow No Low Down Hangin' Around" in 1928, the exact source of this skiffle song is unknown. The melody is quite popular and has been used in a variety of songs from both black and white sources including "Mama Don't'low no Easy Riders Here," "The Crawdad Song," version of "Frog Went a Courtin'," Woody Guthrie & the Almanacs "Pittsburgh Town" and Mississippi Fred McDowell's "My Babe." Alan Lomax collected a version entitled "Cap'n Don't 'Low no Truckin'" in his 1939 field recording trip.

Mama don't 'low no banjo playing 'round here

Mama don't 'low no banjo playing 'round here

We don't care what mama don't 'low. Gonna pick my banjo anyhow,

Mama don't 'low no banjo playing 'round here.

Mama don't 'low no guitar playing 'round here
Mama don't 'low no guitar playing 'round here
I don't care what mama don't 'low. Gonna play my guitar anyhow,
Mama don't 'low no guitar playing 'round here

Mama don't 'low no talking 'round here
Mama don't 'low no talking 'round here
I don't care what mama don't 'low. Gonna shoot my mouth off anyhow,
Mama don't 'low no talking 'round here

Mama don't 'low no singing 'round here
Mama don't 'low no singing 'round here
I don't care what mama don't 'low. Gonna sing my head off anyhow.
Mama don't 'low no singing 'round here

Man Of Constant Sorrow

Traditional Song and White "Blues;" **DATE:** 1913 Burnett; 1917 Sharp. Earlier through the "Drowsy Sleeper" branch (1812); **CATEGORY:** Early Country and Bluegrass Songs; **RECORDING INFO:** The best-known period version for "I Am A Man of Constant Sorrow" was Emry Arthur's 1928 recording (Vo 5208). The Stanley Brothers; Roscoe Holcomb; Frank Proffitt; **OTHER NAMES:** Farewell Song; I Am a Man of Constant Sorrow; **NOTES:** The first published version of Man Of Constant Sorrow is the Farewell Song from a 1913 songbook printed by Richard Burnett of Monticello, Ky and In Old Virginny from Sharp's English Folk Songs from the Southern Appalachians. Both The Farewell Song and Sharp's In Old Virginny Version C are early versions of The Man of Constant Sorrow, which is a branch of East Virginia Blues. Richard Burnett was born in 1883, married in 1905, and blinded in 1907. The second stanza of Farewell Song mentions the singer has been blind six years, which would date it at 1913. in later years, Richard Burnett was asked about the song. He himself could not remember, at that time, if he had composed it, or copied it, or-perhaps most likely-adapted it from something traditional. With the O Brother Where Art Thou?" phenomena The Man of Constant Sorrow has become a crossover pop hit.

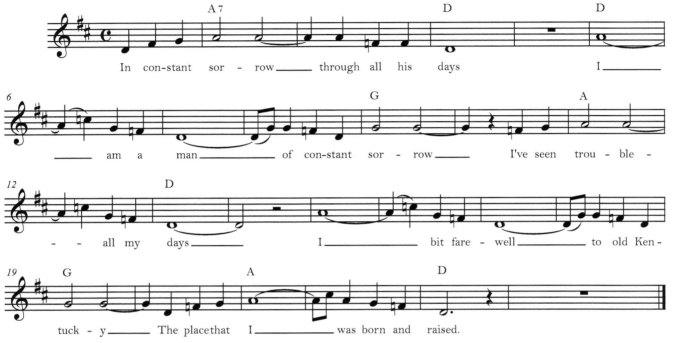

(In constant sorrow through all his days)

I am a man of constant sorrow

I've seen trouble all my days

I bid farewell to old Kentucky

The place where I was borned and raised
(The place where he was borned and raised)

For six long years I've been in trouble
No pleasure here on earth I find
For in this world I'm bound to ramble
I have no friends to help me now
(He has no friends to help him now)

It's fare thee well my own true lover
I never expect to see you again
For I'm bound to ride that northern railroad
Perhaps I'll die upon this train
(Perhaps he'll die upon this train)

You can bury me in some deep valley
For many years where I may lay
Then you may learn to love another
While I am sleeping in my grave
(While he is sleeping in his grave)

Maybe your friends think I'm just a stranger
My face you'll never see no more
But there is one promise that is given
I'll meet you on God's golden shore
(He'll meet you on God's golden shore)

Meet Me in the Moonlight/Prisoner's Song

Traditional Old-time and Bluegrass Song; Very well known; **DATE:** 1800's Broadside; **OTHER NAMES:** Meet Me in the Moonlight Alone; The Prisoner's Song; New Prisoner's Song Kilby Jail; **RECORDING INFO:** Vernon Dalhart, 1924; Clarence Ashley & Tex Isley; Wilf Carter; Buell Kazee; Bill Monroe & his Bluegrass Boys; Stanley Brothers; **NOTES:** Marion Slaughter known as Vernon Dalhart (1883-1948) recorded a 78 with Wreck of the Old 97 and on the flip side was The Prisoner's Song. Estimates of Dalhart's record sales (including millions for The Prinsoner's Song) ran as high as 50 million and vaulted Dalhart to stardom. The origin of the song is unknown despite claims by Dalhart and his cousin, Gary Massey. Perhaps it originated from a popular poem by Joseph Augustine Wade (1796-1845) entitled Meet Me by the Moonlight. Several broadsides appeared in the late 1800's both here and abroad with the Wade lyrics "Meet me by moonlight alone/And then I will tell you a tale/Must be told by the moonlight alone/ In the grove at the end of the vale!"

Meet me in the moonlight love, meet me
Meet me in the moonlight alone
I have a sad story to tell you
All down by the moonlight alone.

I've always loved you my darling
You said I've never been true
I'd do anything just to please you
I'd die any day just for you.

I have a ship on the ocean
All lined with silver and gold
And before my little darling shall suffer
I'll have the ship anchored and sold.

If I had wings like an angel
Over these prison walls I would fly
I'd fly to the arms of my darling
And then I'd be willing to die.

147

Michael, Row the Boat Ashore

Old-time Gospel song from Beaufort, SC-Sea Islands area; **DATE:** 1867; **RECORDING INFO:** Jane Hunter & Moving Star Hall singers; Pete Seeger; **NOTES: T**he song with 29 verses appears in print in 1867. The song is a rowing song from the African-Americans that lived in isolation and spoke Gullah on the East Coast Barrier Islands area (South Carolina and Georgia).

Michael r$\overset{C}{o}$w the boat ashore, Hallelu$\overset{F.\ C}{j}$ah!

Michael r$\overset{Em}{o}$w the boat ash$\overset{Dm}{o}$re, Hallel$\overset{G.\ C}{u}$jah!

Michael boat a gospel boat, Hallelujah!
Michael boat a gospel boat, Hallelujah!

Gabriel blow the trumpet horn...

Brother, lend a helping hand...

Sister help for trim that boat...

Jordan stream is wide and deep...

Jesus stand on t'oder side...

When the river overflow...

River run and darkness comin'...

Sinner row to save your soul...

Motherless Children

Old-Time Spiritual and Blues; S.C. Bown words, Charle Dryscoll music; **DATE:** 1904; **RECORING INFO**: Blind Willie Johnson, 1927; Rev. Gary Davis; Carter family, 1936; Roscoe Holcomb; The Blind Pilgrim; Eric Clapton; Steve Miller; **NOTES**: Since Blind Willie Johnson recorded "Motherless Children" in 1927, dozens of versions of this traditional gospel song have been recorded and the song has crossed into rock.

Moth-er-less chil-dren have a hard time when their mo-ther is dead, Lord.

They get hun-gry, they get cold and wan-der from door to door.

No-bo-dy treats you like your moth-er would when your moth-er is dead, Lord.

Ṁotherless children have a h̊ard time when their m̊other is dead, Lord.
   G   C   G

Motherless children have a hard time when their mother is dead, Lord.
(G)   (C)   (G)

They get hungry, they get cold and wander from door to door.
(G)   (D)   (C)   (Eb)

Nobody treats you like your mother would when your mother is dead, Lord.
(G)   (C)   (G)   (D)

Father will do the best he can when your mother is dead, Lord.
Father will do the best he can when your mother is dead, Lord.
Father will do the best he can, so many things he can't understand.
Nobody treats you like your mother would when your mother is dead, Lord.

Sister will do the best she can when your mother is dead, Lord.
Sister will do the best she can when your mother is dead, Lord.
Sister will do the best she can, so many things she can't understand.
Nobody treats you like your mother would when your mother is dead,.
(Repeat first verse)

Mountaineer's Love Song/Goodbye Liza Jane (Liza Jane)

Old-time Bluegrass, Western Swing Breakdown, Widely Spread; **DATE:** Late 1800's; **OTHER NAMES:** Goodbye Liza Jane; Liz Jane; Susan Jane; Miss Liza Poor gal; **RECORDING INFO;** Old Liza Jane-Uncle Am Stuart, 1924; Liza Jane-Riley Puckett, 1924; Liza Jane-Henry Whitter, 1925; Goodbye Liza Jane-Fiddlin' John Carson, 1926; Mountaineer's Love Song-The Hillbillies, 1926; Miss Liza Poor Gal; Tempera Ramblers, 1928; Liza Jane-Carter Brothers and Son, 1928; Old Eliza Jane-Doc Roberts and Ava Martin, 1928; Liza up the 'Simmon Tree-Bradley Kincaid, 1928; Poor Mary Jane-Charlie Craver 1928; Liza Up the 'Simmon Tree-Bradley Kincaid, 1929; Liza Jane-Kessinger Brothers, 1931; **NOTES:** "Mountaineer's Love Song" is the title given to this song by the Hill Billies which is part of the large family of Goodbye Liza Jane/Liza Jane songs. Eddie Cox, a minstrel show performer, published Good-by, Liza Jane in the 1880's. He didn't claim any credit for writing it, just arranging it. In 1903, the Tin Pan Alley composer, Harry von Tilzer, published Good-Bye, Eliza Jane, which was a different song altogten. Charlie Poole did a cover of the Tilzer version leading some to assume that it was a folk version.

VERSE: I went up on that mountain To give my horn a blow

I thought I heard my Liza say Yonder come my beau

CHORUS: Oh Miss Liza po' gal Oh Miss Liza Jane

Oh Miss Liza po' gal I'm ridin' on that train

I took old Dick and Dinah I hooked 'em to our train;
To get a pile o' (mo)lasses To sweeten Liza Jane

I asked her for to marry me She said, "Ain't you ashamed."
I stuck my head through the crack a bit To kiss my Liza Jane

I've traveled on a steamboat I traveled on a train;
But when I get married I'll marry Liza Jane.

Nine Hundred Miles/Train Forty-Five

Old-Time Bluegrass Song and Breakdown, USA, widely known; **DATE:** Earliest printed date 1909 (JAFL); **RECORDING INFO:** Fiddlin' John Carson, 1924; Grayson & Whitter, 1927 as "Train 45;" Volo Bogtrotters; Woody Guthrie; **RELATED TO:** Ruby (Are You Mad at Your Man?); Longest Train I Ever Saw; Long Steel Rail; **OTHER NAMES:** Train 45; Reuben/Reuban; Old Reuben; I'm Nine Hundred Miles from My Home; **NOTES:** Hedy West arranged the song Five Hundred Miles based on a Nine Hundred Miles variant she learned from her grandmother in Georgia. Her arrangement became a huge hit in the sixties and was sung by Peter, Paul and Mary and many other commercial folk groups.

I am wal-kin' down the track, I got tears in—my eyes. Try'n to read a let-ter from my

home. If his train runs me right, I'll be home by Sat-ur-day night. For I'm

nine hun-dred miles from my home. And I hate to hear that lone-some whis-tle blow.

Well I'm walkin' down the track, I got tears in my eyes (D)

Tryin' to read a letter from my home. (Am) (Dm)

CHORUS: If the train runs me right, I'll be home Saturday night,

For I'm nine hundred miles from my home.

And I hate to hear that lonesome whistle blow. (A7) (D)

Well the train I ride on is a hundred coaches long
You can hear the whistle blow a hundred miles.

I will pawn you my watch, I will pawn you my chain
Pawn you my gold diamond ring.

Well if you say so, I will railroad no more,
Sidetrack my train and come home.

Nine Pound Hammer

Old-time Song; **DATE:** Late 1800's-Early 1900's; **CATEGORY:** Early Country and Bluegrass Songs; **RECORDING INFO:** Al Hopkins & his Buckle Busters (Brunswick 177, 1927); Frank Blevins & his Tar Heel Rattlers; Grayson and Whitter-1928; Flatt & Scruggs & the Foggy Mountain Boys; Greenbriar boys, Jim & Jesse and the Virginia Boys; Monroe Brothers; Don Reno and Bill Harrell with the Tennessee Cutups; Merle Travis; OTHER NAMES: Spikedriver Blues; Roll On, John; Roll On Buddy, Roll On; Take This Hammer; NOTES: Nine Pound Hammer is one of the few work songs to ever enjoy popularity. Early string bands such as Frank Blevins' Tar Heel Rattlers and Al Hopkins Buckle Busters were the first to introduce it as a performance piece. Bluegrass pioneers Bill and Charlie Monroe and fingerpicker Merle Travis brought it to a wider audience and are largely responsible for its continuing popularity. Some versions use a second part that echoes the melody.

This nine pound hammer is a little too heavy, For my size, buddy for my size

Roll on buddy, don't you roll too slow, How can I roll when the wheels won't go.

It's a long way to Harlan, it's a long way to Hazard
Just to get a little booze just to get a little booze
Oh, the nine pound hammer killed John Henry
Ain't gonna kill me, ain't gonna kill me.

There ain't one hammer down in this tunnel
That can ring like mine, that can ring like mine
Rings like silver, shines like gold,
Rings like silver, shines like gold.

Buddy when I'm long gone, won't you make my tombstone
Out of number nine coal, out of number nine coal
I'm going on the mountain, just to see my baby
And I ain't coming back, no I ain't coming back.

Nobody's Darling On Earth

Old-time Song by Will S. Hays **DATE**: 1870; **RECORDING INFO**: Kelly Harrell 1927; North Caroline Cooper Boys; Grayson and Whitter; Uncle Dave Macon; Wade Mainer; **NOTES:** Not to be confused with the 1935 Jimmie Davis song "Nobody's Darlin' But Mine."

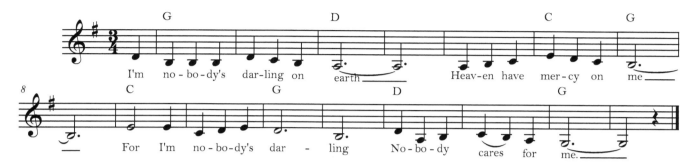

Out in this cold world alone,
Wand'ring about on the street,
Asking a penny for bread
Or begging for something to eat.

CHORUS: I'm nobody's darling on earth;
(G)   (D)

Heaven have mercy on me
        (C)   (G)

For I'm nobody's darling;
(C)   (G)

Nobody cares for me.
(D)   (G)

When I was but a young lad,
Mother was taken from home;
Now I have no one to love me,
No one to call me her own.

While others are sleeping so sound
Or dreaming of silver and gold,
I'm out in this old world alone,
Wand'ring about in the cold.

If I am fortunate enough
To get to that heavenly home,
I will have someone to love me,
Someone to call me her own.

Oh, Dem Golden Slippers/Golden Slippers

Old-time Song and instrumental Tune by James A. "Jimmy" bland; **DATE:** Very popular minstrel tune in the 1880's. Composed in 1870. **OTHER NAMES:** Oh Dem Golden Slippers; **RECORDING INFO:** Carson Robinson; Clark Kessinger; The Tweedy Brothers; Curly Ray Cline; Kenny Hall and the Sweets Mill String Band; **NOTES:** Originally a song composed by prominent black minstrel songwriter and banjo player (with Haverly' Minstrels) James A. Bland in 1870 as "Oh! Dem Golden Slippers," which later passed into folk and fiddling tradition. Bland also wrote "Carry Me Back to Old Virginny" and "In the Evening by the Moonlight."

Oh, my ol' banjo hangs on the wall,
'Cause it ain't been tuned since way last fall,
But the folks all say we'll have a good time,
When we ride up in the chariot in the morn.
There's old Brother Ben an' his sister Luce,
They will telegraph the news to Uncle Bacco Juice
What a great camp meetin' there will be that day
When we ride up in the chariot in the morn.

Oh, my ^G golden slippers are laid away,

'Cause I don't 'spect to wear them till my ^D wedding day

And my long tail coat that I love so well,

I will wear up in the chariot in the ^G morn.

And my long white robe that I bought last June

I'm gonna get changed 'cause it ^D fits too soon,

And the old grey horse that I used to drive,

I will hitch him to the chariot in the ^G morn.

CHORUS: Oh, dem ^G golden slippers, Oh, dem ^C golden slippers,

^D
Golden slippers I'm gonna wear, Because ^G they look so neat,

Oh, dem golden slippers, Oh, dem ^C golden slippers,

^D
Golden slippers I'm a-gonna wear To walk the golden ^G street.

So, it's good-bye, children, I will have to go,
Where the rain don't fall and the wind don't blow
And your ulster coats, why, you will not need,
When you ride up in the chariot in the morn;
But your golden slippers must be nice and clear
And your age must be just sweet sixteen,
And your white kid gloves you will have to wear
When you ride up in the chariot in the morn.

Oh, Susanna

Popular minstrel song by Stephen Foster; Widely know; **DATE:** 1846; **RECORDING INFO:** Riley Puckett; Chubby Parker; Vernon Dalhart; **NOTES:** A song composed by Stephen Foster that became a popular song tune. Foster finished only two songs during his bookkeeping days in Cincinnati. Down South Where the Cane Grows was entered in a context for minstrel songs, but did not win a prize. The second, O, Susanna, was considered a lesser effort and not considered very successful at all. Foster was delighted for eventually recovering $100 for the song. Lyrics edited by Richard Matteson.

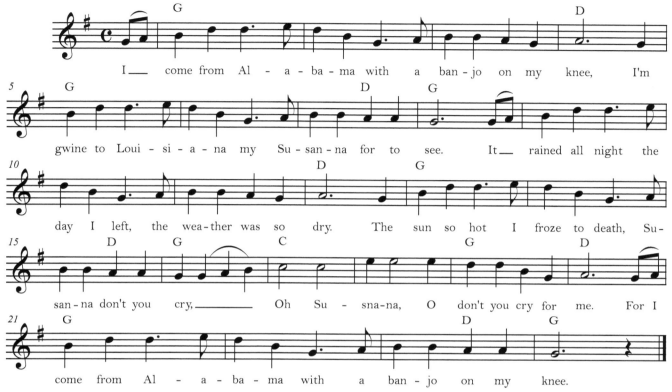

I come from Alabama with a banjo on my knee, I'm gwine to Loui-si-a-na my Su-san-na for to see. It rained all night the day I left, the wea-ther was so dry. The sun so hot I froze to death, Su-san-na don't you cry, Oh Su-sna-na, O don't you cry for me. For I come from Al-a-ba-ma with a ban-jo on my knee.

G
I come from Alabama with a banjo on my knee
G   D   G
I'm gwine to Louisiana Susanna for to see.

It rained all night the day I left
                    D
The weather it as dry
           G
The sun so hot, I froze to death
           D   G
Susanna, don't you cry
           C   G   D
CHORUS: O Susanna, O don't you cry for me
            G
For I come from Alabama
                    D   G
    with my banjo on my knee.

I had a dream the other night when everything was still
I thought I saw Susanna a-coming down the hill
The buckwheat cake was in her mouth
The tear was in her eye
Says I, I'm coming from the south
Susanna, don't you cry.

I jumped abourd de telegraph and trabbled down de wire,
De 'lectric fluid magnified
    and killed hundreds in de fire.
De bull-gine bust, de horse run off,
    I really thought I'd die
I shut my eyes to hold my breah,
Susanna, don't you cry.

I soon will be in New Orleans, and then I'll look around
And when I find Susanna
    I will fall upon de ground.
And if I do not find her, I know I'll surely die,
And when I'm dead and buried,
    Susanna don't you cry.

155

Old Bell Cow

Traditional Old-Time Song; **DATE:** Early 1900's; **OTHER NAMES:** Bell Cow; the Squirrel Hunters; Squirrel Hunting; Rooshian Rabbit; **RECORDING INFO:** Dixie Crackers; John Hartford; Indian Creek Delta Boys; **NOTES:** Bayard (1981) collected this tune and a version appears in American Mountain Songs. This is similar to the version sung by the Dixie Crackers.

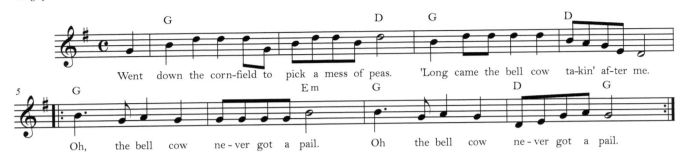

Went down the cornfield to pick a mess of peas
    G   D

'Long came the bell cow takin' after me.
 G   D

CHORUS: Oh, the bell cow never got a pail
        G   Em

Oh, the bell cow never got a pail.
 G   D   G.

One of these days when I learn how,
I'm gonna milk the darned old cow. CHORUS:

The milk tastes good 'til the butter ain't fat
Darned old cow ain't my best pat.

One of these days when I learn how,
I'm gonna milk the darned old cow. CHORUS:

The old bell cow never knew how to court
Sold the milk and I got me a horse.

The old bell cow she had a couple horns
Ain't been milked since I been born.

Way down yonder in Arkansas
The bell cow goofed her mammy and pa.

Some of these days when I learn how,
I'm gonna milk the darned old cow.

ALT CHORUS: Oh the bell cow catch her by the tail
Oh, the bell cow milk her in the pail.

Old Chisholm Trail

Old-time Cowboy Song; Widely Known; **DATE:** 1910 **RECORDING INFO:** Harry McClintock 1928; Jules Allen 1929; Tea Hardin 1933; **NOTES**: According to Meade, the s ong was adapted from Stephen Foster's "Old Uncle Ned."

Come along, boys, and listen to my tale,

I'll tell you of my troubles on the Old Chisholm Trail.

CHORUS: Coma-ti yi yippee, yippee yea, yippee yea

Coma-ti yi yippee, yippee yea

I was born in Texas in the year '89,
I can ride anything this side the state line.

Went down to San Antone and went to workin' cattle,
And here come the sheep men and we had a battle.

It's I an' Bill Jones was good old cronies,
We was always together on our sore-backed ponies.

We left Nelson Ranch on June twenty-third,
With a drove of Texas cattle, two thousand in the herd.

Slicker in the wagon and pouring down hail,
Goin' round the herd with a doggie by the tail.

I'm on my best orse and I am goin' on a run,
I'm the quickest-shootin' cowboy that ever pulled a gun.

I flushed them left, couldn't get 'em to stop,
I can run as long as an eight-day clock.

My seat in the saddle and I gave a little shout
The lead cattle broke an' the herd went about.

Some of 'em we captured without half tryin',
They was so damned scared
    they didn't need hog-tyin'.

We strung 'em out next mornin',
    and the boss made a count
And he said, "Boys, we are just a few out."

"Make a circle, boys, and don't lose no time,
I am sure they will be easy to find."

It's bacon and beans 'most every day
I'd as soon been eatin' prairie hay.

Old Dan Tucker

Old-Time and bluegrass Song; Daniel Decatur Emmett; **DATE:** 1832; Published in 1843; **CATEGORY:** Early Country and Bluegrass Song: **RECORDING INFO**: Fiddlin' John Carson, 1924; Uncle Dave Macon, 1925; Homer and the Barnstormers; **OTHER NAMES:** Dan Tucker: **NOTES:** In Richard Walser's North Carolina Legends, 1980, is the legend of Old Dan Tucker, Where it is said that he was born in London in 1714 and moved with his parents to Bath town, North Carolina six years later. He is said to have married Margaret DeVane in 1740 and moved to what is now Randolph County and built a cabin there. Daniel Decatur Emmett wrote the song from black sources and published it in 1843. The Dan Tucker melody used was by Bob Wills in "Stay All Night" and is similar to the Johnny Booker songs.

Old Dan Tucker's a fine old man, Washed his face in a frying pan.

Combed his hair with a wagon wheel. Died with a toothache in his heel.

CHORUS: Get out the way, old Dan Tucker, You're too late to get your supper,

Supper's gone and dinner's a-cookin', Old Dan Tucker just stands there lookin'.

Old Dan Tucker he comes to town, Riding on a billygoat, leading a hound,
Hound dog bark and the billygoat jump, throwed Dan Tucker on top of a stump.

Old Dan Tucker, he got drunk, Fell in the fire and he kicked up a chunk.
Red hot coal got in his shoe, Oh my Laudy how the ashes flew.

Old Dan Tucker, he come to town, Swinging the ladies round and round,
First to the right and the to the left, And then to the gal that he loved best.

And now old Dan is a dead gone sucker, And never will go home to his supper,
Old Dan he has had his last ride, And the banjo's buried by his side.

Old Gray Mare/Down in Alabam'

Old-time Song; **DATE:** 1858; **OTHER NAMES:** Old Gray Horse; Out of the Wilderness; Down in Alabam; Ain't I Glad I Got Out De Wilderness; Little Black Bull; **RECORDING INFO:** Henry Whitter, 1926; Gid Tanner and His Skillet Lickers, 1927; Earl Johnson and His Clodhoppers, 1927; Bill Monroe; **NOTES:** Nothing is known about J. Warner. The tune may be older than the 1858 date since it closely resembles a revivalist hymn. The Original Chorus is sung to the melody of the verse.

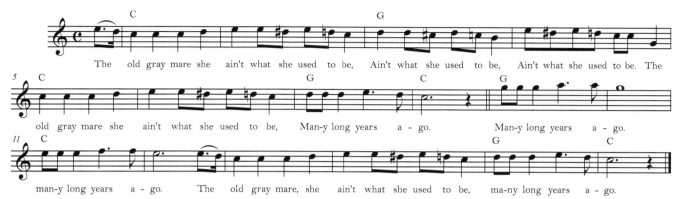

ORIGINAL CHORUS: Ain't I glad I got out de wilderness,
Got out de wilderness, Got out de wilderness,
Ain't I glad I got out de wilderness Down in Alabam'.

ORIGINAL VERSE: Old blind horse come from Jerusalum,
Come from Jerusalum, Come from Jerusalum,
He kicks so high dey put him in de museum, Down in Alabam'.

      C
The old gray mare, she ain't what she used to be

G
Ain't what she used to be, ain't what she used to be

      C
The old gray mare, she ain't what she used to be

G   C
Many long years ago.

G   C
Many long years ago, Many long years ago

They old gray mare she ain't what she used to be

G   C
Many long years ago

The old gray mare, she kicked on the whiffletree...

Little black bull come down in the wilderness...

Ain't you mighty glad to get out o' the wilderness...

The old gray mare stood, under the apple tree...

Oh! The old gray mare was burning up the track...

Oh! The old gray mare she lost a tooth or two...

Oh! The old gray mare she chewed tobacco too...

Old Jimmy Sutton

Old-Time Breakdown; **DATE**: 1888 in The Journal of American Folk-lore, page 93 by American Folklore Society, Project Muse says, "The songs are typical hillbilly numbers: dance tunes ("Hop Up Ladies," "Western Country," "Old Jimmy Sutton," "Shoo Fly"); **RECORDING INFO**: Grayson and Whitter, 1928; Ballard Branch Bogtrotters; Original Bogtrotters; Carolina Tar Heels; Vester Jones; Wade Ward; **OTHER NAMES**: Jimmy Sutton; Old Buck Ram; **NOTES**: Bascom Lamar Lundsford says Old Jimmy Sutton is a tune "played in the Piedmont North Carolina region" that is similar to "Walking in the Parlor." Vester Jones calls Old Jimmy Sutton an old song from "the time of covered wagons." As "Old Jimmy Sutton" the song/tune was in the repertoire of Grayson & Whitter who recorded it first in 1928.

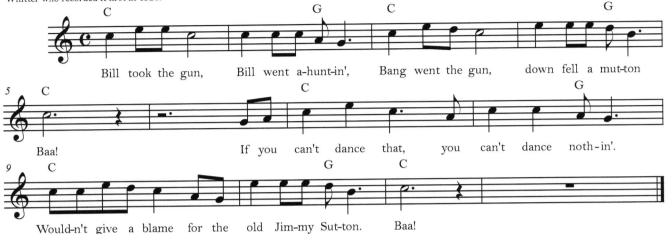

Bill took the gun, Bill went a-huntin', Bang went the gun, down fell a mut-ton Baa! If you can't dance that, you can't dance noth-in'. Would-n't give a blame for the old Jim-my Sut-ton. Baa!

    C   G
Bill took the gun, Bill went a-huntin',

    C   G   C
Bang went the gun, down fell a mutton. Baa!

               C   G
If you can't dance that, you can't dance nothin'.

       C   G   C
Wouldn't give a blame for the old Jimmy Sutton. Baa!

Bill, he took the wagon went after a load of peaches
He run *agin a gatepost and tore him all to pieces and Baa!
The old Jimmy Sutton,
If you can't dance that, you can't dance nothin' Baa!

You can eat the sheep and I'll eat the mutton,
Wouldn't give a thought for the old Jimmy Sutton.

*against

Old Joe Clark

Traditional Old-Time and Bluegrass Song; **DATE:**Late 1800's, Journal of American Floklore 1912; **CATEGORY**: Early Country and Bluegrass Songs; **RECORDING INFO:** Fiddlin' John Carson 1923; Carter Family; Dillards; Kentucky Colonels; Clark Kessinger; Kingston Trio; NOTES: Bayard thinks it was originally a song tune that later became a fiddle standard and play party tune. Mike Seeger relates the local story of the origins of the tune where he lives in Rockbridge County, VA. Joe Clark's father settled around Irish Creek, near South River, in the early 1800's. Joe Clark had a daughter and a jilted beau is said to have written the song, out of jealousy, in the late 1800's. The Clarks have been family-style strong musicians right down through the years. Another investigation determined the source of the tune to be the murder in Maryland of a traveling salesman named Herbert Brown by Joe Clark and Brown's wife Betsy sometime after the Civil War. Joe and Betsy attempted to cover up the crime by asserting the Brown was on a trip up North. This perhaps explains the verse: "Old Joe Clark killed a man/Layed him in the sand" and the chorus which includes "goodbye Betsy Brown." Virginia family band "Fiddlin'" Cowan Powers and Family's recording of the piece was the third best-selling country music record of 1924, while the Skillet Lickers (north Georgia) 1926 recording was the fourth best-selling for that year. Typically it is played A A B B form.

G
Old Joe Clark was a good old man, Never did no harm
F

G
Said he would not hoe my corn, Might hurt his fiddling arm.
D   G

I went down to Old Joe's house, Never been there before
He slept on a feather bed, And I slept on the floor.

CHORUS: Fare the well Old Joe Clark, Fare thee well I say
G   F

Fare thee well Old Joe Clark, I am going away
G   D   G

I went down to Old Joe's house, Old Joe wasn't home
Ate up all of Old Joe's meat, And left Old Joe the bone.

I went down to Old Joe's house, He invited me to supper
Stumped my toe on a table leg, And stuck my nose in the butter.

Old Molly Hare/Hair/Old Granny Blare/Blair

Old-Time and Bluegrass Breakdown; **DATE:** "De Old Hare" circa 1850; 1881 (Uncle Remus: His Songs and His Sayings) Two sets of the tune appear in "Henry Beck's Flute Book [1786]," entitled "Anson's Voyage" and "Farewell to Country Friends" as The Fairy Dance. **RECORDING INFO:** W.E. Bird's as Old Granny Hare 1925; Fiddlin' Powers & Family 1928; Riley Puckett; New Lost City Ramblers; Tommy Jarell; **OTHER NAMES:** Molly Hair/Hare; Old Molly Hair/Hare; Old Granny Blair/Blare; Old Granny Hare; Old Mother Hare; Old Sow; **NOTES:** The song, "Old Molly Hare" evolved from the Scottish melody "Largo's Fairy Dance." The "Old Molly Hare" lyrics are from the US in origin and a set of words were published in Uncle Remus in 1881. The earliest printed source is listed by Meade as "De Old Hare" circa 1850 in Christy's Panorama Songster. Old Molly Hare was the first song Earnest Stoneman learned from his grandmother (Mrs. Bowers) in 1903 to play on the auto harp.

D   G   D
Old Molly Hare what you doing there?

                A7   D
Running down the road just as hard as I can tear

           G   D
Run down one, run down two

           A7   D
Run down one, and give it to you

                  G   D   A7
Step back step back, daddy shot a bear

D   A7   D
Shot him in the eye and he never touched a hair

Old Molly Hare, What you doing there
Sitting on the hillside, eating on a bear
Jump up, jump up, yonder comes a bear
Coming down the hillside as hard as he can tear

Look back, look back daddy shot a bear
Shot him in the eye and he never touched a hair.

Old Molly Hare, if you don't care
Leave my liquor jug setting right there
Old Molly Hare, she took a spell
Kicked my liquor jug all to -----

Look back, look back daddy shot a bear
Shot him in the eye and he never touched a hair.

Old Molly Hare, what you doing there
Running through the briar patch as hard as I can tear
I'd rather be here than to be back there
Big ball of cuckleberries tangled in my hair

Look back, look back daddy shot a bear
Shot him in the eye and he never touched a hair.

Old Time Religion

Traditional Old-Time and Bluegrass Song; **DATE:** 1880; **CATEGORY:** Early Country and Bluegrass Songs; **RECORDING INFO:** Red Ellis and the Huron Valley Boys; Jim and Jesse; EC and Eona Ball; Clyde Moody; Johnson Family Singers; **OTHER NAMES:** Give me That Old Time Religion; Give Me Old Time Music; **NOTES:** This piece was copyrighted in 1891 by Charlie D. Tillman but given that the text sung by the Fisk Jubilee Singers was printed in 1880, the claim is in error. First recorded by Homer Rodenheaver in 1923 on Co A3856, this spiritual has been popular among black and white performers. Give Me Old Time Music was recorded by Arthur Smith & His Dixie Liners on October 1, 1938, which is a parody of That Old Time Religion.

CHORUS: Gimme that old time religion, Gimme that old time religion

Gimme that old time religion, It's good enough for me.

It was good for the Hebrew children
It was good for the Hebrew children
It was good for the Hebrew children
It's good enough for me.

It will do when the world's on fire
It will do when the world's on fire
It will do when the world's on fire
It's good enough for me.

It was good for Paul and Silas
It was good for Paul and Silas
It was good for Paul and Silas
It's good enough for me.

It makes me love everybody
It makes me love everybody
It makes me love everybody
It's good enough for me.

On Top of Old Smoky

Traditional Old-time Song; **DATE:** 1911 (Belden); **RECORDING INFO:** George Reneau, 1925; Bradley Kincaid, 1929; **NOTES:** Some of the lyrics appear in a British broadside named The Young Man's Lamentation that mention a "False-hearted lover" and was printed by Busby, Deacon,, Blare and Back between 1690 and 1696. Meeting's a pleasure/But parting's a grief/An Unconstant Lover/Is worse than a Thief/A Thief he can Rob me/And take what I have/But an Unconstant Lover/Will bring me to the Grave. The song is closely related to "The Cuckoo" and especially "The Wagoner's Lad."

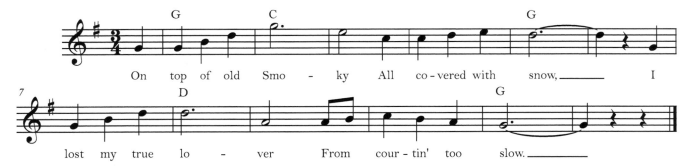

On top of old Smoky, all covered with snow
(G   C   G)

I lost my true lover from courtin' too slow.
(D   G)

Though courtin's a pleasure and parting is grief
A false-hearted lover is worse than a thief.

For a thief will just rob you and take what you have
But a false-hearted lover will lead you to the grave.

The grave will decay you and turn you to dust,
Not one boy is a thousand a poor girl can trust.

He'll hug you and kiss you and tell you more lies,
Than cross-ties on a railroad or stars in the skies.

Over the Garden Wall

Old-time song by Harry Hunter and George D. Fox; **DATE:** 1879; **RECORDING INFO:** Carter Family, 1933; **NOTES:** Sara Carter said "that was an old ballet (sic) given to us by an old lady in Tennessee." The song was actually written by the minstrel showmen harry Hunter and George D. Fox. The song was popularized by the vaudeville singer Tony Pastor and then moved into the folk tradition. The Carters sang only two verses, the first and fourth, with only slight alterations.

Oh, my love stood under the walnut tree, Over the garden wall,

She whispered and said she'd be true to me, Over the garden wall,

She's beautiful eyes and beautiful hair, She was not very tall so she stood in a chair,

And many a time have I kissed her there, Over the garden wall.

CHORUS: Over the garden wall, The sweetest girl of all,

There never were yet such eyes of jet, And you can bet I'll never forget

The night our lips in kisses met, Over the garden wall.

But her father stamped and her father raved, Over the garden wall,
And like an old madman he behaved, Over the garden wall,
She made a bouquet of roses red, But immediately I pooped up my head,
He gave be a bucket of water instead, Over the garden wall. CHORUS

One day I jumped down on the other side, Over the garden wall,
And she bravely promised to be my bride, Over the garden wall,
But she screamed in a fright, "Here's father quick,
I have an impression he's bringing a stick."
But I brought the impression of half a brick, Over the garden wall. CHORUS

But where there's a will, there's always a way, Over the garden wall,
There's always a night as well as the day, Over the garden wall,
We hadn't much money, but wedding's are cheap,
So while the old fellow was snoring asleep,
With a lad and ladder, she managed to creep Over the garden wall. CHORUS

Paddy, Won't You Drink Some Good Ol' Cider?/Cider Mill

Old-Time Breakdown and Song; **DATE**: Early 1900's; **OTHER NAMES**: Cider; Cider Mill; Down To the Stillhouse to Get a Little Cider; Stillhouse; **RECORDING INFO**: Fiddlin' Bob Larkin 1928; Ernest Stoneman 1928; Skillet Licker 1929; Riley Puckett & Clayton McMichen; Tommy Jarrell; **NOTES**: This song is from a large family of songs popular in the Blue Ridge Mountains. Tommy Jarrell called the song "Cider." The Camp Creek Boys issued a torrid rendition of the song calling it "Stillhouse." This version is similar to the Skillet Lickers versions.

C
You be the horse,

And I'll be the rider,

G   C   G C
Going to Paddy Watson's to get a little cider.

              C
CHORUS: Paddy won't you drink some,

F
Paddy won't you drink some,

C   G C
Paddy won't you drink some good ol' cider.

Got a little cider last night
A little night before, sir,
Going out tomorrow night to get a little more, sir.
CHORUS

166

Pallet on the Floor (Atlanta Blues)

Old-time Blues Tune; **CATEGORY:** Early Country and Bluegrass Songs; **DATE:** Early 1900's; 1923 by W.C. Handy; **RECORDING INFO:** Leake County Revelers in 1928 on Columbia 15264-D; Bogtrottters; Original Bogtrotters; Mississippi John Hurt; Mike Seeger and Paul Brown; Doc Watson; **RELATED TO:** "Ain't No Tellin'"; **OTHER NAMES:** Make Me a Pallet on Your Floor; Atlanta Blues; Make Me a Bed on Your Floor; **NOTES:** The title was recorded for the Library of Congress by musicologist/folklorist Vance Randolph from Ozark Mountain fiddlers in the early 1940's. The first printed version by W.C. Handy in under the title, "Atlanta Blues" in 1923 with lyrics by Dave Elman. The song is referenced in the Journal of American folklore XXIV 278 in 1911. A favorite amongst blues players, it was remembered as one of the Bolden Band's specialties. W.C. Handy used it as a strain in his 1917 recording "Sweet Child."

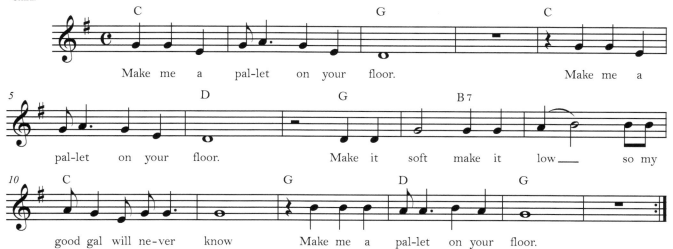

Make me a pallet on your floor

Make me a pallet on your floor

Make it soft, make it low so my good gal will never know

Make me a pallet on your floor.

These blues are everywhere I see
These blues are everywhere I see
Blues all around me, everywhere I see
Nobody's had these blues like me CHORUS

Come all you good time friends of mine
Come all you good time friends of mine
When I had a dollar you treated me just fine
Where'd you go when I only had a dime CHORUS

I'd be more than satisfied
If I could catch a train and ride
When I reach Atlanta and have no place to go
Won't you make me a pallet on your floor CHORUS

Papa's Billy Goat

Traditional Country and Old-Time ballad; **DATE**: Early 1900's (collected in 1913 by Brown); **OTHER NAMES**: The Billy Goat; Joey Long's Goat; The Goat; Papa's Billy Goat; Rosenthatl's Goat; Goat Song; **RECORDING INFO**: Fiddlin' John Carson 1923; Uncle Dave Macon; Sarah Ogan Gunning; Riley Puckett; **NOTES**: Papa's Billy Goat was recorded by Fiddlin' John Carson and Uncle Dave Macon in the early 1920's. The story for the song is found in a poem, "The Ballad of Casey's Billy Goat," by Robert Service. Carson's version is a medley and he breaks into "Turkey in the Straw," adding two floating verses at the end. Carson's song is set to the familiar tune of Reuben and Rachel (now generally mistitled "Reuben, Reuben") a ditty written by Harry Bush and William Gooch and copyrighted in 1871.

C
Papa bought him a great big billy goat
               G

C
Mama she washed most ev'ry day
                         G

      C   G   F   C
She hung her clothes out on the line

                      G   C
Well the derned goat, he come that way.

He pulled down the red flannel shirt.
You just ought'a heard them buttons crack
I'll get even with the son-of-a-gun
Gonna tie him across that railroad track.

I tied him 'cross the railroad track
An' the train was a-comin' at a powerful rate
He belched up that old red shirt
Then he flagged down the derned train

Well, I went to the depot, I bought me a ticket
And I walked right in an' I sat right down
Stuck the ticket in the brim o' my hat
An' the dog-gone wind blowed out on the ground.

Big conductor come around, he said, give me your ticket
I'd have t' pay again or be left on the track
I'll get even with that son-of-a-gun
I got a round-trip ticket and I ain't a-comin' back.

Then I acted an old fool, married me a widow (sung "wid-er")
And the widow had a daughter and her name was Maude
Father being a widower married her daughter
And now my daddy is my own son-in-law.

Paper of Pins, A

Old-time Love Ballad; England and USA; **DATE:** 1849 (Hallwell) **OTHER NAMES:** The Keys of Canterbury; The Keys of Heaven; I'll Give to You a Paper of Pins **RECORDING INFO:** Bradley Kincaid; Vass Family; Linda Brown & Donnie Stewart; **NOTES:** Versions with "if you will marry me" appeared more recently. In both of Sharp's versions; the lady accepts something and that's the end.

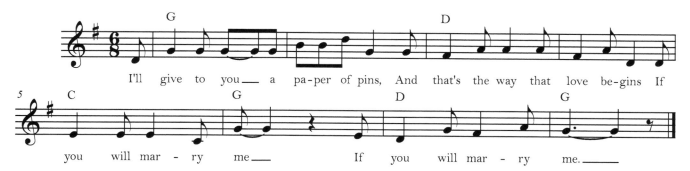

I'll give to you a paper of pins,

And that's the way that love begins,

If you will marry me,

If you will marry me.

I'll not accept a paper of pins,
If that's the way that love begins,
And I won't marry you,
And I won't marry you.

I'll give to you a coach and four,
That you may ride from door to door, etc.

I'll give to you a little lap dog,
To carry with you when you go abroad, etc.

I'll give to you a pacing horse,
That paced these hills from cross to cross, etc.

I'll give to you a coach and six,
With every horse as black as pitch, etc.

I'll give to you a gown of green,
That you may shine as any queen, etc.

I'll give to you a blue silk gown,
With golden tassels all around, etc.

I'll give to you my hand and heart,
That we may marry and never part, etc.

I'll give to you the keys of my chest,
That you may have gold at your request,
If you will marry me,
If you will marry me.

Oh, yes, I'll accept the key to your chest,
That I may have gold at my request, etc.
And I will marry you,
And I will marry you.

And now I see that money is all,
And woman's love is nothing at all.
So I'll not marry you,
So I'll not marry you.

I'm determined to be an old maid,
Take my stool and live in the shade,
And marry no one at all,
And marry no one at all.

Pass Around the Bottle/John Brown's Body/Battle Hymn

Old-time Song-Melody Battle Hymn, **DATE:** 1855 "She Had Such Wheedling Ways" at The Lester S. Levy Collection, 1857 "Say, Brothers, Will You Meet Us," 1861 "John Brown's Body," First recording "Old Aunt Peggy Won't You Set 'Em Up Again" by Fiddlin' John Carson 1924, Pass around the Bottle 1926, Gid Tanner & his Skillet Lickers; **RECORDING INFO:** Fiddlin' John Carson, 1924; Gid Tanner & his Skillet Lickers, 1926; Georgia Yellow Hammers, 1927; Al Bernard, 1930; Sim Harris, 1927; North Carolina Hawaiians, 1928; Ernest Stoneman, 1929; **RELATED TO:** Say, Brothers, Will you Meet Us; John Brown's Body; The Battle Hymn of the Republic; Marching On; **OTHER NAMES:** Old Aunt Peggy Won't You Set 'Em Up Again; Pass Around the Bottle and We'll All Take a Drink; **NOTES:** My Brother Will You Meet Me, a gospel song is one of the earliest sources of the melody. The tune to Pass Around the Bottle is the same as The Battle Hymn of the Republic. The poetry by Julia Ward Stowe of the Battle Hymn of the Republic was first published in the Atlantic magazine in February, 1862. The tune was based on the song, John Brown's Body.

Pass around the bottle and we'll all take a drink (G)

Pass around the bottle and we'll all take a drink (C ... G)

Pass around the bottle and we'll all take a drink (B7 ... Em)

As we go marching on. (Am D G)

CHORUS: Glory, glory to old Georgia (G)

Glory, glory to old Georgia (C ... G)

Glory, glory to old Georgia (B7 Em)

As we go marching on. (Am . D G)

Hang Jeff Dais on a sour apple tree
Hang Jeff Dais on a sour apple tree
Hang Jeff Dais on a sour apple tree
As we go marching on. CHORUS

Old Aunt Peggy won't you fill 'em up again
Old Aunt Peggy won't you fill 'em up again
Old Aunt Peggy won't you fill 'em up again
As we go marching on.

Paul and Silas Bound In Jail

Old-time and Bluegrass Gospel Song; **DATE:** Early 1900's; 1927 Sandburg; **OTHER NAMES:** Paul and Silas; All Night Long; **RELATED TO:** Keep Your Hand on the Plow; **NOTES:** Paul and Silas's stay in prison is related in Acts 16: 19-40. This gospel song is not the same as the blues oriented All Night Long even though it has the same tag.

G
Paul and Silas bound in jail, all night long

C
Paul and Silas bound in jail, all night long

G   C
Paul and Silas bound in jail, all night long

            G   D   G
Cryin', "who shall deliver me?"

Paul and Silas bound in jail, all night long
Paul and Silas bound in jail, all night long
Paul and Silas bound in jail, all night long
Cryin', who shall deliver me?

They cried glory, glory halleloo...

Oh, the lightning flashed and the thunder roared...

The old jail house began to rock...

One jailer cried, "What must I do?"

(Repeat 1st verse)

Payday at Coal Creek

Traditional Old-time Song; **DATE**: Circa 1911; Collected in 1928; **OTHER NAMES**: Payday; Last Payday at Coal Creek; **RECORDING INFO**: Pete Steel, 1938; Pete Seeger; **NOTES**:
Several traditional songs were written about the horrible conditions in the Coal Creek mines. In 1877, the state of Tennessee chose to relieve its shortage of prisons by putting miners to
work in the Coal Creek mines. This song was written about the second of two mining disasters in 1902 and 1911. Easy Rider was a name hobo's called a freight car with good wheels
running on smooth track.

Payday, it's payday, oh, payday,

Payday at Coal Creek tomorrow,

Payday at Coal Creek tomorrow.

Payday, it's payday, oh, payday,
Payday don't come at Coal Creek no more,
Payday don't come no more.

Bye bye, bye bye, oh, bye bye
Bye bye, my woman, I'm gone,
Bye bye, my woman, I'm gone.

You'll miss me, you'll miss me, you'll miss me,
You'll miss me when I'm gone,
You'll miss me when I'm gone.

I'm a poor boy, I'm a poor boy, I'm a poor boy,
I'm a poor boy and a long way from home,
I'm a poor boy and a long way from home.

Easy rider, oh easy rider, oh easy rider,
Oh, easy rider, but she'll leave that rail sometime,
Easy rider, but she'll leave that rail sometime.

Peg and Awl

Old-time Song; **DATE**: Early 1900's; **OTHER NAMES**: Peg An' Awl; **RECORDING INFO**: Kelly Harrell, 1925; Carolina Tar Heels, 1928; Hobart Smith; Clarence Ashley & Doc Watson; **NOTES**: The title and tag refer to a "Peggin' Awl."

In the year of eighteen and one; (Peg and awl)
C

In the year of eighteen and one; (Peg and awl)

In the year of eighteen and one; Peggin' shoes was all I done
F   C

(Hand me down my peg, my peg, my peg and awl.)
G   C

In the year of eighteen and two; (Peg and awl)
In the year of eighteen and two; (Peg and awl)
In the year of eighteen and two; Peggin' shoes was all I'd do.
(Hand me down my peg, my peg, my peg and awl.)

In the year of eighteen and three; (Peg and awl) (REPEAT)
In the year of eighteen and three; Peggin' shoes is all you'd see.
(Hand me down my peg, my peg, my peg and awl.)

In the year of eighteen and four; (Peg and awl) (REPEAT)
In the year of eighteen and four; I said I'd peg them shoes no more.
(Throw away my pegs, my pegs, my pegs and awl.)

They've invented a new machine, peg and awl (REPEAT)
They've invented a new machine. The prettiest thing you've ever seen
(Throw away my pegs, my pegs, my pegs and awl.)

Make one hundred pair to my one, peg and awl (REPEAT)
Make one hundred pair to my one, peggin' shoes it ain't no fun
(Throw away my pegs, my pegs, my pegs and awl.)

Policeman

Old-time Song; **DATE:** 1917 (Sharp);1915 (Brown) **RELATED TO:** Tell Old Bill; How Many Biscuits Can You Eat?; This Morning, This Evening So Soon; Ain't No Use in Workin' So Hard; Red Hot Breakdown; Settin' in the Chimney Jamb; Wagon; **RECORDED BY:** Gid Tanner and his Skillet Lickers; Tommy Jarrell; Kenny Hall; Reed Martin; **NOTES:** This song is closely related to "This Morning, This Evening, So Soon" that is related to a large group of songs including "Crawdad Song." Most of these songs are very similar and use a tag at the end of each verse (sugar babe/baby mine/this morning etc.) Sharp & Karpeles collected a version of Sugar Babe by Eliza in 1917 which has a verse found in most versions of The Policeman: Shoot your dice and have your fun, Sugar Babe (2x)/Ran like the devil when the police come, sugar babe.

G
Police come I didn't want to go this mornin',

C   G
Police come I didn't want to go this mornin',

C
Police come I didn't want to go,

G
Shot him down with a forty-four this mornin'.

Down went the trigger and band went the gun this mornin'
Down went the trigger and band went the gun this mornin'
Down went the trigger and band went the gun,
I wish I had my wagon I'd of hauled him home this mornin'.

Big police sittin' on a log this mornin'
Big police sittin' on a log this mornin'
Big police sittin' on a log,
Finger on the trigger and eye on a log this mornin'

I know something I won't tell this mornin'
I know something I won't tell this mornin'
I know something I won't tell,
We'll all go to heaven in a coconut shell this mornin'

Two old maids in a foldin' bed this mornin'
Two old maids in a foldin' bed this mornin'
Two old maids in a foldin' bed,
One turned over and the other one said, "Good mornin'"

Two old maids a-sittin' in the sand this mornin'
Two old maids a-sittin' in the sand this mornin'
Two old maids a-sittin' in the sand,
Each one wishin' the other was a man this mornin'

Two old maids a-sittin' in the snow this mornin'
Two old maids a-sittin' in the snow this mornin'
Two old maids a-sittin' in the snow
What they're doin' there I don't know this mornin'

I got drunk and fell on the floor this mornin'
I got drunk and fell on the floor this mornin'
I got drunk and fell on the floor
Good corn liquor and I want some more this mornin'

Bull frog jumped from bank to bank this mornin'
Bull frog jumped from bank to bank this mornin'
Bull frog jumped from bank to bank,
Skinned his back from shank to shank this mornin'

Shoot your dice and have your fun this mornin'
Shoot your dice and have your fun this mornin'
Shoot your dice and have your fun,
Run like hell when the police come this mornin'

Shoot your dice and roll 'em in the sand this mornin'
Shoot your dice and roll 'em in the sand this mornin'
Shoot your dice and roll 'em in the sand,
Ain't gonna work for no boss man this mornin'

Polly Wolly Doodle

Traditional Old-time Song Well known; **DATE**: 1882; **OTHER NAMES**: Sing Polly Wolly Doodle; **RECORDING INFO**: Gid Tanner & his Skillet Lickers 1926; Vernon Dalhart 1929; Louise Massey & the Westerners 1939; **NOTES**: The style of this song suggests a minstrel origin (some of the lyrics are from minstrel songs) but no sheet music has been found before the 1880's.

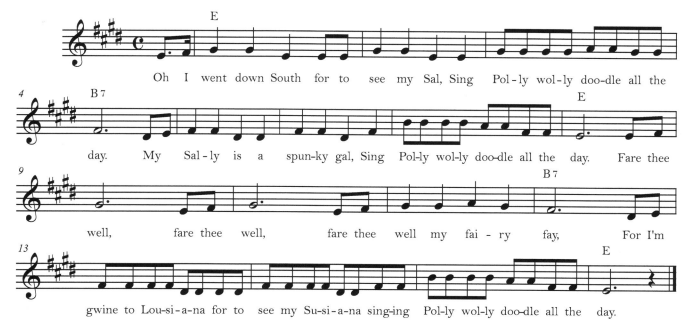

Oh, I went down south for to see my Sal, Sing Polly Wolly Doodle all the day

My Sally is a spunky gal, Sing Polly Wolly Doodle all the day.

CHORUS: Fare thee well, Fare thee well, Fare thee well, my fairy fay,

For I'm goin' to Lousiana, For to see my Susyanna, Sing Polly Wolly Doodle all the day.

Oh, my Sal, she is a maiden fair...
With curly eyes and laughing hair...

Behind the barn, down on my knees
I thought I heard a chicken sneeze

He sneezed so hard with the whooping cough,
He sneezed the head and the tail right off

There's a bullfrog sitting by the railroad track
Picking his teeth with a carpet tack

Well I went to the river and I couldn't get across
So I floated on a fish 'cos I thought it was a horse

Poor Wayfaring Stranger

Traditional Gospel Song; **DATE:** 1858; **CATEGORY:** Early Gospel Songs; **RECORDING INFO:** Vaughn's Texas Quartet, 1929; Bill Monroe, 1958; Roscoe Holcomb; **OTHER NAMES:** Poor Wayfaring Pilgrim; I Am a Poor Wayfaring Pilgrim; NOTES: The hymn text (tune as Judgement in Kentucky Harmony, 1816) was first published in Bever's 1858 Christian Songster. Versions printed in Dett 1927 (Jackson 1933), in Hymns for the Camp, 1862; and The Southern Zion's Songster, 1864. This tune, set with these words, continues in the present editions of both the Cooper and the Denson Sacred Harps and the Primitive Baptist songbook Old School Hymnal. Related to Lady of Carlisle, John Riley.

I know dark clouds will gather 'round me, I know my way is rough and steep;
Am   E   Am   Dm   E7

But beauteous fields lie just beyond me, Where souls redeemed their vigil keep.
Am E   Am   Dm E   Am

CHORUS: I'm going there to meet my father, I'm going there no more to roam
F   G   C   F   G   E

I'm just a-going over Jordan, I'm just a-going over home.
Am E   Am   Dm   E   Am

I'm going there to meet my mother, She said she's meet me when I come
I'm just a-going over Jordan, I'm just a-going over home.

I want to wear a crown of glory, When I get home to that bright land.
I want to shout Salvation's story, In concert with that bloodwashed band.

I'm going there to meet my Savior, To sing His praises forevermore
I'm only going over Jordan, I'm only going over home.

Prettiest Little Gal in the County-O

Old-Time Song and Breakdown; **DATE:** 1843 as "Dandy Jim from Caroline;" **RECORDING INFO:** Gid Tanner and His Skiller Lickers, 1924; Norman and Nancy Blake; Clyde Davenport; Clayton McMichen; Kenny Hall and the Long Haul String Band; **RELATED TO:** Wouldn't Give Me Sugar in My Coffee-O; She Wouldn't Give me Sugar in my Coffee; Old Aunt Jenny; Turkey Buzzard; Prosperity Breakdown; Goin' Down to Georgie-O; What'll I Do With the/this Baby-O; **OTHER NAMES:** Prettiest Little Baby in the County-O; Prettiest Little Girl/Gal in the Country-O; **NOTES:** "Prettiest Little Girl/Gal in the County-O" is one of a large group of songs that originated from the chorus of Dandy Jim from Caroline, a minstrel song written in 1843. Dandy Jim was published by at least six publishers in New York and Boston as well as in Baltimore. It was attributed it to Chas. Reps, Dan Emmet, Geo F. Bristow and J.T. Norton.

G
Prettiest girl in the county-o,

D   G
Watch her sway, do-see-doe.

G
Prettiest girl in the county-o,

D   G
Watch her sway, do-see-doe.

G
CHORUS: Prettiest girl in the county-o,
                         C   G

D
I like sugar in the coffee-o.

G   C   G
Prettiest girl in the county-o,

D
Pass that sugar with the coffee-o.

Prettiest girl in the county-o,
I can't get her in the morning-o.
Prettiest girl in the county-o,
I can't get her in the evening-o.

Swing 'em like you love 'em,
Boys ain't above 'em.
Prettiest girl in the county-o.
I can't get her in the morning-o.

Pretty Little Pink/Fly Around

Old-Time; Bluegrass Play-Party Song and Breakdown; Widely Known; **DATE:** 1929 From "The Scots Muscial Museum: 1787-1803" by Robert Burns; Appears in Baring-Gould Mother Goose 1895; **RECORDING INFO:** Bradley Kincaid 1929; Lily May Ledford; Hobart Smith; Tennessee Ernie Ford **OTHER NAMES:** Blue Eyes Ran Me Crazy; My Pretty Little Pink; Little Pink; All Around Those Pretty Little Pinks; Long the Days of Sorrows; Fly Around My Pretty Little Miss/Pink; We're Marching Down to Old Quebec; Charley He's a Good Old Boy/Man; Charlie's Neat and Charlie's Sweet; Western Country; Susannah Gal; Blue Eyed Gal; Charlie He's My Darling; Four in the Middle; Coffee Grows on White Oak Trees; Old King Cole was a Jolly Old Soul (Jean Ritchie) **NOTES:** "Pink" is a nickname for girl/miss/love. pink is also the color traditionally identified with the female gender. The "Pretty Little Pink" lyrics also appear in "We're Marching to Quebec(sometimes New Orleans etc.)" "Fly Around My Pretty Little Miss" is also titled "Fly Around My Pretty Little Pink" and appears under that latter title frequently. The earliest reference is taken from a poem by Robert Burns between 1787-1803 entitled "Here's to the Health My Bonnie Lass"; O dinna think my pretty pink?But I an live without thee/I vow and swear, I dinna care/How long ye look about ye.

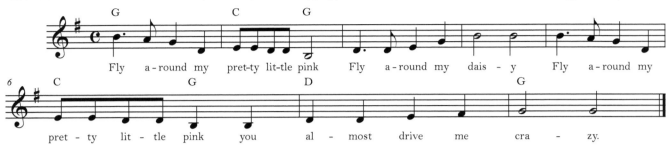

Lord, Lord, my pretty little Pink

Lord, Lord, I say

Lord, Lord, my pretty little Pink

I'm going to stay away.

Cheeks as red as a red, red rose
Her eyes as a diamond brown
I'm going to see my pretty little miss
Before the sun goes down

CHORUS: Fly around my pretty little pink

Fly around my daisy

Fly around my pretty little pink

You almost drive me crazy.

I reckon you think my pretty little miss
That I can't live without you
But I'll let you know before I go
That I care very little about you

It's rings upon my true love's hands
Shines so bright like gold
Gonna see my pretty little miss
Before it rains or snows

When I was up in the field of work
I sat down and cried
Studying about my blue eyed girl
Thought to my God I'd die

CHORUS II: Fly around me pretty little pink
Fly around my dandy
Fly around my pretty little pink
I don't want none of your candy

Every time I go that road
It looks so dark and cloudy
Every time I see that girl
I always tell her howdy.

Coffee grows on white oak trees
The river flows with brandy
Rocks on the hills all covered with gold
And the girls all sweeter than candy.

I'll put my knapsack on my back
My rifle on my shoulder
I'll march away to Spartanburg
And there I'll be a soldier

Charlie is a nice young my
Charlie is a dandy
Every time he goes to town
He buys the ladies candy

I don't want none of your weevily wheat
I don't want none of your barley
Want some flour in half an hour
To bake a cake for Charlie

Every time I go that road
It looks so dark and hazy
Every time I see that girl
She almost drives me crazy

I asked that girl to marry me
And what did she say?
She said that she would marry me
Before the break of day (CHORUS II)

Pretty Saro

Traditional Old-Time Song; **DATE:** 1911; **RELATED TO:** In Eighteen Forty-Nine; Lone Valley; At the Foot of Yonder Mountain; **OTHER NAMES:** Pretty Sarah;
RECORDING INFO: Ritchie Family; Horton Baker; Doc Watson; Bluegrass Messengers; **NOTES:** This song can be traced back to England as "The Maid of Bonclody"
printed c. 1867 by P. Brereton, 56 Cook Street, Dublin. It's closely related to "At the Foot of Yonder Mountain."

Down in some lonesome valley, in such a lone place,
(G) (D) (C) (D)

Where the wild birds do whistle, their notes to increase;
(G) (D) (Em) (D)

Farewell Pretty Saro I bid you adieu,
(G) (C Am) (D)

And I'll dream of Pretty Saro, where ever I go.
(Em) (D) (C) (G)

I came to this country in eighteen forty-nine,
I saw so many lovers, but I never saw mine;
I looked all around me, and I saw I was alone,
And me a poor stranger, a long way from home.

My love she won't have me, so I, I understand,
She wants a freeholder who owns house and land,
I can not maintain her with silver and gold,
Or buy all fine things a big house can hold.

Putting On the Style

Old-time Song by George Wright words and music; **DATE**: 1875; **RECORDING INFO**: Vernon Dalhart 1925; Dixie Mountaineers with Earnest Stoneman 1927; **NOTES**: The lyrics to this moralistic song could easily be updated by substitution: Young man with his new car, driving like he's mad/With a set of car keys/ he's borrowed from his dad/He guns the engine so loudly/just to see his lady's smile/But she knows he's only putting on the style.

D   A7   D
Young man in a carriage, driving like he's mad With a team of horses, he's borrowed from his dad

                                                A7   D
He cracks his whip so lively, just to see his lady's smile But she knows he's only putting on the style

               D   A7   D
CHORUS: Putting on the agony, putting on the style That's what all the young folks are doing all the while

                                          A7   D
And as I look around me, I'm very apt to smile To see so many people putting on the style

Sweet sixteen, she goes to church, just to see the boys She laughs and she giggles at every little noise
She turns this way a little, she turns that way a while But everybody knows she's only putting on the style

Young man in a restaurant smokes a dirty pipe Looking like a pumpkin that's only halfway ripe
Smoking, drinking, chewing and thinking all the way There is nothing equal to putting on the style

Preacher in the pulpit shooting with all his might Gory Hallelujah, puts the people in a fright
You might think that Satan's coming up the aisle But it's only preacher putting on the style

Young man just back from college makes a big display With a great big jawbreak that he can hardly say
It can't be found in Webster, and won't be for a while But everybody knows he's only putting on the style

Doctor comes to see you, just to hold your hand Feeds you pills and medicines and tells you you'll feel grand
And all the times he's talking, he wears a great big smile Thinks he'll make a lot of money putting on the style

Ragged But Right

Traditional Old-time and Bluegrass Song; **DATE:** Early 1900's; **RECORDING INFO:** Blue Harmony Boys (Rufus and Ben Quillian) 1929; Riley Puckett 1934; Buddy Jones 1937; George Jones; Johnny Cash; **NOTES:** This is a jug band/blues song that Riley Puckett recorded in 1934. It has been reworked by country artists like George Jones and has become a country standard.

Folks, I'm here to tell you that I'm ragged but I'm right (G ... D)

I'm a thief and a gambler, and I stay up late at night (G)

Gonna have a Porterhouse steak three times a day for my board (C ... G ... E)

More than any loafer in this town can afford. (A7 ... D)

A big electric fan to keep me cool while I sleep
A pretty little woman plays around at my feet
I'm a ramblin' and a gambler and I leave every night
People, I tell you I'm ragged but I'm right.

I hopped on a frieght train in North Caroline
Rode down to Atlanta and bought me some 'shine
Went into a card game with thirty-nine cents
Came out with enough for another month's rent

Well you may think I'm bragging but don't get me wrong
I can't run for office while I'm singing this song
I'm a thief and a gambler and I'm drunk every night
I tell you boys I'm ragged but right

I left a pretty little gal layin' there on the floor
Gave her all my love, and who could ask me for more?
Gave her my last quarter just to buy her a drink
Showed her to the door, and then what do you think?

I said, "Go home to your mother, and tell her for me
I'm hittin' the road just 'cause I want to be free
'Cause I'm a ramblin' man, a gamblin' man, and Lord am I tight
I just called up to tell you that I'm ragged but right."

Railroad Bill

Old-time Song and Blues; **DATE:** 1909 Perrow; **RECORDING INFO:** Riley Puckett 1924; Georgia Crackers 1927; 1927; Frank Hutchison 1929; Etta Baker; **NOTES:** Morris Slater was a train robber known as "Railroad Bill," who roamed Florida and Alabama from 1894 to 1897. After an Alabama deputy was killed, Slater was surrounded in a grocery store, "eating crackers and cheese." He probably could have been arrested, but the posse shot him instead. Four versions were collected by Perrow in 1909 and I have included verses from these as well as the standard verses. The last verse is sometimes "Ride, ride, ride."

C
Railroad Bill, Railroad Bill

E7   F
He never works and he never will and it's

C   G   C
Ride, Railroad Bill.

Railroad Bill, he was a mighty mean man
He shot the midnight lantern out of the brakeman's hand
Ride, Railroad Bill.

I'm going up on a mountain, I'm going out West
A thirty-eight special stickin' out of my vest
Ride, Railroad Bill.

Railroad Bill is a mighty band man,
Come skipping and dodging through this land.
Ride, Railroad Bill.

Railroad Bill he was a mighty bad man
Kill anybody that he think he can
Ride, Railroad Bill.

Railroad Bill he done stole my wife
I'm gonna find him, I'm gonna take his life
Ride, Railroad Bill.

Railroad Bill, up on a hill
Lightin' a seegar with a ten-dollar bill.
Ride, Railroad Bill.

Raise a Ruckus Tonight

Old-time Song by HG Wheeler and JW Wheeler 1884; **OTHER NAMES:** Come Along Little Children; We're Gonna Have a Good Time Tonight; Hawk and Buzzard; Going To Raise a Ruckus Tonight; **RECORDING INFO:** Norfolk Jubille Quartet; Raise a Ruckus Tonight, 1923; The Georgia Yellow Hammers, Going to Raise a Ruckus Tonight, 1928; Bill Chitwood & his Georgia Mountaineers, Raise Rough House Tonight, 1928; Cliff Carlisle, Gonna Raise a Ruckus Tonight, 1939; Hugh Cross & Riley Puckett, Gonna Raise Ruckus Tonight, 1928; **NOTES:** A popular old-time song with floating lyrics from different sources like You Shall Be Free.

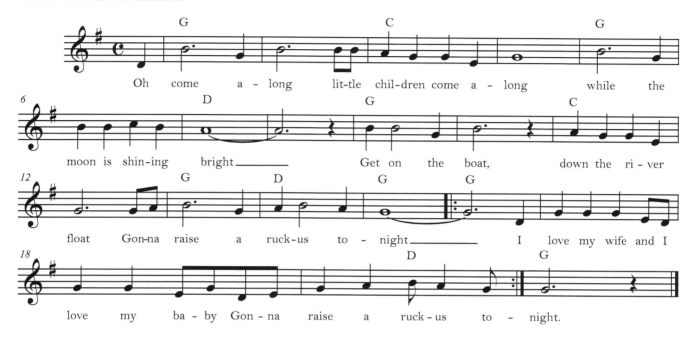

CHORUS: Oh, come along, little children come along,

While the moon is shining bright,

Get on the boat, down the river float,

Gonna raise a ruckus tonight

VERSE: I love my wife and I love my baby

Gonna raise ruckus tonight,

I love my biscuits sopped in gravy,

Gonna raise a ruckus tonight.

Well she brings me chicken and she brings me pie
Gonna raise a ruckus tonight,
I eat some of everything the rich folks buy
Gonna raise a ruckus tonight.

Well there ain't no use in me working so hard
Gonna raise a ruckus tonight,
When I've got a woman in the rich folks' yard
Gonna raise a ruckus tonight.

Well, every evening about half past eight
Gonna raise a ruckus tonight
I'll hang my bucket on the rich folks' gate
Gonna raise a ruckus tonight.

Old hen sitting on the fodder stack,
Gonna Raise a ruckus tonight,
Hawk came along and struck him in the back,
Gonna raise a ruckus tonight.

Old hen flew and the biddies too,
Gonna raise a ruckus tonight,
What in the world is the rooster gonna do?
Gonna raise a ruckus tonight.

Red Apple Juice

Old-time and Bluegrass Song; Widely know; **DATE:** 1909 from E.C. Perrow as "Done All I Can Do;" Early 1900's as "Red Apple Joice" (Lunsford 1927 recording); **OTHER NAMES:** Red Rocking Chair; Sugar Baby; Honey Baby; I Ain't Got no Honey Baby Now; **RECORDING INFO:** Bascom Lamar Lunsford 1927; James F. Leisy; Ralph McTell; **NOTES:** This white blues is found throughout the Southeast and Appalachians. The confusion between the Sugar Babe/Crawdad songs and the Sugar Baby/Red Rocking Chair songs continues. The problem is that some Red Apple Juice/Red Rocking Chair songs continues. The problem is that some Red Apple Juice/Red Rocking Chair songs are named Sugar Babe. Compilation of different lyrics, edited by Richard Matteson. This is a different version from the one in my Bluegrass Picker's Tune Book.

Ain't got no use,
F   C

Ain't got no use for your red apple juice.
F   C   Am

Ain't got no honey baby now,
C   Am

Ain't got no honey baby now.
C   G   C

CHORUS: You'll rock the cradle,
You'll rock the cradle, and I'll sing the song,
You'll rock the cradle when I'm gone,
You'll rock the cradle when I'm gone.

Ain't got no use
Ain't got no use for your red rocking chair
Ain't got no honey baby there,
Ain't got no honey baby there.

*Done all I can do
Done all I can do to try to live with you,
Send you back to your mama next pay day,
Send you back to your mama next pay day.

Gave her all I made,
Gave her all I made then I laid her in the shade.
What more can a poor boy do?
What more can a poor boy do?

*lyrics from the 1909 version

Rock Island Line

Traditional Old-time song; **DATE:** Early 1900's; **RECORDING INFO:** Kelly Pace & group of prisoners, Rock Island Line 1934; Leadbelly; The Weavers; **NOTES:** The earliest version was collected at Cummins Prison Farm, Arkansas in 1934 by John & Ruby Lomax. Leadbelly learned the song around 1934 from the Pace version and adapted it.

I may be right, I may be wrong

I know you're gonna miss me when I'm gone

CHORUS: Oh the Rock Island Line is a mighty fine line

Oh the rock Island Line is the road to ride,

Oh the Rock Island Line is a might fine line,

If you want to ride it, got to ride it like you're flyin'

Buy your ticket at the station on the Rock Island Line.

Jesus died to save our sins
Glory to God I'm gonna see Him again.

Moses stood on the Red Sea shore
Smotin' the water with a two-by-four.

Roll in My Sweet Baby's Arms

Traditional Old-Time and Bluegrass Song; **DATE:** Early 1900's; **CATEGORY:** Early County and Bluegrass Songs; **RECORDING INFO:** The Monroe Brothers, 1936; Flatt & Scurggs, 1950; The Stanley Brothers; Doc & Merie Watson; **OTHER NAMES:** Rollin' In My Sweet Baby's Arms; **NOTES:** A bluegrass standard originating from the textile mills area in the mountains of NC and VA. Roll in My Sweet Baby's Arms was popularized by the Monroe Brothers in 1936. The song is now performed by everyone from parking lot pickers to Buck Owens and Leon Russell.

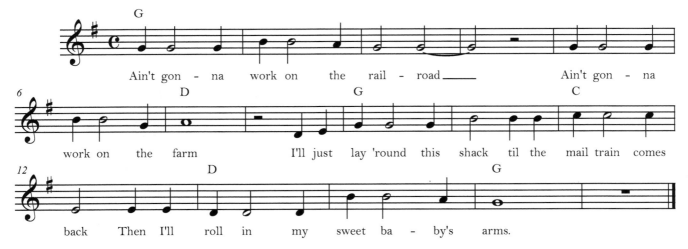

Ain't gon - na work on the rail - road_____ Ain't gon - na work on the farm I'll just lay 'round this shack til the mail train comes back Then I'll roll in my sweet ba - by's arms.

Ain't $\overset{G}{\text{gonna}}$ work on the railroad, Ain't gonna work on the $\overset{D}{\text{farm}}$.

I'll just $\overset{G}{\text{lay}}$ 'round this shack til the $\overset{C}{\text{mail}}$ train comes back

Then I'll $\overset{D}{\text{roll}}$ in my sweet baby's $\overset{G}{\text{arms}}$.

CHORUS: $\overset{G}{\text{Roll}}$ in my sweet baby's arms, Roll in my sweet baby's $\overset{D}{\text{arms}}$,

$\overset{G}{\text{Lay}}$ 'round this shack til the $\overset{C}{\text{mail}}$ train gets back, Then I'll $\overset{D}{\text{roll}}$ in my sweet baby's $\overset{G}{\text{arms}}$.

Now where were you last Friday night, While I was layin' in the jail?
Were you walkin' the streets with another man? You wouldn't even go me bail. CHORUS

Sometimes there's a change in the ocean, Sometimes there's a change in the sea,
Sometimes there's a change in my own true love, But there's never a change in me. CHORUS

I know your parents don't like me, They turn me away from your door,
If I had my life to live over, Oh well, I'd never go back anymore. CHORUS

Roll On the Ground/Big Ball's in Town

Traditional Old-Time Song; **DATE:** Late 1800's Billy Golden 1896; **OTHER NAMES:** Big Ball in Town; Big Ball in Memphis/Boston; **RECORDING INFO**: Billy Golden 1896; Warren Capliner's Cumberland Mountain Entertainers 1928; Georgia Yellow hammers 1929; All Hopkins & his Buckle Busters; Gid Tanner & His Skillet Lickers; J.E. ,Mainer; **NOTES**: The traditional Ballad Index as well as Meade categorizes the "Big Ball in Town" songs with "roll on the ground." Recorded by Billy Golden as "Roll on the Ground" in 1899 (Meade has 1896), the lyrics appear in later in the Al Hopkins 1927 versions. "Roll on the Ground" and "Roll 'Em on the Ground" are similar songs.

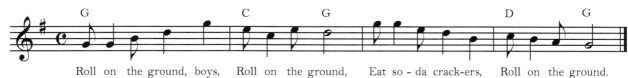

Roll on the ground, boys, Roll on the ground, Eat so-da crack-ers, Roll on the ground.

CHORUS: Roll on the ground, boys, Roll on the ground

Eat soda crackers, Roll on the ground

Workin' on the railroad
Dollar a day,
Eat soda crackers
And the wind blows 'em away.

Get on your big shoes,
Get on your gown,
Shake off those sad blues,
Big Ball's in town.

I'll stay in Asheville,
I'll stick around,
I'll stay in Asheville
When Big Ball's in town.

Get drunk in Asheville,
Dance 'round the town,
Board up your windows,
Big Ball's in town.

Let's have a party,
Let's have a time
Let's have a party,
I've only a dime.

CHORUS 2: Roll 'em boys roll 'em
Roll 'em on the ground
Shootin' seven, eleven,
Roll 'em all around.

Salty Dog Blues

Traditional Old-Time and bluegrass Song; **DATE:** Early 1900's ; **CATEGORY:** Early Country and Bluegrass Songs; **RECORDING INFO:** Allen Brothers, 1927; Flatt & Scruggs & the Foggy Mountain Boys; Erik Darling; Mississippi John Hurt; Osborne Brothers; Morris Brothers; Do Reno and Bill Harrell; **OTHER NAMES**: Salty Dog Blues; Old Salty Dog Blues; **NOTES:** The first commercially successful self-accompanied artist in the "race field" was African-American Papa Charlie Jackson, who played a banjo strung like a guitar. The classic Morris Brothers recording "Let me By Salty Dog" in 1938 was based on papa Charlie Jackson's 1924 recording. Flatt & Scruggs based their version on the earlier Morris Brothers version. The term "salty dog" suggests an off-color meaning for the chorus.

Standing on the corner with the low down blues

Great big hole in the bottom of my shoes

Honey let me be your Salty Dog.

CHORUS: Let me be your Salty Dog, or I won't be your man at all

Honey let me be your salty dog.

Now look a-here Sal, I know you
Run down stocking and worn out shoes
Honey let me be your Salty Dog. CHORUS

I was down in the wildwood setting on a log
Finger on the trigger and an eye on the hog
Honey let me be your Salty Dog. CHORUS

I pulled the trigger and the gun said go
Shot fell over in Mexico
Honey let me be your Salty Dog. CHORUS

Scarborough Fair

Old English and US Ballad; Widely known **DATE:** 1673 (broadside) **OTHER NAMES:** The Elfin Knight; The Cambric Shirt; A True Lover of Mine
RECORDING INFO: Ewan MacColl Brian Withycombe; Michelle McLaughlin; Simon and Garfunckel **NOTES:** This song as commonly known as The
Elfin Knight (Child #2). The now well-known refrain "Parsley, sage, rosemary and thyme" was added in 1784, when a version appeared in Gammer Gurton's
Garland.

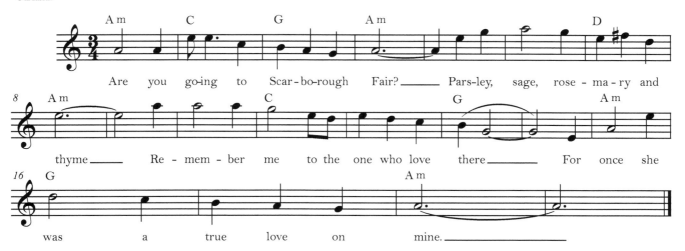

Am   C   G   Am
Are you going to Scarborough Fair?

                  D   Am
Parsley, sage, rosemary and thyme

         C   G
Remember me to one who lives there,

     Am   G   Am
For once she was a true love of mine.

Tell her to make me a cambric shirt...
Without any seam or fine needlework...

Tell her to wash it in yonder dry well
Where water ne'er spring nor drop of rain fell

Oh, will you find me an acre of land
Between the sea foam and the sea sand

Oh, will you plow it with a lamb's horn
And sow it all over with one peppercorn

Oh, will you reap it with a sickle of leather
And tie it all up with a peacock's feather

And when you have done and finished your work
Come to me for your cambric shirt

She'll Be Coming Round the Mountain

Traditional Oldtime Song; Widely Known **DATE:** Adapted from Old Ship of Zion circa 1876; 1924 recording by Henry Whitter **OTHER NAMES:** She's Comin' Round the Mountain; Comin' Round the Mountain **RECORDING INFO:** Henry Whitter 1924; Vernon Dalhart 1925; Al Hopkins & his Buckle Busters 1927; Uncle Dave Macon & Sam McGee 1930 **NOTES:** The song originated as a parody of "The Old Ship of Zion" or "When the Charion Comes" in the late 1800's.

She'll be com-ing 'round the moun-tain when she comes_____ She'll be com-ing 'round the moun-tain when she comes_____ She'll be com-ing 'round the moun-tain she'll be com-ing 'round the moun-tain she'll be com-ing 'round the moun-tain when she comes._____

She'll be coming 'round the mountain when she comes
<small>C</small>

She'll be coming 'round the mountain when she comes

She'll be coming 'round the mountain
<small>G</small>

She'll be coming 'round the mountain
<small>C</small>

She'll be coming 'round the mountain
<small>F</small>

She'll be coming 'round the mountain when she comes
<small>C</small>

She'll be huffin' and a puffin' when she comes...

Oh, we'll all come out to meet her when she comes...

We will kill to old red rooster when she comes...

She'll be wearing pink pajamas when she comes...

Oh she'll have to sleep with Grandma when she comes...

She'll be riding six white horses when she comes...

Shenandoah

Old-Time Song; **DATE**: Circa 1903 (recording, Minster Singers); **OTHER NAMES**: World of Misery; Across the Wide Missouri; The Rolling River; **RECORING INFO:**
Minster Singers, 1903; Campbell & burr, 1917; Paul Robeson, 1941; Pete Seeger; **NOTES**: This popular shanty is a favorite of mine.

Oh,   C   Am   F C
Oh, Shenandoah, I long to hear you,

    F   C
Away, you rolling river.

       F   Am
Oh, Shenandoah, I long to hear you

   C   Em   F   G .C
Away, we're bound away, 'cross the wide Missouri

Oh, Shenandoah, I love your daughter
Away, you rolling river.
Oh, Shenandoah, I love your daughter
Away, we're bound away 'cross the wide Missouri

Missouri she's a mighty river...
When she rolls down, her topsails shiver...

Seven years, I courted Sally...
Seven more, I longer to have her...

Farewell, my dear, I'm bound to leave you...
Oh, Shenandoah, I'll not deceive you...

Shorty George Blues

Old-Time Blues Song; **DATE:** Early 1900's; **RECORDING INFO:** James "Iron Head" Baker 1933; Leadbelly; Mance Lipscomb; **NOTES:** "Shorty George" was the name of a train that carried convicts' wives and sweethearts to and from the penitentiary for conjugal visits. It was in the repertoire of Iron Head Baker and Leadbelly.

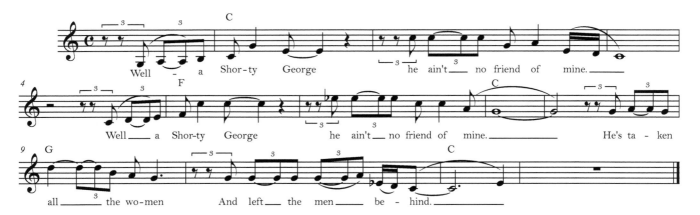

CHORUS: Well-a, Shorty George, he ain't no friend of mine,
(C)

Well-a, Shorty George, he ain't no friend of mine,
(F)   (C)

He's taken all the women and left the men behind.
(G)   (C)

CHORUS 2: Well-a, Shorty George done been here and gone,
Well-a, Shorty George done been here and gone,
Lord he left many a man a long ways from his home.

Well-a, Shorty George travelin' through the land,
Well-a, Shorty George travelin' through the land,
Always lookin' to pick up some woman's man.

Well, my papa died when I was just a lad,
Well, my papa died when I was just a lad,
And ever since that day, I been to the bad.

Got a letter from my baby, couldn't read from crying,
Got a letter from my baby, couldn't read from crying,
She said my mama weren't dead yet but she was slowly dying.

Well, I took my mama to the burying ground,
Well, I took my mama to the burying ground,
I never knowed I loved her till the coffin sound.

Yes, I went down to the graveyard, peeped in my mama's face,
Yes I went down to the graveyard, peeped in my mama's face,
"Ain't it hard to see you in this lonesome place?"

Shout Mourner/You Shall Be Free

Old-time Song and Spiritual; **DATE**: 1911; **OTHER NAMES**: Poor Moaner (Po' Mourner) ; Shout Monah; You Shall Be Free; Mourner; You Shall Be Free, When the Good Lord Sets You Free; **RELATED TO**: Moanish Lady; **RECORDING INFO**: Land Norris, 1924; Uncle Dave Macon, 1927; Four Dusty Travelers; Carolina Tar Heels; Bill Boyd's Cowboy Ramblers; John All; Bill & Belle Reed; **NOTES**: These songs are classified under the African-American spiritual "Mourner, You Shall Be Free." After each line of the verse, you can sing ("shout mourner" or "oh Monah"). Vocal fills can also be used before each chorus line ("In the murnin' You shall be free).

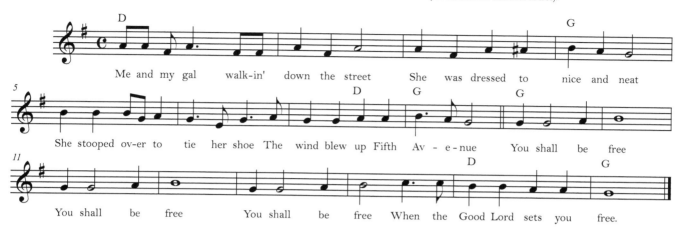

D

Me and my gal walkin' down the street

She was dressed so G nice and neat

She stooped over to tie her shoe

The wind blew up D Fifth Avenue. G

CHORUS: (In the mornin')

You G shall be free, You shall be free,

You shall be free,

When the G Good Lord sets you free. G D

I went to see my girl last night
It was dark and I had no light
Her bulldog met me at the gate
He jumped on me with all of his weight.

I was down in the hen house the other night.
Awful dark, I didn't have no light.
I reached for a chicken, I got me a goose.
A man come out, I had to turn him loose.

I came to the river and I couldn't get across
Jumped on the gater 'cause I thought he was a horse
The horse wouldn't go and I sold it for a hoe
The hoe wouldn't dig and I sold it for a pig.

Oh, some folks say, time is hard
Preacher says, "Put your trust in God."
Man knows the difference, don't you see
A hog can't run just as fast as me.

The pig wouldn't squeal and I sold it for a wheel
The wheel wouldn't run and I sold it for a gun
The gun wouldn't shoot and I sold it for a boot
The boot wouldn't wear and I sold it for a bear.

Behind the barn down on my knees
I thought I heard a chicken sneeze
He sneezed so hard, with the whooping cough
He sneezed his head and tail right off.

Silver Dagger [Laws G21]

Traditional Old-Time and Bluegrass Song; **DATE:** Earliest text: Drowsy Sleeper-Bodelian Library 1817; Appears in The Social Harp 1855 (first verse only); Earliest complete version in US "Awake, Awake!" sung by Mary Sands at Allamstand, NC Aug 1, 1916; **CATEGORY:** Early Country and Bluegrass Songs; **RECORDING INFO:** Oh Molly Dear (be 35667-3) Kelly Harrell 1926; Oh Molly Dear (be 39725-2); BF Shelton 1927; Sleepy Desert (Paramount 3282); Wilmer Watts & the Lonely Eagles 1929; Wake Up You Drowsy Sleeper (BE 62575-2) Oaks Family 1930; Katie Dear (14524-2) Callahan Brothers (vcl duet w. gtrs) 1934; Katie Dear (BS 018680-1) Blue Sky Boys (vcl duet w/ mndln & gtr) 1938; Sarah Ogan Gunning; Joan Baez; Old Crowe Medicine Show; Dave Van Ronk; **OTHER NAMES:** Oh Molly Dear (Go Ask Your Mother); Katie Dear; Awake, Awake; Julianne; **RELATED TO:** Greenback Dollar; Old Virginny/East Virginia Blue/Dark Holler Blues; Darling think of What You've Done; **NOTES:** Silver Dagger has the same basic plot as Drowsy Sleeper but the silver dagger is used as the suicide weapon. The relationship of Drowsy Sleeper with Old Virginny/East Virginia Blues/Dark Holler Blues/Man of Constant Sorrow has been well documented. The Callahan Brothers learned Katie Dear (Silver Dagger) from their mother. This would probably bring the date back to the late 19th century at least.

Oh Katie dear, go ask you mama, if you can be a bride of mine

If she says yes, then we'll be married, if she says no, we'll run away.

Oh Willie dear, there's no need in asking, she's in her room taking her rest
And by her side is a silver dagger, to slay the one that I love best.

Oh Katie dear, go ask your papa, if you can be a ride of mine
If he says yes, come back and tell me, if he says no, we'll run away.

Oh Willie dear, there's no need in asking, he's in his room taking a rest
And by his side is a silver dagger, to slay the one that I love best.

So he picked up that silver dagger, and plunged it through his troubled heart
Saying, "Goodbye Katie, goodbye darlin', it's now forever we must part."

So she picked up that bloody dagger, and plunged it through her lily-white breast
Saying, "Goodbye papa, goodbye mama, I'll die for the one that I love best."

Spike Driver Blues

Old-Time Blues Song; **OTHER NAMES:** Take this Hammer; Take It to the Captain; **DATE:** Take This Hammer, 1909; Perrow; **RECORDING INFO:** Frank Blevins & his Tar Heel Rattlers, 1928; Mississippi John Hart; Doc Warson; **NOTES:** This song is closely related to the Nine Pound Hammer songs like Swannnanoa Tunnel, Take This Hammer, Roll On Buddy and I Got a Bulldog (in this collection). Each verse may be repeated like Mississippi John Hart's versions.

Take this hammer and carry it to the captain

Tell him I'm gone, tell him I'm gone, tell him I'm gone.

I don't want your cold iron shackles
Round my leg, round my leg, round my leg.

It's a long way from East Colorado
To my home, to my home, to my home.

This is the hammer that killed John Henry
Won't kill me, won't kill me, won't kill me.

John Henry, was a steel drivin' boy
But he went down, he went down, he went down.

John Henry, left his hammer
All painted in red, painted in red, painted in red.

Saint Louis Blues

Old-time Blues Song by W.C. Handy; **DATE:** 1914; **RECORDING INFO:** Sophie Tucker 1917; Marion Harris 1920; Virginia Childs 1926; Callahan Brothers 1934; Milton Brown; Bill Boyd; Bob Wills; **NOTES:** One of the most popular blues songs ever written. Handy found his inspiration for the song while wandering the streets of St. Louis. One afternoon he met a black woman tormented by her husband's absence. She told Handy, "Ma man's got a heart like a rock cast in de sea." After Sophie Tucker recorded it in 1917, it became the first blues song to sell a million copies.

VERSE: I hate to see the ev'nin' sun go down

I hate to see the ev'nin' sun go down

'Cause my baby, he done left this town

Feelin' tomorrow like I feel today,
Feelin' tomorrow like I feel today.
I'll pack my trunk, make my get away.

BRIDGE: St. Louis woman with her diamond rings

Pulls that man round by her apron strings.

'Twant for powder an' for store both hair

De man I love would not gone nowhere.

CHORUS: Got the St. Louis blues just as blue as I can be.
That man go a heart like a rock cast in the sea.
Or else he wouldn't have gone so far from me.
(Doggone it!)

VERSE: Been to the Gypsy to get my fortune told,
Been to the Gypsy to get my fortune told,
'Cause I'm most wild 'bout my Jelly roll.

Gypsy done told me, "Don't you war no black,"
Yes, she done told me, "Don't you wear no black."
Go to St. Louis, you can win him back.

BRIDGE: Help me to Cairo, make St. Louis by myself,
Get to Cairo, find my old friend Jeff.
Going to pin myself close to his side,
If I flag his train, I sure can ride.

CHORUS: I loves that man like a schoolboy loves his pie,
Like a Kentucky Col'nel loves his mint an' rye.
I'll love my baby till the day I die.

VERSE: You ought to see that stovepipe brown of mine,
Like he owns the Diamond Joseph line.
He'd make a cross-eyed man go stone blind.

Blacker than midnight, teeth like flags of truce,
Blackest man in the whole St. Louis.
Blacker the berry, sweeter is the juice.

BRIDGE: About a crap game he knows a pow'ful lot,
But when work-time comes he's on the dot.
Going to ask him for a cold ten-spot.
What it takes to get it, he's certainly got.

CHORUS: A black-headed gal make a freight train jump the track.
Said a black-headed gal make a freight train jump the rack,
But a long tall gal makes a preacher ball the jack.

EXTRA CHORUSES: Lord, a blonde-headed woman makes a
        good man leave the town,
I said the blonde-headed woman makes a good man leave the town,
But a red-head woman makes a boy slap his papa down.

O ashes to ashes and dust to dust,
I said ashes to ashes and dust to dust,
If my blues don't get you my jazzing must.

Stagolee/Stackerlee [Laws 115]

Old-Time Blues Ballad; **DATE**: 1903; **OTHER NAMES**: Stack O'Lee Blues; Stagger Lee; **RECORDING INFO**: Senter Boyd; Fruit Jar Guzzlers, 1928; Cab Calloway & his Orchestra; Cliff Edwards; Tennessee Ernie Ford; Mississippi John Hurt; **NOTES**: "On Dec. 29, 1895, William Lyons and Lee Sheldon (nicknamed "stag" Lee) were drinking together at a tavern in St. Louis, Missouri. A political discussion began; in the heat of the argument, Lyons knocked off Sheldon's stetson hat, and Sheldon promptly pulled a pistol and shot him dead. He was arrested and tried; the first trial ended in a hung jury, but he was convicted in a second trial and served time in prison, dying in 1916." The number of versions and artists that have recorded this song is staggering-over 200 different recording artists. This is compilation of several versions.

G
I remember one September,

On one Friday night,

C
Stagolee and Billy Lyons,

G
Had a great fight,

D   G
That bad man, oh, cruel Stagolee.

Now you talking about
        some gamblers,
Oughta seen Richard Lee,
Shot one thousand dollars,
And come out on a three,
That bad man, oh, cruel Stagolee.

Billy Lyons shot six bits,
Stack he bet he passed,
Stackerlee out with a forty-five,
Said you've done shot your last,
That bad man, oh, cruel Stagolee.

Billy Lyons told Stagolee,
"Please don't take my life,
I got two little babies,
And a darlin' lovin' wife"
That bad man, oh, cruel Stagolee.

God'll take care of your
        two little children
And I'll take care of your wife
You done stole my stetson hat
And I'm bound to take your life.
That bad man, oh, cruel Stagolee.

Lord, a woman came a running,
Fell down on her knees,
Crying, O Mister Stagolee,
Don't shoot my brother please,
That bad man, oh, cruel Stagolee.

Boom boom boom boom
With the forty-four
When I spied Billy Lyons,
He was lyin' down on the floor
That bad man, oh, cruel Stagolee.

The judge told the sheriff,
We want him dead or alive,
"How in the world can
        we bring him in,
When he totes a forty-five,"
That bad man, oh, cruel Stagolee.

"Gentleman's of the jury,
What do you think of that?
Stagolee killed Billy Lyons
For a five-dollar Stetson hat!"
That bad man, oh, cruel Stagolee.

Standin' on the gallows,
Head way up high,
At twelve o'clock they killed him,
They're all glad to see him die.
That bad man, oh, cruel Stagolee.

Stack grabbed the devil
        by the collar,
Throwed him up on the shelf,
Said, get out of here,
        you son of a gun,
I'll run this place myself.
That bad man, oh, cruel Stagolee.

Step It Up and Go

Old-time Jug Band Blues; **DATE:** Early 1900's **OTHER NAMES**: Bottle Up and Go; Shake It Up and Go; **RECORDING INFO:** Blind Boy Fuller 1935; Brownie McGhee 1942; Maddon Bros. & Rose 1947; Tommy McClennan 1944; Bob Dylan; **NOTES**: Bottle Up and Go was recorded in 1932 by the Picaninny Jug Band. Apparently Fuller changed the lyrics slightly for the classic 1932 recording.

Now she may be, ninety years But she ain't too old, to shift them gears
G

CHORUS: You gotta step it up and go, yes go, You can't stay here, you gotta step it up and go.
C   G   D   G

Now, my mama killed a chicken, She thought it was a duck
She put him on the table, With the legs stickin' up CHORUS

Now looky here, baby, Where'd I stay last night?
Ain't none a yo' business, You don't do me right CHORUS

Now, told my girl, week 'fore last
The gate she jus' came in, Just a little too fast CHORUS

I used to have a gal, she was little and low
She used to love me but she don't no mo'

I went downtown to have a little fun,
Up stepped a sheriff with a big shotgun

I know a woman she lives way upstairs
She makes her living by putting on airs

A nickel is a nickel, a dime is a dime
You shake yours and baby I'll shake mine

I went to the river and I couldn't get across
So I jumped on a gater 'cause I thought it was a horse

Sugar Hill

Old-Time Breakdown; **DATE**: Earliest recording 1928 by Crockett Ward & his Boys; Composed by George Washington Dixon some time prior to 1827, and a version's of Dixon's song is included in a collection of Minstrel songs that was published in New York, in 1855; **RELATED TO:** Liza Jane; Chicken in the Bread Tray; Jenny Get Around; Angeline the Baker; **OTHER NAMES**; Sailing on the Ocean; **RECORDING INFO:** Crockett Ward & his Boys 1928; The Original Bogtrotters; Tommy Jarrell & Fred Cockerham; **NOTES:** Sugar Hill is a term used to denote the wild part of town where anything is available. In 1827 George Washington Dixon began singing a song called "My Long Tail Blue." The song was printed in 1855. The basic tune and some of the lyrics are used in Sugar Hill today. The song was collected in 1911 by EC Perrow.

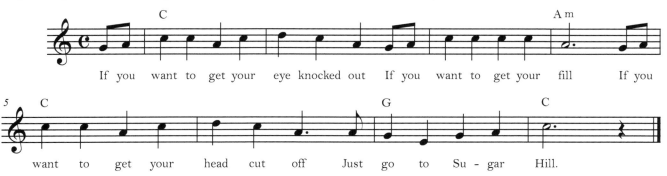

If you
                C
If you want to get your eye knocked out If you want to get your fill.
                                                                          Am

         C   G   C
If you want to get your head cut off Just go to Sugar Hill.

Jaybird on the mountain top The Redbird on the ground.
Blackbird in the sugar tree A-shaking that sugar down.

They said she got mighty sick And what do you reckon ailed her.
She drink three quarts of sugar top And then her stomach failed her.

Ten Cents in my pocket book And don't you hear it jingle.
I'm gonna court them pretty gals As long as I stay single.

Jaybird pulled a big plow Sparrow a-why not you?
Your legs so slim and slender I'm 'fraid they'll break in two.

Yonder comes my old true love And how do you reckon I know
Tell her by her shoo fly dress That comes from sugar store.

Swannanoa Tunnel

Traditional Old-Time Song; **DATE:** 1913 in JAFL 26; 1916 in Cecil Sharp collection; **RELATED TO:** Take This Hammer; Nine Pound Hammer; **RECORDING INFO:** Bascom Lamar Lunsford; Erik Darling; **NOTES:** Anther of the closely related song to Take This Hammer. This is known as a work song and the hammer would strike on the 3rd beat of each measure. Other similar songs in this collection are I've Got Bulldog and Spike Driver's Blues.

Asheville   Junc-tion,   Swan-nan-no-a   tun-nel,   All caved   in, babe,   all caved   in.

Asheville Junction, Swannanoa tunnel
          G   C

All caved in, babe, all caved in.
        G   D   G

I'm goin' back to Swannanoa tunnel
That's my home, babe, that's my home.

When you hear that hoot owl squallin'
Somebody's dyin', babe, another man's gone.

If I could gamble like Bill Dooley
I'd leave my home, honey, I'd leave my home.

Reilly Gardner killed my partner,
Couldn't kill me, couldn't kill me.

Ain't no hammer in these mountains
Out rings mine, baby, out rings mine.

Take a Drink on Me

Old-Time Song; **DATE**: Early 1900's; **RECORDING INFO**: Charlie Poole and the North Carolina Ramblers 1927; New Lost City Ramblers; Old Crowe Medicine Show; **NOTES**: This old-time song is directly based on Take A Whiff On Me. Another old-time bawdy song Take Your Leg Off Mine is a direct variant.

Now, what did you do with the gun in your hand,
_A

You gave it to a rounder and he shot a good man,
_D

Oh, Lord, honey, take a drink on me!
_E _A

CHORUS: Take a drink on me, take a drink on me,
_A

All you roudners, take a drink on me
_D

Oh, Lord, honey, take a drink on me.
_E _A

If you keep on stalling, you'll make me think
Your daddy was a monkey and your mama was an ape,
Oh, Lord, honey, take a drink on me.

You see that gal with a hobble on
She's good looking just as sure as you're born.
Oh, Lord, honey, take a drink on me. (REPEAT FIRST VERSE)

Take Me Out to the Ball Game

Old-time Song by Jack Norworth and Harry Von Tilzer **DATE:** 1908; **RECORDING INFO:** Kerry Kearney; Curtis Stingers; Wayne Henderson; **NOTES:** One of the all-time popular songs from Tim-Pan Alley by Jack Norworth and Harry Von Tilzer written in 1908.

202

out   at   the   old   ball   game. _____

D
Katie Casey was baseball made Had the ^Gfever and had it bad.
(chords: G Em   G   Em)

A   Em   A   D
Just to root for the home town crew, Ev'ry sou, Katie blew;

On a Saturday, her young beau Called to see if she'd like to go
(chords: G   Em   G   Em)

To see a show, but Miss Katie said "No! I'll tell you what you can do."
(chords: E   A   B7   E   A)

CHORUS: Take me out to the ball game Take me out with the crowd,
(chords: D   A   D   A)

B7   Em   E   A
Buy me some peanuts and Cracker Jacks, I don't care if I never get back.

Let me root, root, root for the home team, If they don't win it's a shame;
(chords: D   A   D   D7   G)

For it's one, two, three strikes you're out At the old ball game.
(chords: G/B Bb7   D   E A D)

Katie Casey saw all the games, Knew the players by their first names;
Told the umpire he was wrong All along, good and strong.
When the score was just two to two Katie Casey knew what to do,
Just to cheer up the boys she knew She made the gang sing this song:

Tear It Down

Traditional Jug Band Song. **DATE:** Early 1900's; **OTHER NAMES:** Tear it Down Bed Slats and All; Bed Slats; **RECORDING INFO:** King David's Jug Band 1930; Sam Jones; Memphis Jug Band; Bob Coleman & Cincinnati Jug Bad; Old Crow Medicine Show; **NOTES:** This jug band song was recorded by a number of groups in the late 1920's and 1930's. The lyrics have been edited and a new verse is added.

I had a girl and her name was Eve *Every time I looked she had something up her sleeve

She cooked them biscuits, she cooked brown Started workin' when I was turned around

When you catch another mule kicking in your stall Go on and tear it down

CHORUS: Keep tearin' it down, (Bed slats and all) Keep tearin' it down, (Bed slats and all)

Keep tearin' it down, (Bed slats and all) Keep tearin' it down, (Bed slats and all)

When you catch another mule kicking in your stall Go on and tear it down

Mr. Evans Mr. Evans, oh ain't it a shame To see that monkey on a chain
Went upstairs to ring the bell Police in the alley well well well....
When you catch another mule kicking in your stall Go and tear it down CHORUS:

Had me a girl she was little and low Every time I see her wanted mo', mo, mo.
When I got up and went downtown Started workin' when I wasn't around
When you catch another mule kicking in your stall Go on and tear it down CHORUS:

*Every time I looked at her she hollered, "Police."

204

Tell Old Bill

Old-Time and Bluegrass Song, widely known; **DATE:** Carl Sandburg first heard this grim blues-ballad from Nancy Barnhart of St. Louis back in the 1920's. Related to: Baby Mine, Words Charles Mackay; Music Achiblald Johnson in 1874; **OTHER NAMES:** Old Bill **RELATED TO:** The Policeman; How Many Biscuits Can You Eat?; This Morning, This Evening So Soon; This Morning, This Evening Right now; Ain't No Use in Workin' So Hard; Red Hot Breakdown; Settin' in the Chimney Jamb; The Wagon; **RECORDING INFO:** Carolina Tar Heels; Dave Von Ronk; Bob Gibson; **NOTES:** The song, "This Morning, This Evening So Soon," is a branch of songs closely related to the "Crawdad Song" (You get a line I'll get a pole). "Tell Old Bill," "The Policeman" and "How Many Biscuits Can You Eat?" are versions of "This Morning."

G
Tell old Bill when he comes home this morning,

Tell old Bill when he comes home this ev'ning,
D

Tell old Bill when he comes home, to leave them downtown gals alone;
G   C

This morning, this ev'ning, so soon.
G   D   G

Bill left by the alley gate this morning,
Bill left by the alley gate this ev'ning,
Bill left by the alley gate, and old Sal says, "Now don't be late."
This morning, this ev'ning, so soon.

Bill's wife was a-baking bread this morning,
Bill's wife was a-baking bread this evening,
Bill's wife was a-baking bread, when she found out that her Bill was dead,
This morning, this evening, so soon.

Oh no, that cannot be this morning,
Oh no, that cannot be this ev'ning,
Oh no, that cannot be, they killed my Bill in the first degree,
This morning, this ev'ning, so soon.

They brought Bill home in a hurry-up wagon this morning
They brought Bill home in a hurry-up wagon this ev'ning,
They brought Bill home in a hurry-up wagon, poor dead Bill how his toes were a-dragging,
This morning, this ev'ning, so soon.

The Fox

Traditional Old-Time and Bluegrass Song; **DATE**: 1810 (Gammer Gurton's Garland); **CATEGORY**: Songs From Oversees; **RECORDING INFO**: Burl Ives; Pete Seeger; Blue Sky Boys; Nickel Creek; OTHER NAMES: Daddy Fox; Old Mother Hippletoe; Fox Went Out on a Chilly Night; **NOTES:** The earliest version of this piece appears to have been a middle English poem found in a British Museum dating from the fifteenth century. It has become popular in some bluegrass circles after a recording by Nickel Creek.

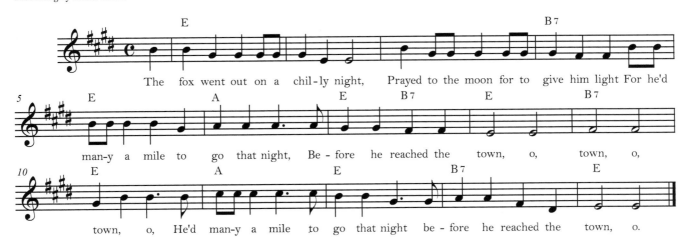

The fox went out on a chilly night And he prayed for the moon to give him light

He had many a mile to go that night Before he reached the town, o, town, o, town, o,

He'd many a mile to go that night before he reached the town, o.

Well the fox he ran till he came to the pen Where the ducks and the geese were kept there in

He said a couple of you are gonna grease my chin Before I leave this town, o, town, o, town, o,

A couple of you are gonna grease my chin before I leave this town, o.

Well he grabbed the old grey goose by the neck Swung her up and across his back
He didn't mind her quacky quack quack, And her legs all hanging down, o, down, o down, o,
He didn't mind her quacky, quack, quack, and her legs all hanging down, o.

Old mother Flipper Flopper jumped out of bed Looked out the window and cocked her head
She said John the grey goose is gone, And the fox is on the town, o, town, o, town, o.
She said John the grey goose is gone, and the fox is on the town, o.

So John he scampered to the top of the hill Blew his horn both loud and shrill
Fox, he said, "I better flee with my kill or they'll soon be on my trail, o, trail, o, trail, o,
Fox, he said, "I better flee with my kill or they'll soon be on my trail, o.

Well the fox he ran till he came to the den There were little ones 8, 9, and 10
They said daddy better go back again Cause it must be a mighty fine town, o, town, o, town, o.
They said daddy better go back again, cause it must be a mighty fine town, o.

Thompsons Old Grey Mule/Old Thompson's Mule

Old-time Song by Thomas Westendorff; **DATE:** 1884; **OTHER NAMES:** "Thompson's Old Grey Mule;" "Jim Thompson's Old Grey Mule;" "Kicking Mule," Braying Mule;" "Yodeling Mule;" **RELATED TO:** "Whoa Mule;" "Kickin' Mule;" **RECORDING INFO:** Riley Puckett 1924; Earnest Thompson; J.E. Mainer's Mountaineers; Georgia Yellow Hammers 1927; Gid Tanner & his Skillet Lickers; Earl Johnson and his Clodhoppers; Shelton Brothers; **NOTES:** "Johnson's/Thompson's Old Grey Mule" was written by Thomas Westendorff in 1884 as "Old Thompson's Blue." This is a different song that "Whoa Mule" (by W.S. Hays) and is characterized by mule sounds (either sung or played on the fiddle) in the chorus. The original sheet music can be viewed on-line at American Memory.

Old Thompson had a big gray mule,

And he drove him 'round in a cart.

Oh! He loved that mule and the mule loved him,

With all his mulish heart.

When the rooster crowed, Ole Thompson knowed,

That the day was going to break,

Then he'd clean that mule with the leg of a stool,

Or scratch him down with a rake.

CHORUS: And the mule would say

"Eh-aw, eh-aw, eh-aw, eh-aw

Eh-aw, eh-aw, eh-aw, eh-aw,"

When he scratched him down with a rake.

He find that mule on ole boot legs And chunks of yellow clay,
Some shavings and some wooden pegs, That was his oats and hay.
That mule would chaw with him iron jaw, On a pir of dirty socks.
And he'd wink his eye like he had some pie
   With his big mouth chuck full of rocks.
CHORUS 2: And the mule would say "Eh-aw, eh-aw, eh-aw, eh-aw
Eh-aw, eh-aw, eh-aw, eh-aw," With his big mouf full of rocks.

That mule could kick like a ton o' brick, And his both hind legs was loose,
He throwed 'em back at wild man Jack And cooked his royal goose.
Old Jack thought he had been caught, In an awful big cyclone.
And you may bet that he wish he'd let That ol' gray mule alone.

CHORUS 3: And the mule would say "Eh-aw, eh-aw, eh-aw, eh-aw
Eh-aw, eh-aw, eh-aw, eh-aw," Let that ol' gray mule alone.

One day while roaming 'round the field, He found a old hoop skirt,
And commenced at once for to make a meal, Of ol' wire, rust and dirt.
That night he took a awful cramp And it settled in his feet,
But before de dawn dat mule was gone To walk a bright golden street.

CHORUS 4: And the mule would say "Eh-aw, eh-aw, eh-aw, eh-aw
Eh-aw, eh-aw, eh-aw, eh-aw," To walk a bright golden street.

Tom Dooley

Traditional Old-Time and Bluegrass Song; **DATE:** Late 1800's; **CATEGORY:** Early Country and Bluegrass Songs; **RECORDING INFO:** First recorded Grayson and Whittier 1929; Frank Prolffin; Doc Watson; Kingston Trio; **OTHER NAMES:** Murder of Laura Foster; Tom Dula; **NOTES:** It 1856 Laura Foster was murdered by Thomas C. Dula and his sweetheart Ann Melton. On May 1, 1868 Tom Dula is hanged for the murder. The details and various versions about this famous love triangle could fill a short book. After Frank Warner collected the song from Frank Proffit in NC, the Kingston Trio picked up Warner's version, and made a huge bit of it in 1958.

Verse 2: Hang your head, Tom Dooley, Hand your head and cry

You killed poor Laura Foster. You know you're bound to die.

You took her on the hillside, as God Almighty knows.
You took her on the hillside, and there you hid her clothes.

You took her by the roadside, where you begged to be excused.
You took her by the roadside, where there you hid her shoes.

You took her on the hillside, to make her your wife.
You took her on the hillside, where there you took her life.

Take down my old violin, play it all you please.
This time tomorrow, it'll be no use to me.

I dug a grave four foot long, I dug it three foot deep.
Poured cold clay o'er her, and tromped it with my feet.

This world one more morning, then where you reckon I'll be?
Hadn't 'a been for Grayson, I'd 'a been in Tennessee.

(Here is the Kingston Trio's version)
Met her on the mountain, there I took her life.
Met her on the mountain, stabbed her with my knife.

This time tomorrow, reckon where I'll be?
Hadn't have been for Grayson, I'd been in Tennessee.

This time tomorrow, reckon when I'll be?
Down in some lonesome valley, hanging from a white oak tree.

Uncle Bud

Bawdy Old-time Song, widely known; **DATE:** Early 1900's; **RELATED TO:** Birmingham; Froggie Went A-Coutrtin'; **OTHER NAMES:** Ol' Bud; Uncle Joe; Uncle Budd;
NOTES: Meade lists Uncle Bud as a subtitle under Froggy Went A-Courting'. The standard old-time melody and form of Uncle Bud are based on Froggie Went A-courting songs which first appear in 1549 as Wedderbum's Complaynt of Scotland. The first recording of Uncle Bud was done in 1926 by Gid Tanner & his Skillet Lickers. Typical bawdy lyrics include Uncle Bud's sexual exploits and anatomy. A great blues version can be heard online at the The Library of Congress American Memory Collection features a recording of Zora Neale Harston in 1939. Most blues versions are typically bawdy and have a different form and melody.

G
I got a gal and she's like you Uncle Bud I got a gal and she's like you Uncle Bud

G   C   D
I got a gal and she's like you She don't wear no- yes she do, Uncle Bud

Where will the wedding supper be? Uncle Bud
Where will the wedding supper be? Uncle Bud
Where will the wedding supper be?
Way down yonder in the holler tree, Uncle Bud.

Uncle Bud gets married on Sunday morn, Uncle Bud
Uncle Bud gets married on Sunday morn, Uncle Bud
Uncle Bud gets married on Sunday morn,
He's gonna bring back a gallon of corn, Uncle Bud

I know a man they called Bud, Uncle Bud
I know a man they called Bud, Uncle Bud
I know a man they called Bud,
He carried his whiskey in jug, Uncle Bud

See my gal come 'cross the road, Uncle Bud
See my gal come 'cross the road, Uncle Bud
See my gal come 'cross the road,
Soon that baby give sugar in the gourd, Uncle Bud

Big cat, little cat playin' in the sand, Uncle Bud
Big cat, little cat playin' in the sand, Uncle Bud
Big cat, little cat playin' in the sand,
Little cat yelled like a natural man, Uncle Bud.

Oh, Uncle Bud goin' down the road, Uncle Bud
Oh, Uncle Bud goin' down the road, Uncle Bud
Oh, Uncle Bud goin' down the road
Haulin' women by the wagon load, Uncle Bud

Viola Lee Blues

Old-time Jug Band Song; **DATE**: Early 1900's; **RECORDING INFO**: Memphis Jug Band; Canon's Jug Stompers; Julius Daniels; Grateful Dead; **OTHER NAMES**: The Judge He Pleaded; **NOTES**: A standard blues in the repertoire of early jug bands.

The judge he pleaded, the clerk he wrote it

G

The clerk he wrote it down indeed-ah

The judge he pleaded, the clerk he wrote it down

                 C   G

If you miss jail sinner, you'll be Nashville bound.

     D   G

Some got six months, some got one solid

Some got one solid year, indeed-ah

Some got six months, some got one solid year

But me and my buddy, we got lifetime here

I wrote a letter, mailed it in the

Mailed it in the air, indeed-ah

I wrote a letter, mailed it in the air

You may know my brother, I've got a friend somewhere

Fix my supper, mama, let me go to

Let me go to bed, indeed Lord

Fix my supper, let me go to bed

I've been drinking white lighting and it just gone to my head.

Wade in the Water

Old-time Gospel; **DATE**: 1800's; **RECORDING INFO**: Sunset Four Jubilee Singers 1925; Lincoln Four Quartette 1928; Empire Jubilee Quartet 1929; Birmingham Jubilee Quartet 1930; **NOTES**: This African-American spiritual became popular in the 1960's by the Ramsey Lewis Trio and later by Eva Cassidy. The standard chords in Em are: Em D/ C B7.

CHORUS: Wade in the water. Wade in the water, children.

Wade in the water. God's gonna trouble the water.

Jordon's water is chilly and cold. God's gonna trouble the water.

It chills the body, but not the soul. God's gonna trouble the water.

If you get there before I do.
God's gonna trouble the water.
Tell all my friends I'm coming too.
God's gonna trouble the water.

Well, who are these children all dressed in red?
God's a-gonna trouble the water
Must be the children that Moses led
God's a-gonna trouble the water.

Who's that young girl dressed in white?
God's gonna trouble the water.
Must be the Children of Israelites
God's gonna trouble the water.

Wagoner's Lad

Old-time Ballad, Widely known; **DATE:** 1907 (JAFL,20); 1908 Campbell; **RELATED TO:** Old Smokey, An Inconstant Lover; I'm a Rambler, I'm a Gambler,
Rye Whiskey/Jack O'Diamonds; **OTHER NAMES**: Loving Nancy; My Horse Ain't Hungry; **RECORDING INFO:** Dock Boggy as "Loving Nancy," Vernon
Dalhart and also Kelly Harrell 1926 as "My Horse's Ain't Hungry," Buell Kazee 1928; Mr. & Mrs. John Sams; Pete Seeger; **NOTES:** This song is related to "On
Top of Old Smokey" and the "Rye Whiskey/Jack O'Diamonds" songs.

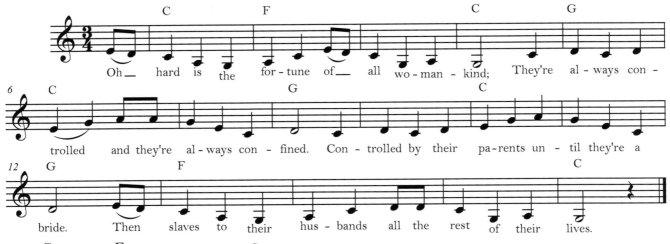

Oh hard is the fortune of all womankind

They're always controlled, they're always confined

Controlled by their parents until they're a bride

Then slaves to their husbands the rest of their lives.

Oh I am a poor girl, my fortune is sad
I have always been courted by the wagoner's lad
He courted me daily by night and by day
And now he is loaded and going away.

Your parents don't like me because I am poor
They say I'm not worthy of entering your door
I work for my living, my money's my own
And if they don't like me they can leave me alone

Your horses are hungry, go feed them some hay
Come sit down beside me as long as you may
My horses ain't hungry, they won't eat your hay
So fare thee well, darling, I'll be on my way

Your wagon needs greasing, your whip's for to mend
Come sit down here by me as long as you can
My wagon is greasy, my whip's in my hand
So fare thee well, darling, no longer to stand

212

Wanderin'

Old-time Blues Song; **DATE:** Early 1900's; 1927 (Sandberg); **RECORDING INFO:** Vernon Dalhart, 1928; Matthew Sabatella, The Boundary Water Boys; Dan Zane;
NOTES: The song appeared in Sandburg's American Songbag in 1927 and was recorded twice by Vernon Dalhart in 1928.

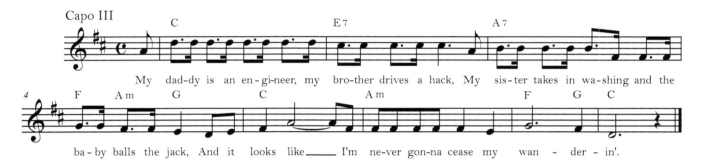

My da^Cddy is an engineer, My bro^{E7}ther drives a hack,

My si^{A7}ster takes in washin', An' the ba^Fby ba^{Am}lls the ja^Gck,

   An' it looks like I'm ^Cnever ^{Am}gonna cease my wa^Fn^Gder^Cin'.

I been a wanderin' Early and late,
New York City To the Golden Gate,
   An' it look like I'm never gonna cease my wanderin'.

Been a-workin' in the army Workin' on the farm,
All I got to show for it Is the muscle in my arm
   An' it looks like I'm never gonna cease my wanderin'.

Snakes in the ocean Fish in the sea,
Took a red-headed woman To make a fool outta me,
   An' it looks like I'm never gonna cease my wanderin'.

Now I've worked in a diner, For nickels and dimes,
And still I keep on waiting For the better times,
   An' it looks like I'm never gonna cease my wanderin'.

Water is Wide, The (O Waly, Waly)

Old-time Ballad; Britain and the US **DATE:** 1765 (Percy) **RECORDING INFO:** Beers Family; Lou and Sally Killen; Pete Seeger, James Taylor **NOTES:** This ballad, as called "O Waly, Waly" is an English folk song that is related to "Jamie Douglas" Child 204.

The water is wide, ^G ^C I cannot get o'er ^G

Nor do I ^{Em} ^C have wings to fly ^D

Build me a ^{Bm} boat that can carry two, ^{Em} ^C

And both shall row, ^G ^D my love and I. ^G

A ship there is and she sails the sea
She's loaded deep as deep can be
But not so deep as the love I'm in
I know not if I sink or swim

I leaned my back against an oak
Thinking it was a trusty tree
But first it bent and then it broke
So did my love prove false to me

I reached my finger into some soft bush
Thinking the fairest flower to find
I pricked my finger to the bone
And left the fairest flower behind

Oh love be handsome and love be kind
Gay as a jewel when first it is new
But love grows old and waxes cold
And fades away like the morning dew

Must I go bound while you go free
Must I love a man who doesn't love me
Must I be born with so little art
As to love a man who'll break my heart

When cockle shells turn silver bells
Then will my love come back to me
When roses bloom in winter's gloom
Then will my love return to me

What'll I Do With The Baby-O

Old-Time Song and Breakdown, Widely known; **DATE:** 1843 as "Dandy Jim from Caroline." **RELATED TO:** Wouldn't Give Me Sugar in My Coffe-O; Cornstalk Fiddle and a Shoestring Bow; Prettiest Little Girl/Gal in the County-O/Country/World; **OTHER NAMES:** She Wouldn't Give Me Sugar in my Coffee; What'cha Goin' to Do with the Baby; Baby-O; **RECORDING INFO:** Hodge Brothers 1928; Grayson & Whitter 1929; Owen Chapman; Tommy Jarrell; Kenny Hall and the Long Haul String Band; Burl Ives; Bradley Kincaid; J.E. Mainer's Mountaineers; Kossoy Sisters; Jean Ritchie; **NOTES:** What'll You Do with the Baby-O is one of a large group of songs that originated from the chorus of Dandy Jim from Caroline in 1843. The first recordings of What are You Going To Do With the Baby? Were made in 1928 by the Hodge Brothers and then by Grayson & Whittier in 1929. Cecil Sharp collected a version in 1917. Most of the lyrics today use dark humor regarding the fate of the poor baby.

Baby, this and baby that

The baby killed my old tom cat.

CHORUS: What're you gonna do with the baby-o?

What're you gonna do with the baby?

Wrap him up with a tablecloth
And put him up in the stable loft. CHORUS:

Wrap him up in calico
Smack his bottom and let him go. CHORUS:

Wrap her up in calico,
Throw her out the window. CHORUS:

Wrap him up in calico
Send it to its Pappy-o. CHORUS:

Dance her north, dance her south,
Pour a little moonshine in her mouth. CHORUS:

When the Saints Go Marching In

Old-time Dixieland Spiritual; **DATE:** 1896 (copyright); **RECORDING INFO:** Paramount Jubilee Singers 1923; Wheat Street Female Quartet 1925; Blind Willie Davis 1928; Pave Jubilee Singers 1928; Fiddlin' John Carson 1934; Monroe Brothers; **NOTES:** Two different versions of this song were published in 1896, one by J.M. Black and the other with words credited to Kathrine E. Purvis and music by Black. It was collected in Nassau by the McCutcheons in 1917 and my haveoriginated in the Bahamas.

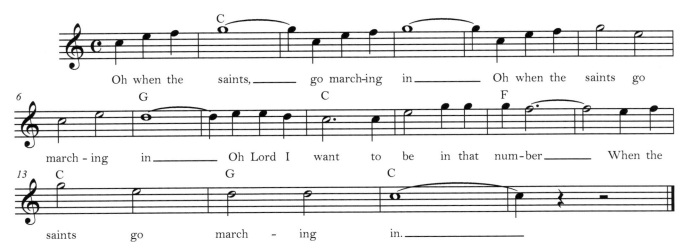

Oh when the saints go marching in
C

Oh when the saints go marching in
G

Oh Lord I want to be in that number
C   F

When the saints go marching in
C   G   C

And on that hallelujah morn
And on that hallelujah morn
Oh Lord I want to be in that number
On that hallelujah morn

And when the stars begin to shine
And when the stars begin to shine
Then Lord, let me be in that number
When the stars begin to shine

When Gabriel blows in his horn
When Gabriel blows in his horn
Oh Lord I want to be in that number,
When Gabriel blows in his horn.

And when the sun refuse to shine
And when the sun refuse to shine
Oh Lord I want to be in that number,
When the sun refuse to shine.

And when the moon has turned to blood
And when the moon has turned to blood,
Oh Lord, I want to be in that number,
When the moon has turned to blood.

And when they gather round the throne,
And when they gather round the throne,
Oh Lord, I want to be in that number,
When they gather round the throne.

White House Blues

Traditional Old-Time and Bluegrass Song; **DATE** Early 1900's; **CATEGORY:** Early Country and Bluegrass Songs; **RECORDING INFO:** Charlie Poole and the North Carolina Ramblers 1926; Flatt & Scruggs & the Foggy Mountain Boys; Greenbriar Boys; Wade Mainer; Stanley Brothers 1927; Bill Monroe 1954; Charlie Monroe & the Kentucky Pardners; Muleskinner; Don Reno; Bill Harrell and the Tenn. Cuttups; Stoneman's Dixie Mountaineers; Doc Watson; **OTHER NAMES:** Mister McKinley; Road to Washington; **NOTES:** White House Blues is based on the shooting death of President William McKinley by anarchist Leon Czolgosz on Sept. 6, 1901. McKinley's wounds should not have been serious, but his inept doctor decided to operate immediately rather than wait for a specialist. The same tune is used for the old-time song, "Battleship of Maine."

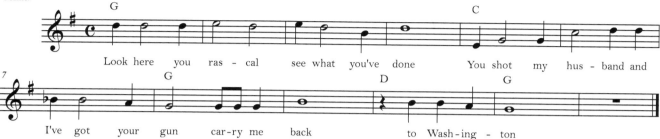

Look here you rascal, see what you've done
You shot my husband and I've got your gun
Carry me back to Washington.

McKinley hollered, McKinley squalled
Doctor said, "McKinley, I can't find the ball
You're bound to die, you're bound to die."

He jumped on his horse, he pulled on his mane
Said, "Listen you horse, you got to out run this train
From Buffalo to Washington."

The doctor come a running, took off his specs
Said, "Mr. McKinley, better cash in your checks
You're bound to die, you're bound to die."

Roosevelt's in the White House, doing his best
McKinley's in the graveyard, taking is rest
He's gone, he's gone, he's gone a long, long time.

Roosevelt's in the White House, drinking out of a silver cup
McKinley's in the graveyard, he'll never wake up.

Who Broke The Lock?

Old-Time Song and Breakdonw, Written by Monroe and Mack as "Who Picked the Lock?"; **DATE:** 1893; **RECORDING INFO:** First recorded as Who Broke the Lock (Unique Quartette, c. 1895); Cousins and DeMoss, 1898; Original Bogtrotters; Otto Gray's Oklahoma Cowboy Band; Dickel Brothers; Kenny Hall and the Long Haual String Band; Joel Mabus; Lonnie Mack; H.M. Barnes & his Blue Ridge Ramblers; **OTHER NAMES:** Who Picked the Lock?; Who Stole the Lock?; Who Stole de Lock on de Henhouse Door?; Riley's Hen House Door; **NOTES:** Monroe and mack were probably inspired by the popular "Dars a Lock on de Chicken Coop Door" by Sam Lucas which was published in Boston by Shas. D. Blake in 1885. The two most influential recordings of "Who Broke The Lock On the Henhouse Door?" were made by Riley Puckett and the Bogtrotters.

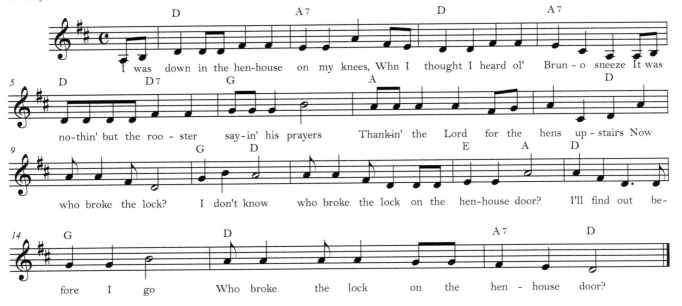

I was down in the hen-house on my knees, Whn I thought I heard ol' Brun - o sneeze It was no-thin' but the roo - ster say-in' his prayers Thankin' the Lord for the hens up - stairs Now who broke the lock? I don't know who broke the lock on the hen-house door? I'll find out be- fore I go Who broke the lock on the hen - house door?

I was down to the henhouse on my knees When I thought I heard ol' Bruno sneeze.
D   A7   D   A7

It was nothin' but the rootser sayin' his prayers Thankin' the Lord for the hens upstairs.
D   D7   G   A   D

CHORUS: Now who broke that lock? (I don't know) Who broke the lock on the henhouse door?
                                    G   D   E   A

I'll find out before I go, Who broke the lock on the henhouse door?
D   G   D   A7   D

I went down to the farmers gate I blowed my horn both seen and late.
The farmer's dog he wouldn't bark or bite But the son of a gun, he could read and write.

Said the barnyard hen to the barnyard rooster Somehow you all don't hear quite as well as you utta
Said the rooster to the hen that may be true But I'd rather be deaf than be dumb like you.

There was a hen and a rooster livin' way out west Said the hen to the roster I love you best
Said the rooster to the hen I know you're tellin' me a lie I done and caught you flirtin' with an old Shanghai.

Said the barnyard rooster to the barnyard hen, "Well, you ain't laid an egg since the Lord knows when."
Said the barnyard hen to the barnyard rooster, "Well, you ain't been around as often as you used-ter."

As I was a-going through the field A black snake caught me by the heel
I turned around to do my best And my left foot slipped in a hornet's nest.

The meat's upon the goose, but the marrow's in the bone. The devil's on the hillside. Don't you hear him groan?
Turkey's playing seven-up on the melon vine, Goose chewing tobacco and the duck is drinking wine.

Whoa Mule

Bluegrass and Old-time Breakdown by William Shakespeare Hays; **DATE:** 1879; **OTHER NAMES:** Whoa Mule, Whoa; The Kicking Mule; Hold onto the Sleigh; I know an Old Canaller; Simon Slick; **RECORDING INFO:** Bill Chitwood & Bud Landress 1924; Clarence Ashley & Tex Isley; Georgia Yellow Hammers; J.E. Mainer's Mountaineers; **NOTES:** Whoa Mule/Kickin' Mule originated from minstrel sources. William Shakespeare Hays "Whoa! I Tell you!" published in 1879 is the one of the original sources and earliest printings. The "hold onto the sleigh" verse comes from Hays and was later adapted by Uncle Dave Macon "Hold on to the Sleigh" appears in many different versions.

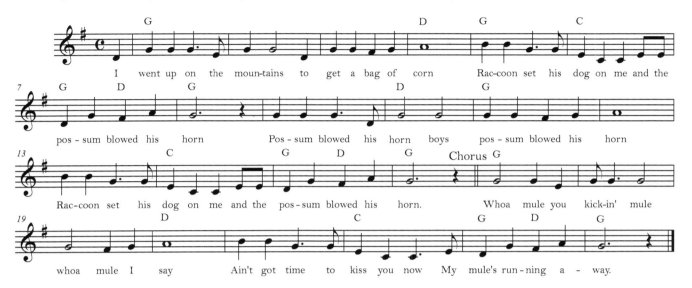

I went up on the mountain to get a bag of corn,

Raccoon set his dog on me and the possum blowed his horn

Possum blowed his horn boys, possum blowed his horn

Raccoon set his dog on me and the possum blowed his horn

CHORUS: Whoa mule, you kickin' mule, Whoa mule I say,

I ain't got time to kiss you now, My mule's runnin' away.

Used to have an old banjo, "Twas all strung up with twine,
And the only song you'd hear me sing, Was I wish that gal was mine.
Well, I wish that gal was mine boys, I wish that gal was mine,
The only song you'd hear me sing, Was I wish that gal was mine.

I took my wife to the barnyard, And I set her down to supper,
Well she got choked on a turkey leg, And stuck her nose in the butter.
Stuck her nose in the butter, Stuck her nose in the butter.
Well she got choked on a turkey leg, And stuck her nose in the butter.

Your face is like a coffee pot, Your nose is like a spout.
Your mouth is like a fireplace, With all the ashes out.
Well, with all the ashes out, boys, With all the ashes out.
You mouth is like a fireplace with all the ashes out.

Wildwood Flower

Old-Time and Bluegrass Song by J.P Webster and Maud Irving; **DATE:** 1895; **CATEGORY:** Early Country and Bluegrass Songs; **RECORDING INFO:** Joan Baez; Norman Blake; Carter Family; Roy Clark; Flatt & Scruggs; New Lost City Ramblers; Stanley Brothers; Keith Whitley & Ricky Skaggs; **OTHER NAMES:** I'll Twine Mid the Ringlets; Frail Wildwood Flower; **NOTES:** Autoharpist Sara Carter sang lead when the Carter Family made "Wildwood Flower" the #3 hit in the nation in 1928. As a parlor tune, the piece went back at least to 1859, as Maud Irving's "I'll Twine Midst the Ringlets." Music historian Charles Wolfe hears "The Pale Amaryllis" entangled in it as well. The actual flower (aronatas) has never been identified.

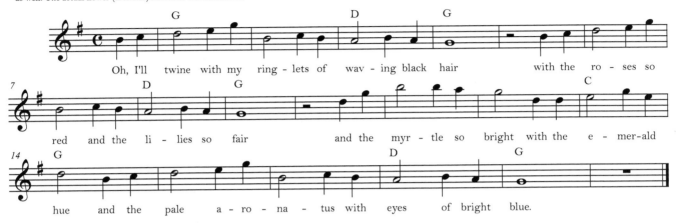

Oh, I'll twine with my ringlets of waving black hair
      G   D   G

With the roses so red and the lilies so fair
                         D   G

And the myrtle so bright with emerald hue
                       C   G

And the pale aronatus with eyes of bright blue.
                   D   G

Oh, I'll dance, I will sing and my laugh shall be gay
I will charm ev'ry heart, in his crown I will sway
When I woke from my dreaming, idols were clay
All portions of love then had all flown away.

Oh, he taught me to love him and promised to love
And to cherish me over all others above
How my heart now is wond'ring misery can tell
He's left me no warning, no words of farewell.

Oh, he taught me to love him and called me his flow'r
That was blooming to cheer him through life's dreary hour
Oh, I'm longing to see him through life's dark hour
He's gone and neglected this pale wildwood flower.

Willie Moore

Old-time Ballad; **DATE:** Early 1900's; **RECORDING INFO:** Burnett & Rutherford 1927; Doc Warson & Gaither Carlton; Joan Baez; **NOTES:** The classic version is Burnett & Rutherford's in 1927. Richard Burnett who played the banjo and sang (Crica 1885-1975) from Monticello, Kentucky was blinded by a robber's gunshot in 1907, and became a musician. He claimed to compose "Ma of Constant Soorow" and it appeared in his collection of songs printed in 1913. It's likely that Burnett arranged "Willie Moore" and added to it. Jean Ritchie learned same melody for "Sweet William and Lady Margaret" from her familyl. There has been some speculation about the initials (in last verse) and who they refer to.

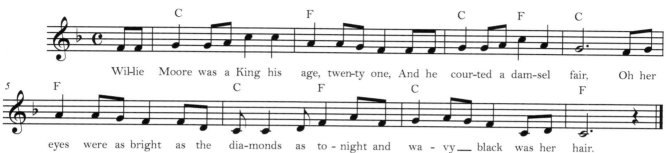

Willie Moore was a king, his age twenty-one

And he courted a damsel fair.

Oh her eyes were as bright as the

     diamonds as tonight

And wavy black was her hair.

He courted her both night and day
Till on marry they did agree.
But when he came to get her parents' consent
They said that could never be.

"I love Willie Moore," sweet Annie replied,
"Better than I love my life,
And I would rather die than weep here and cry,
Never to be his wife."

Oh it was about the tenth of May,
The time I remember well,
That very same night her body disappeared
In a way no tongue could tell.

Sweet Annie was loved both far and near
Had friends most all around
And there she was dressed in a shroud of snowy white
And laid in a lonely tomb.

Her parents now are left alone,
One mourns while the other weeps,
Beneath a grassy mound before the cottage door
The body of sweet Annie sleeps.

Willie Moore scarcely spoke to his friends they say
And at last from them all he did part.
And they last heard from him he was in Montreal
Where he died of a broken heart.

This song was composed in the flowery West
By a man you may never have seen;
O, I'll tell you his name, but it is not in full,
His initials are J.R.D.

Yellow Rose of Texas

Old-Time Song and Breakdown, Widely known **DATE:** Circa 1836, is a handwritten transcript stored in the archive at the University of Texas, Austin. **RECORDING INFO:** Da Costa Woltz's Southern Broadcasters; 1927; The Red Clay Ramblers; Gene Autry; North Carolina Copper Boys Milton Brown & his Musical Brownies **NOTES:** The Yellow Rose of Texas was a hit for Mitch Miller in 1955. A manuscript of a poem, but not music, appeared around 1836 signed "H.B.C." and giving honor to a lover. The earliest known copy of the song The Yellow Rose of Texas appeared soon after the Battle of San Jacinto. This handwritten version was dedicated to E.A. Jones. The debate about the origin of the song and who the "rose" of Texas was, rages on. Certain sites name Emily D. West, called Emily Morgan as the "rose" and credit her with Sam Houston's army victory during the Mexican war by "distracting" Santa Anna. The author of the 1858 first printed version "J.K." has never been identified.

There'sa yel-low rose in Tex-as, That I am going to see, No-bo-dy else could miss her Not half as much as me; She cried so when I left her, It like to broke my heart, And if I e-ver find her, We ne-ver more shall part.

There's a yellow rose in Texas, That I am going to see,

Nobody else could miss her, Not half as much as me.

She cried so when I left her, It like to broke my heart,

And if I ever find her, We never more will part.

CHORUS: She's the sweetest little rosebud that Texas ever knew,
Her eyes are bright as diamonds, They sparkle like the dew;
You may talk about your Clementine, And sing of Rosalee,
But the yellow rose of Texas, Is the only girl for me.

When the Rio Grande is flowing, The starry skies are bright,
She walks along the river In the quiet summer night:
I know that she remembers, When we parted long ago,
I promised to return again, And not to leave her so. CHORUS:

Oh now I'm going to find her, For my heart is full of woe,
And we'll sing the songs together, That we sung so long ago
We'll play the banjo gaily, And we'll sing the songs of yore
And the Yellow Rose of Texas shall be mine forevermore. CHORUS:

UNIQUELY INTERESTING MUSIC!

Made in the USA
Charleston, SC
23 November 2010